PSYCHOLOGICAL MANAGEMENT OF TRAUMATIC BRAIN INJURIES IN CHILDREN AND ADOLESCENTS

THE REHABILITATION INSTITUTE OF CHICAGO PUBLICATION SERIES
Don A. Olson, Ph.D., Series Coordinator

Spinal Cord Injury: A Guide to Functional
Outcomes in Physical Therapy Management

Lower Extremity Amputation: A Guide to Functional
Outcomes in Physical Therapy Management

Stroke/Head Injury: A Guide to Functional
Outcomes in Physical Therapy Management

Clinical Management of Right Hemisphere Dysfunction

Clinical Evaluation of Dysphasia

Spinal Cord Injury: A Guide to Functional
Outcomes in Occupational Therapy

Spinal Cord Injury: A Guide to Rehabilitation Nursing

Head Injury: A Guide to Functional Outcomes in
Occupational Therapy

Speech/Language Treatment of the Aphasias:
An Integrated Clinical Approach

Speech/Language Treatment of the Aphasias: Treatment Materials
for Auditory Comprehension and Reading Comprehension

Speech/Language Treatment of the Aphasias: Treatment Materials
for Oral Expression and Written Expression

Rehabilitation Nursing Procedures Manual

Rehabilitation
Institute of
Chicago
PROCEDURE
MANUAL

PSYCHOLOGICAL MANAGEMENT OF TRAUMATIC BRAIN INJURIES IN CHILDREN AND ADOLESCENTS

Ellen Lehr, PhD

Associate Program Director-Pediatrics
New Medico Community Re-Entry Service of Washington
New Medico Head Injury System
Mountlake Terrace, Washington

AN ASPEN PUBLICATION®
Aspen Publishers, Inc.
Rockville, Maryland
1990

Library of Congress Cataloging-in-Publication Data

Lehr, Ellen.
Psychological management of traumatic brain injuries
in children and adolescents/Ellen Lehr.
p. cm.--(The Rehabilitation Institute of Chicago publication series)
"An Aspen publication."
Includes bibliographical references.
ISBN: 0-8342-0095-3
1. Brain--Wounds and injuries. 2. Children--Wounds and injuries.
3. Teenagers--Wounds and injuries. 4. Brain--Wounds and injuries--Patients--
Rehabilitation. 5. Psychotherapy. I. Title. II. Series.
[DNLM: 1. Brain Injuries--in adolescence. 2. Brain Injuries--in infancy & childhood.
3. Brain Injuries--psychology. 4. Psychotherapy. WS 340 L524p]
RD594.L425 1989 617.4'81044--dc20 DNLM/DLC
for Library of Congress
89-17550
CIP

The authors have made every effort to ensure the accuracy of the information herein, particularly with regard to drug selection and dose. However, appropriate information sources should be consulted, especially for new or unfamiliar procedures. It is the responsibility of every practitioner to evaluate the appropriateness of a particular opinion in the context of actual clinical situations and with due consideration to new developments. Authors, editors, and the publisher cannot be held responsible for any typographical or other errors found in this book.

Editorial Services: Mary Beth Roesser

Library of Congress Catalog Card Number: 89-17550
ISBN: 0-8342-0095-3

Printed in the United States of America

1 2 3 4 5

Table of Contents

Contributors

Ellen Lehr, PhD
Associate Program Director—Pediatrics
New Medico Community Re-Entry Service of Washington
New Medico Head Injury System
Mountlake Terrace, Washington

Joseph A. Lantz, PsyD
Staff Psychologist
Paulson Center for Rehabilitation Medicine
Willowbrook, Illinois

John F. Doronzo, PhD
Clinical Psychologist
Development Associate
HEALTHSOUTH Head Injury Rehabilitation Center
St. Louis, Missouri

All the contributors were employed at the Rehabilitation Institute of Chicago during the development of this book and gratefully acknowledge the support of the institute in this project.

Foreword

More than one million children and adolescents sustain traumatic brain injuries in this country each year. While the vast majority will regain a normal level of functioning without any lasting impairment, approximately 16,000 to 20,000 youngsters will suffer injuries severe enough to leave them with permanent cognitive and physical disabilities.

Although the National Head Injury Foundation (NHIF) has long been aware that this particularly vulnerable population has been neglected by head injury rehabilitation, education, and community-based services, attention is just now being focused on children and adolescents with head injuries. After years of concentration on the rehabilitation of adults with traumatic head injuries, the special needs of head injured children are now being recognized and addressed.

As chairperson of the NHIF Pediatric Task Force and as a member of the NHIF Special Education Task Force, Ellen Lehr has been a vocal advocate for improved systems of care for children and adolescents with head injuries. This book represents her and her colleagues' research and clinical findings and covers the full spectrum of head injury rehabilitation from the acute-care setting to return to home and school. As such, it serves as an important resource for physicians (particularly pediatricians, neurologists, and psychiatrists), educators, allied health clinicians, psychologists, neuropsychologists, insurers, case managers, and most importantly, parents.

In this volume, Dr. Lehr and her colleagues contribute to a deeper understanding of the long-term impact of childhood head trauma by addressing the holistic needs of children and adolescents who have sustained head injuries. In an effort to enhance this population's ability to return to their preinjury course of development and potential, the authors give special attention to the behavioral and psychosocial aspects of head injury, providing crucial insight into the devastating consequences of brain trauma and its far-reaching effects on the professionals, educators, and family members who interact with them.

The book also focuses on minor head injury in children and early identification as a means to reducing the severity of disability. The medical community often dismisses the potential long-term impact of minor head injury on a child's intellectual and psychosocial development. Early recognition and intervention are critical in ensuring the future success and achievement of fullest potential for these children.

This book paves the way for future investigations that will be essential to the well-being of young head injury survivors. We cannot continue to allow advanced medical technology to save this country's young people only to relegate them to unfulfilling and unproductive lives. Educating and disseminating information among medical and rehabilitation professionals, family members, and educators will make a difference.

Finally, as the parent of a daughter who was 15 years old at the time of her injury in 1975, I am especially gratified by the efforts of Dr. Lehr and her colleagues to bring the issues of childhood brain trauma to the forefront of head injury research and rehabilitation.

Marilyn Price Spivack
President, Co-founder
National Head Injury Foundation

Preface

This book is about the psychological issues that children and adolescents face after they have experienced traumatic brain injuries and about the management of the psychological aspects of their injuries. It attempts to integrate existing research findings with the clinical experience of working with these children and adolescents, their families, their friends, and the professionals who treat them. It has grown out of day-to-day clinical experience, especially in a pediatric rehabilitation setting, with several hundred children and adolescents who have had head injuries. More importantly perhaps, it has developed from the need to understand the experience of these children, adolescents, and their families, not only while they are involved in hospital care but especially after they return home and to school.

The book focuses directly on the psychological concerns related to pediatric head injury, that is, the cognitive, learning, behavioral, emotional, and social effects of traumatic brain injuries on the subsequent development of children and adolescents. Although it is not an explicit treatment or therapy manual, the insights and information that are integrated in this book can help to guide the development and application of intervention approaches for use with these children and adolescents. The medical or physical effects of head injuries are presented only in terms of their psychological aspects.

It is hoped that this book will be readable and useful both for professionals who work directly with head-injured children and adolescents and for others who have interests in this area. It attempts to avoid or explain jargon, both medical and neuropsychological, so that those who teach, raise, and help these children and adolescents find the information in this book understandable.

The terms *head injury* and *traumatic brain injury* are used interchangeably. The designation of traumatic brain injury (TBI) is becoming more common because it focuses directly on the brain, rather than the head, as the primary site of injury. It is also helpful in clarifying for children that not only their heads were hurt but more importantly their invisible brain was injured.

It is dedicated to the children, adolescents, and families who insisted directly and indirectly on teaching us about the psychological effects of head injuries.

Chapter 1

Incidence and Etiology

Ellen Lehr

"Did you know I almost died!"
(6-year-old boy 7 months after severe head injury)

"Sometimes I wish it was like in the cartoons where the guy gets hit on the head, he sees stars and gets a big lump, and then gets up and runs around again."
(13-year-old boy 1 1/2 years after severe head injury)

"My life will never be the same."
(14-year-old girl 2 years after severe head injury)

"I could feel sorry for myself when I realize the drastic difference between my life as it was and as it is now. I also can feel very sad for what I've lost, such as the future plans I had dreamed about before I became injured and the friends who couldn't handle my head injury and the changes it brought on. Those feelings could be real downers at times."
(19-year-old young woman 3 years after severe head injury)

INTRODUCTION

Although more and more is known about the effects of head injuries on adult functioning, relatively little is known about the long-term effects of traumatic brain injuries on the subsequent development of children and adolescents. This is a much more complex endeavor, involving not only the effects of head injuries per se but also the interaction of head-injury effects and the process of development. In work with adults, a certain level of baseline functioning can be assumed across many areas, including cognitive abilities, academic achievement, vocational success, psychosocial adjustment, and emotional stability. With children and adolescents, their functioning in all of these areas is a work in progress. Since traumatic brain injuries can impair the substrata from which developmental potential proceeds, that is, the integrity of brain functioning itself, injury effects in children and adolescents are likely to be more profound and more complex than in adults.

It is also more difficult to assess the effects of head injuries in children and adolescents since it is difficult to predict what their potential may have been if they had not sustained head injuries. In adults, one of the primary measures of the effect of head injuries is their capacity after injury to return to preinjury jobs, personalities, cognitive level, etc. However, in

1

children and adolescents, a return to preinjury levels would restrict them to an impaired functional level for the rest of their lives. No parents would want their child to remain at a 3-, 10-, or 15-year-old level indefinitely. Instead, the primary measure of head-injury recovery in children and adolescents involves a return to their preinjury developmental course and potential, with the ultimate measure of good recovery that of attaining independent adult-level functioning in all areas.

INCIDENCE

Although it has been estimated that more than 1 million children sustain traumatic head injuries each year in the United States, with 3 million head injuries overall, until the past 9 years, with the founding of the National Head Injury Foundation, this has been a silent epidemic. Yet, in childhood and adolescence, accidents are the leading cause of both death and disability, with head injuries predominating. In fact, the number of children who die in accidents comprises half of all deaths in childhood (1–14 years of age) (National Center for Health Statistics, 1982) and is twice that of children who die of cancer and congenital defects combined (Gross, Wolf, Kunitz, & Jane, 1985). Approximately 28% of severe head injuries occur in children and adolescents 19 years and under (Gross et al., 1985). As the mortality rates for diseases that previously accounted for most childhood deaths have decreased, due to advances in medical science, the importance of injuries in childhood as the primary cause of death and disability has increased.

Despite the critical nature of the high incidence of death and disability related to traumatic brain injuries in childhood and adolescence, there are surprisingly few comprehensive studies in this area. Those few usually focus on data from a few hospitals and rarely on a compilation of data from a wide network of hospitals, emergency rooms, doctor's office visits, and death statistics. Most of the statistics on head injuries in children and adolescents have been gathered through those patients seen in emergency rooms or admitted to hospitals. They do not include children who were killed at the scene of the accident and therefore usually underestimate fatalities. In addition, the statistics often do not include children who were treated in settings other than emergency rooms or who did not receive medical attention and therefore also may underestimate mild injuries. However, many statistical studies may inflate the number of mild injuries since all injuries to the face and head may be included, whether brain function was affected or not. Another method of determining incidence is to ask parents if their children had ever suffered a blow to the head severe enough to cause them serious worry. When parents of more than 5,000 children in a Swedish town were asked this question, their responses indicated that 15% of their children had had at least one such injury, with 5% having been in coma (Rune, 1970).

Death and Survival Rates

In the United States, approximately 200 of every 100,000 children sustain traumatic brain injuries each year, and approximately 10 of every 100,000 children between birth and 14 years of age die each year from these injuries (Annegers, 1983; Kraus, Fife, Cox, Ramstein, & Conroy, 1986). For comparison purposes, the next highest cause of death in childhood is leukemia, at a rate of 1.9 per 100,000. Since the incidence of head injuries increases dramatically in adolescence, the fatality rate through 19 years of age is considerably higher, reaching a peak of more than 500 per 100,000 at 19 years of age (Klauber, Barrett-Conner, Marshall, & Bowers, 1981). Even though the mortality rate is lower for children, one-third of children (0–14) who were hospitalized in coma after injury died; whereas for those injured over the age of 15, 48% died (Gross et al., 1985). When examined from the opposite perspective, two-thirds of children who become comatose after traumatic brain injuries survive, while only half of those older than 15 years of age survive. The higher rate of children who live after sustaining significant head injuries, combined with their generally more adequate potential for physical recovery, makes the importance of appropriate services all the more crucial.

Effect of Acute Medical Management on Morbidity and Mortality

In the past 15 years, the mortality from head injuries has been decreasing as the management of these patients in trauma centers and emergency rooms has improved. Medical treatment improvements have included the use of CT (computed tomography) scans, monitoring of intracranial pressure, and use of steroids to control brain swelling after injury. Because of this, a decline in deaths from severe head injuries and a subsequent increase in the number of disabled survivors were predicted (Jennett, 1972). In terms of the physical recovery of severely injured children and adolescents, this increase has not resulted (Brink, Imbus, & Woo-Sam, 1980). In a study of more than 300 children and adolescents who were comatose at least 24 hours after head trauma (median length of coma between 5 to 6 weeks) and treated in a pediatric rehabilitation program, 73% regained independence in ambulation and self-care after a 1-year period (Brink, Imbus, & Woo-Sam, 1980). Even though the mortality rate decreased, the chances of achieving physical recovery remained the same as in the previous 10-year period (Brink, Garrett, Hale, Woo-Sam, & Nickel, 1970). However, the outcome in terms of cognitive, emotional, and psychosocial sequelae appears less favorable.

Severity of Injury

Although it is well known that most traumatic brain injuries are mild in nature, incidence studies rarely are conducted in such a way as to indicate clearly the relative frequency of injuries of varying levels of severity. In one of the few studies that examined severity levels, 88% of head injuries in children were mild in nature with 44% involving no evidence of loss of consciousness (Kraus et al., 1986). In another comprehensive incidence study, approximately 5.1% of children who were injured had sustained severe injuries and 5.4% died from their injuries (Annegers, Grabow, Kurland, & Laws, 1980).

Sex Differences

The incidence of head injuries in boys is significantly higher than that in girls at all but the earliest age ranges (Annegers, 1983; Gross et al., 1985) (see Figures 1-1 and 1-2). Other than in infancy, boys are 2 to 4 times more likely to sustain head injuries than girls, with the greatest difference in adolescence. Even though this has been well known for many years and is true of all accidents, not only those involving cerebral injuries, the reasons for it are still not clearly known. Hypotheses as to why this occurs are usually related to the higher level of activity, exploration, and risk taking in boys than girls (Maccoby & Jacklin, 1974).

CAUSATION AND ETIOLOGY

The causes of head injuries in children and adolescents vary with the age of the child and are closely related to their developmental capabilities. For example, falls are more common in infancy and toddler years; pedestrian accidents, in preschool and early school years; and driver and passenger injuries (often related to alcohol and drug use) and sports injuries, in adolescence. However, throughout all age groups, automobile-related

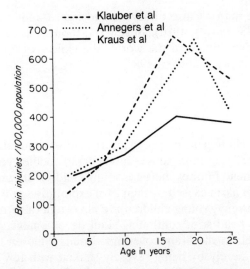

Figure 1-1 Number of Brain Injuries to Males per 100,000 Population. *Source:* From "The Epidemiology and Prevention of Pediatric Head Injury" by Frederick P. Rivara and Beth A. Mueller, 1986, *The Journal of Head Trauma Rehabilitation*, *1*(4), p. 9. Copyright 1986 by Aspen Publishers, Inc.

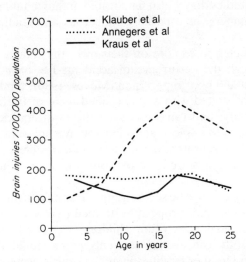

Figure 1-2 Number of Brain Injuries to Females per 100,000 Population. *Source:* From "The Epidemiology and Prevention of Pediatric Head Injury" by Frederick P. Rivara and Beth A. Mueller, 1986, *The Journal of Head Trauma Rehabilitation*, *1*(4), p. 10. Copyright 1986 by Aspen Publishers, Inc.

accidents are a major cause of severe and fatal traumatic brain injuries (Annegers, 1983; Moyes, 1980). In general, though, as the child becomes a more active participant in the world, the child's world becomes more dangerous (Matheny & Fisher, 1984).

Infancy

In infancy, excluding birth-related injuries, most traumatic brain injuries are related to falls or child abuse. Infancy and toddler years are a high-risk period for head injuries, because young children are unable to protect themselves from harm caused by their own exploration or by other people. In terms of anatomy, young children are also vulnerable because of their relatively large head size, continuing skull development, and fragility of the blood vessels in the brain coverings. Young children can sustain significant injury merely by being severely shaken with few or no external signs of injury or abuse (Duhaime, Gennarelli, Thibault, Bruse, Margulies, & Wiser, 1987). In addition, the outcome for infants who are severely abused may be significantly worse than for those who are accidentally injured (Brink, Imbus, & Woo-Sam, 1980). Very young infants are at risk when placed on high surfaces, such as changing tables, highchairs, infant carriers, furniture, and counters, or when dropped—a fear of most parents. Recent studies have also implicated infant equipment, especially walkers and jumpers, as especially dangerous and leading to accidental injuries.

As children begin to explore on their own, the chance of accidents increases. Although the occurrence of accidents has been associated with parental neglect and poor supervision (Moyes, 1980), toddlers can require the attention associated with a well-trained team of traffic controllers to ensure their safety, and can stress even the most conscientious of caretakers. Their need to explore and their relative unawareness of the dangerousness of their actions make supervision of toddlers a full-time occupation. At this age, falls are the most common cause of head injuries and the most common cause of fatalities.

Young children can also be severely injured as passengers in automobiles, especially if they are not properly restrained (Karwacki & Baker, 1979). Because of their small size, young children are more likely to be thrown around or out of the car, even in accidents with minimal impact. The high rate of infant and toddler fatalities in motor vehicle accidents provided the impetus for mandatory restraints in approved car seats designed specifically for young children.

Preschool Years

The preschool-age period continues to be one of high risk for traumatic head injuries. In fact, it is often reported as the second highest period (Hendrick, Harwood-Hashe, & Hudson, 1964; Klonoff, 1971), next only after adolescence. The primary cause of the injuries continues to be related to falls, but an increasing number of injuries are sustained in pedestrian accidents. This is not unexpected since in this period of development children are beginning to experience a wider world more independently. They are able to walk, run, and ride tricycles with ease; they are more frequently away from home and cross streets to playgrounds, stores, and preschool programs. However, their awareness of safety and their judgment, including prediction of the speed and closeness of cars, are not as fully developed as their physical capacities.

At this time, behavioral characteristics of the child may begin to be increasingly related to a greater propensity for injury risk. Hyperactivity, attention difficulties, decreased compliance, and a sense of "do-it-myself" may contribute to a greater risk of injury. However, parents continue to assume primary responsibility for their children's accidents at this age (Klonoff, 1971).

School-Age Children

The school-age years are one of the lowest in terms of incidence of head injuries when compared with the rates in the infancy, preschool, and adolescent years. Motor vehicle accidents continue to cause most of the severe injuries, including those in which children are either passengers or pedestrians. Sports-related injuries increase during this period, with many accidents related to bicycles, skateboards, and baseball bats. At this time, parents begin to take less responsibility and begin to attribute the cause of injury to the children themselves (Klonoff, 1971).

Adolescence

The incidence of head injuries, which remains relatively stable throughout childhood, increases dramatically in adolescence. The number of severe injuries in the 15- to 19-year-old age range equals that of all the previous 14 years combined (Gross et al., 1985). Since most injuries in adolescence are related to motor vehicles, either as the driver or passenger, it is not surprising that this increase occurs when adolescents are getting their driver's licenses and spending much of their time in cars and other vehicles. Many adolescents also are experimenting with the use of alcohol and drugs, which are often implicated in motor vehicle and other accidents. It is not at all uncommon for adolescents to have had a friend, relative, or classmate who was seriously injured or killed in a car accident. Despite the severity of the problem of adolescent accidents and injuries, little is known about which adolescents are at higher risk, the relationship of adolescent behavior to injuries at this age, or how to prevent injuries in adolescence.

Geographic and Time Considerations

Although head injuries occur in all parts of the United States and indeed the world, the circumstances of injury can vary according to the locale. Motor vehicle accidents are the most frequent causes of injury, but these can involve tractors, snowmobiles, jeeps, motorcycles, and mopeds, as well as automobiles. In rural areas, injuries from accidents involving horses and cows can be a common cause of injuries in rural farming communities, whereas in urban areas injuries may be more frequently related to falls from windows, assaults, and gunshot wounds (Cataldo, Dershewitz, Wilson, Christophersen, Finney, Fawcett, & Seekins, 1986).

Injuries are more likely to occur in afternoon and early evening hours regardless of the cause. Although there have been no indications that injuries occur more frequently on certain days of the week, this is probably confounded by children being out of school during the high-injury summer months (Kraus et al., 1986).

Children at High Risk for Head Injuries

Accidents will occur in the best-regulated families: and in families not regulated . . . they may be expected with confidence and borne with philosophy. (Charles Dickens, *Pickwick Papers*)

Unquestionably, many poisonings and accidents are due to carelessness, but the more carefully one takes the history of what actually happened the more one feels that those writers who merely blame the parent for carelessness, and assume with proper care all these accidents would be avoided, either have no children of their own, or, if they have had children, have forgotten their capacity for getting into trouble (Illingworth, 1974).

Although most research studies with children who have sustained head injuries are specific about the age and cause of the injuries, few attempt to explore the behavior of the injured children or the nature of the injury situation with a focus on possible prevention. It is difficult therefore to delineate if there are high-risk groups of children or high-risk situations that increase the possibility of injury. This difficulty includes understanding possible family and parenting characteristics that may contribute to childhood injuries. Most of the efforts in studying children who have sustained head injuries have focused exclusively on their postinjury functioning, rather than on preinjury characteristics that may have contributed to the likelihood of accident occurrence.

In addition, in studies of the effects of traumatic brain injuries on subsequent development, those children who have had a previous history of learning or intellectual difficulties, or a history of behavior or emotional disorders, are often excluded from research studies in order to assess better the effect of the head injury with the fewest confounding factors. Interestingly, in one survey of children in special education programs in Vermont, many of those receiving special education services had a history of head injury noted in their school records (Savage, 1985). From this research it is not possible to determine if their learning and behavior difficulties predated or postdated their head injuries, or if they are a combination of both.

Whether some children and adolescents are more likely to sustain injuries is an area of conflicting information. Specific behaviors have been related to an increased likelihood of accidents (Matheny & Fisher, 1984; Bijur, Stewart-Brown, & Butler, 1986). There is relative agreement as to which behaviors are more likely to be implicated: impulsivity, inattention, emotional lability, higher levels of activity, risk taking, competitiveness, and aggressiveness. Correspondingly, the opposite of these behaviors has not been associated with accident occurrence. This has been confirmed in a well-designed study with adults in which bus drivers with more accidents were characterized by poorly focused or poorly sustained attention to clearly perceptible signals, hastiness, lack of sustained control in motor action, and excessive tension (Hakkinen, 1958). However, simple reaction time and intelligence did not appear to be significant factors.

In research with children who have had head injuries, the findings are much less clear. Somewhat conflicting results have emerged from two longitudinal studies. Klonoff and his group (Klonoff, 1971; Klonoff, Crockett, & Clark, 1984) have found that an increased incidence of pediatric head injuries was associated with environmental factors such as congested residential areas, lower-income housing, marital instability, and lower occupational status of the father. Developmental anomalies, hyperactivity, mental deficiency, brain damage, and emotional disturbance were not associated with head injuries. However, the findings of the research by Michael Rutter's group (1980) indicated that there were behavioral differences between children who sustained mild injuries and those with severe injuries. Those with mild injuries were described as "less intelligent, behaviorally deviant children" who were more likely to "behave in ways which lead to accidents and hence to head injuries" (Rutter, 1980). In support of this, the circumstances surrounding mild injuries were described as different from severe injuries. Those children who sustained mild injuries were more likely to be engaging in prohibited activities at the time of injury (41% of mild injuries versus 16% of severe injuries), with the cause of injury less likely to be related to road traffic accidents (33% of mild injuries versus 80% of severe injuries) and more likely to be related to falls, sports, and assaults (Rutter, Chadwick, Shaffer, & Brown, 1980).

It is also not clear if children who have had one head injury are more susceptible to another or are more likely to have had a previous head injury. Unfortunately there is little information in comparing the incidence for injury in children who have had a head injury with those who have not. In Klonoff's (1971) study, 23% of those children who had been treated in the emergency room for head trauma had a subsequent head injury or accident within the following year, but no data on the control group were available to help assess if this was an increased risk. In a comprehensive study of the incidence of traumatic brain injury in childhood, the increased risk for subsequent injury was 2 times greater than that of children who had not been injured and was equal for both boys and girls (Annegers, 1983).

A current prospective study being conducted in Britain (Butler & Golding, 1986) is especially important in clarifying some of the accident issues for children 5 years and younger. This research avoids many of the previous criticisms since it involves a comprehensive follow-up of all children born in a 1-week period of time (April 5–11, 1970). Approximately 80% of the children were located; data were collected through interviews with their parents (usually the mother), and a questionnaire was completed by the parents on medical, social, and family background. In addition, child health clinic records were reviewed.

Of the approximately 16,000 children studied after birth, 17 had died from accidents or violence by the age of 5. Of these 17 deaths, 12 were related to head injuries (7 motor vehicle accidents, 2 objects falling on children, and 3 nonaccidental injury). Considering the prevalence of injury (43% of the children had received medical care for at least one accidental injury), there was a low incidence of death and disability (8 children).

Although accidents were rare in the first year of life, the mortality rate was higher than in the succeeding 4 years. The peak of the accident rate during the first 5 years of life was at 3 years of age. Interestingly the incidence of head injuries was comparable with that of lacerations and superficial injuries and far exceeded the other types of accidents.

Boys not only had more accidents than girls but also were more likely to have repeated accidents. Children who had a single accident were similar to those who had no accidents. However, children with more than one accident showed marked differences: they were more likely to be described as disobedient, destructive, hyperactive, and fighting with other children. Their mothers were likely to be young, employed, heavy smokers, and living in urban areas. Interestingly, despite the frequent low reported incidence of somatic complaints related to head injuries in this age range, children with more than one accident by the age of 5 were more likely to have headaches, bite their fingernails, and have persistent sleep problems.

However, it would probably be unwise to assume that the greatest proportion of traumatic brain injuries are directly related only to children's or adolescents' behavior. Instead many factors are probably involved, including environmental factors (road and intersection design, play spaces close to traffic, design of play equipment including bicycle design), parental and caretaker awareness and anticipation of possible dangers (gates on stairs, use of car seats and seat belts), teaching of safety behavior to children, driver's education of adolescents, sporadic behaviors (being in the wrong place at the wrong time), and being the victim of other people's behavior. Because of the extremely high rate of pediatric head injuries, all of these are probably as or more important overall than a simple focus on identifying accident-prone individuals.

In addition, there are major concerns about focusing only on child and adolescent or parent behavior when dealing with pediatric head injury in the clinical setting. If this helps to focus on behavior change to limit future or repeat injuries, it can have a positive effect. However, it can have a negative effect if the professionals treating the child and family perceive behavioral aspects of accidents as an area that is not only resistant to change but a return to preinjury functioning. In this case, the child and family are likely to receive less than appropriate services.

It is easy to overgeneralize from *more prevalent* to *always is the case.* Even though certain behaviors can lead to an increase in the incidence of injuries, they are not necessarily the most frequent cause. It is unwise to assume that children or adolescents with known behavioral control difficulties are always responsible for their own injuries. For example, an overactive, risk-taking boy may be injured as a passenger in a car accident when the driver of the other car is at fault. Even though he is at greater risk for injury related to climbing trees, jumping from heights, and riding his bicycle like Evel Knievel, his actual injury was not a result of his behavior.

In conclusion, research and more complete information about incidence and etiology needs to be focused on preventing injuries, not only on treating injuries. Even though this information and research are not necessarily crucial for those children and adolescents who have had traumatic brain injuries, it is vital for attempts to curb this mounting health hazard. Much more needs to be known about the precise characteristics of the causative factors in traumatic head injuries in children and adolescents in order to develop workable strategies for reducing disability and death and the emotional and financial expense to children, their families, and society.

REFERENCES

Annegers, J.F. (1983). The epidemiology of head trauma in children. In K. Shapiro (Ed.), *Pediatric head trauma.* Mt. Kisco, NY: Futura Publishing Co.

Annegers, J.F., Grabow, J.D., Kurland, L.T., & Laws, E.R. (1980). The incidence, causes, and secular trends of head trauma in Olmsted County, Minnesota, 1935–1974. *Neurology, 30,* 912–919.

Bijur, P.E., Stewart-Brown, S., & Butler, N. (1986). Child behavior and accidental injury in 11,966 preschool children. *American Journal of Diseases of Childhood, 140,* 487–492.

Brink, J.D., Garrett, A.L., Hale, W.R., Woo-Sam, J., & Nickel, V.L. (1970). Recovery of motor and intellectual function in children sustaining severe head injuries. *Developmental Medicine and Child Neurology, 12*(5), 565–571.

Brink, J.D., Imbus, C., & Woo-Sam, J. (1980). Physical recovery after severe closed head trauma in children and adolescents. *Journal of Pediatrics, 97,* 721–727.

Butler, N.R., & Golding, J. (Eds.). (1986). *From birth to five: A study of the health and behavior of Britain's 5-year-olds.* New York: Pergamon Press.

Cataldo, M.F., Dershewitz, R.A., Wilson, M., Christophersen, E.R., Finney, J.W., Fawcett, S.B., & Seekins, T. (1986). Childhood injury control. In N.A. Krasnegor, J.D. Arasteh, & M.F. Cataldo (Eds.), *Child health behavior: A behavioral pediatrics perspective.* New York: John Wiley & Sons.

Duhaime, A., Gennarelli, T.A., Thibault, L.E., Bruce, D.A., Margulies, S.S., & Wiser, R. (1987). The shaken baby syndrome: A clinical, pathological, and biomedical study. *Journal of Neurosurgery, 66,* 409–415.

Gross, C.R., Wolf, C., Kunitz, S.C., & Jane, J.A. (1985). Pilot Traumatic Coma Data Bank: A profile of head injuries in children. In R.G. Dacey, R. Winn, & R. Rimel (Eds.), *Trauma of the central nervous system.* New York: Raven Press.

Hakkinen, S. (1958). *Traffic accidents and driver characteristics: A statistical and psychological study.* Helsinki: Finland's Institute of Technology (Scientific Researches No. 13).

Hendrick, E.B., Harwood-Hashe, D.C.F., & Hudson, A.R. (1964). Head injuries in children: A survey of 4465 consecutive cases at the Hospital for Sick Children, Toronto, Canada. *Clinical Neurosurgery, 11,* 46–65.

Illingworth, C.M. (1974). Childhood poisonings: Who is to blame? *The Practitioner, 213*, 73–78.

Jennett, B. (1972). Head injuries in children. *Developmental Medicine and Child Neurology, 14*, 137–143.

Karwacki, J.J., & Baker, S.P. (1979). Children in motor vehicles: Never too young to die. *Journal of the American Medical Association, 242*, 2848–2851.

Klauber, M.R., Barrett-Conner, E., Marshall, L.F., & Bowers, S.A. (1981). The epidemiology of head injury: A prospective study of an entire community—San Diego County, California, 1978. *Journal of Epidemiology, 112*, 500–509.

Klonoff, H. (1971). Head injuries in children: Predisposing factors, accident conditions, accident proneness, and sequelae. *American Journal of Public Health, 61*(12), 2405–2417.

Klonoff, H., Crockett, D.D., & Clark, C. (1984). Head injuries in children: A model for predicting course of recovery and prognosis. In R.E. Tarter and G. Goldstein (Eds.), *Advances in clinical neuropsychology, Vol. 2*. New York: Plenum Press.

Kraus, J.F., Fife, D., Cox, P., Ramstein, K., & Conroy, C. (1986). Incidence, severity, and external causes of pediatric brain injury. *American Journal of Diseases of Childhood, 140*, 687–693.

Maccoby, E.E., & Jacklin, C.N. (1974). *The psychology of sex differences*. Stanford, CA: Stanford University Press.

Matheny, A.P., Jr., & Fisher, J.E. (1984). Behavioral perspectives on children's accidents. *Advances in Developmental and Behavioral Pediatrics, 5*, 221–264.

Moyes, C.D. (1980). Epidemiology of serious head injuries in childhood. *Child Care, Health and Development, 6*, 1–9.

National Center for Health Statistics. (1982). Advance report, final mortality statistics. In *Monthly Vital Statistics Report*, Vol. 31, No. 6, Suppl. [DHHS Publ. No. (PHS)82-1120]. Hyattsville, MD: U.S. Public Health Service.

Rune, V. (1970). Acute head injuries in children. *Acta Paediatrica Scandinavica* (Suppl.), 209.

Rutter, M. (1980). Raised lead levels and impaired cognitive/behavioral functioning: A review of the evidence. *Developmental Medicine and Child Neurology 22* (Suppl.), 21.

Rutter, M., Chadwick, O., Shaffer, D., & Brown, G. (1980). A prospective study of children with head injuries: I. Design and methods. *Psychological Medicine, 10*, 633–645.

Savage, R. (1985). *A survey of traumatically brain injured children within school-based special education programs*. (pp. 1–6) Rutland, VT: Head Injury/Stroke Independence Project, Inc.

Chapter 2

Measurement and Process of Recovery

Ellen Lehr

INTRODUCTION

There are two sections in this chapter. The first is a discussion of the differences between pediatric and adult traumatic brain injuries and the effect of these differences on the measurement of injury severity. The second is a clinically based presentation that attempts to capture the experience of traumatic brain injury over time from three points of view: the injured child or adolescent, the family members, and the professionals who care for them.

One of the primary differences between head injury in children and adolescents and in adults, according to research literature on adults, is that children usually sustain generalized injuries. The predominance of older research on adults often focused on soldiers who had penetrating, focal injuries received in military combat. This emphasis has changed recently since the major cause of injuries in both the pediatric and adult population currently involves motor vehicle accident-related injuries.

The characteristics of generalized traumatic brain injuries consist of the effects of rapid acceleration and deceleration on the brain including shearing (tearing) of nerve fibers, contusion (bruising) of brain tissue against the skull, brain stem injuries, and edema (swelling). These injuries are often called *closed head injuries* since they do not involve penetration of the skull or the coverings of the brain. At times, skull fractures may also be present as well as a combination of closed and open head injuries. Focal injuries do occur in the pediatric population, though less frequently. For instance, children can sustain gunshot injuries, usually as the victims of violence or play with loaded guns.

Injury that occurs in reaction to the initial impact is called *primary damage*. This can consist of bleeding within the brain (hematomas), which is less common in younger children but increases in adolescence. It also

15

involves diffuse injury to the nerve fibers as they get stretched and torn when the brain is rapidly accelerated and then decelerated (for example, a person's head hitting the windshield in a car).

Secondary injury consists of the brain's response to the initial injury. This is especially important in children younger than 10 years. Secondary diffuse injury is common in young children with severe injuries and seems to be related to pervasive cerebral swelling causing injury to nerve fibers. However, this swelling may not be due to the same causes as in adult injuries. It may be related to increased blood volume after injury, rather than to edema or retention of fluid in the tissues. This difference in neurological reaction to injury may be a factor in the better outcome in children. Diffuse swelling is common in children who are immediately comatose after injury but can also be delayed and occur in those who were initially lucid after injury.

DIFFERENCES BETWEEN PEDIATRIC AND ADULT TRAUMATIC BRAIN INJURIES

Much more is known about the nature of traumatic brain injuries in adults than about injuries in children or adolescents. In adults, the nature of the brain is more of a unitary phenomenon, whereas in children the brain is continually in a process of developmental change. It cannot therefore be assumed that injury at any one point from infancy to young adulthood has the same effect since the brain is not the same across this time span.

In the infant and young child, the brain is considerably larger in comparison with body size than at later ages. The immature skull is thinner, more pliable, and more easily deformed by trauma. Although this allows for increased brain growth, it is not clear how it affects the skull's ability to protect the brain from external trauma (Shapiro, 1985). The developing brain is also closer to the brain coverings (the dura), has a smaller cushioning space between itself and the skull, and is able to move around more freely. All of these differences between the adult and developing brain may actually increase the likelihood of certain traumatic effects such as subarachnoid hemorrhages (bleeding in the small area between the brain covering, the dura, and the brain itself) and diffuse injury to the nerve fibers through increased brain movement. However, it is not clear how the changes in brain and skull anatomy over the developmental period are affected by traumatic injuries.

Interestingly the presentation of coma in children and adults is not identical either. Even with little or no loss of consciousness, traumatically brain-injured children can show abnormalities, which are sometimes severe, on CT scans (Zimmerman & Bilanuik, 1981). It is less likely for infants and young children to experience immediate loss of consciousness or loss of memory subsequent to significant injuries. This is especially important since these two symptoms are heavily relied on in assessing the severity of injury in adults but may be less predictive of severity of injury in infants and young children. As children become older, the incidence of amnesia and unconsciousness as a reaction to traumatic brain injury increases (Brink, Garrett, Hale, Woo-Sam, & Nickel, 1970; Hendrick, Harwood-Hash, & Hudson, 1964; Klonoff & Low, 1974).

CLASSIFICATION AND MEASUREMENT OF INJURY SEVERITY

No one classification scheme of injury severity is widely used and accepted. Rather several classification systems may utilize different sources of data, such as behavioral information, presence of skull fractures, CT findings, and physiological factors (Jennett & Teasdale, 1981). An example of a classification schema that attempts to combine data from several sources in order to describe injury severity was developed by Annegers (1983). The specific levels of severity and their definitions are presented in Table 2-1.

Injury severity is classified behaviorally by the length of altered consciousness—most clearly the period of unconsciousness (nonresponsiveness to stimuli)—and the length of post-traumatic amnesia (the period after

---

Table 2-1 Injury Severity Classification

1. *Mild*
   Loss of consciousness or post-traumatic amnesia of less than ½ hour without a skull fracture
2. *Moderate with fracture*
   Linear or basilar skull fracture with or without documentation of loss of consciousness
3. *Moderate without fracture*
   Loss of consciousness or post-traumatic amnesia greater than ½ hour
4. *Severe*
   Intracranial hematoma, brain contusion, or loss of consciousness or posttraumatic amnesia of greater than 24 hours
5. *Fatal*
   Death within 28 days of injury

Source: From *Pediatric Head Trauma* by K. Shapiro (Ed.), 1983, Mt. Kisco, NY: Futura Publishing Company. Copyright 1983 by Futura Publishing Company.

injury before the individual begins to remember ongoing events). Several objective observation approaches that have primarily been developed for use with adults are discussed. These techniques, especially the Glasgow Coma Scale, have been used extensively in research on adult injuries. However, even the phenomena of coma and post-traumatic amnesia have been less precisely defined when assessing and studying the effects of head injury in children (Goethe & Levin, 1984).

Measurement of Loss of Consciousness

Since the clinical impressions of emergency and medical staff appear to differ in assessing the depth and length of the period of unconsciousness, attempts have been made to quantify their observations accurately (Teasdale, Knill-Jones, & Van Der Sande, 1978). Asking the patient about the period of loss of consciousness is not feasible, regardless of age, since the individual is not aware of what has occurred. Information derived from family members or others at the scene of injury may also be unreliable.

In an attempt to structure and quantify observations of unconsciousness, the Glasgow Coma Scale (GCS) was developed (Teasdale & Jennett, 1974). The GCS defines *coma* as the absence of eye opening, the inability to obey commands, and the failure to speak recognizable words. It is a commonly used, easily applied observational scale developed to assess the level of consciousness of patients after suspected traumatic brain injury. The wide application of GCS ratings of patients in a variety of settings, including the scene of injury, outpatient medical settings, and hospital emergency rooms, has made it possible to equate the status of injured individuals for both clinical and research purposes.

The GCS consists of ongoing observations of the patient that are summarized into a numerical score. They are usually recorded at the arrival of emergency medical personnel or admission to the emergency room and then at stated intervals (such as once during each nursing shift) until the patient recovers consciousness. The items of the scale and score levels are presented in Table 2-2.

The Glasgow Coma Scale score is equal to the total of the three catagories of response. Maximum score is 15 and minimum score is 3, with more severely injured individuals scoring lower. Through the use of the total scores, the severity of injury as measured by loss of consciousness can be quantified: mild injury = GCS score of 13–15, moderate injury = GCS score of 9–12, severe injury = GCS score of 3–8 (Jane & Rimel, 1982).

Although the GCS has been a major improvement in the reliable assessment of loss of consciousness, it has been developed and utilized pri-

Table 2-2 Glasgow Coma Scale Ratings

Eye Opening
Spontaneous 4
To speech 3
To pain 2
None 1
Best Motor Response
Obeys commands 6
Localizes 5
Withdraws 4
Abnormal flexion 3
Extensor response 2
None 1
Verbal Response
Oriented 5
Confused conversation 4
Inappropriate words 3
Incomprehensible sounds 2
None 1

Source: From "Assessment of Coma and Impaired Consciousness: A Practical Scale" by G. Teasdale and B. Jennett, 1974, *Lancet, 2*, pp. 81–84. Copyright 1974 by The Lancet. Reprinted by permission.

marily with individuals in their late teens and with adults and less so with children (Levin & Eisenberg, 1979). The relationship between GCS scores and outcome has been little studied in children of varying ages. It is not clear that the classification of injury severity using GCS scores is as reliable with children as with adults. Because of the differences in presentation of coma in children and adults, it is not even clear if it is measuring the same phenomenon. The verbal response part of the GCS is clearly not appropriate for preverbal children and may primarily reflect the fear of older children in reaction to injury and the hospital environment. Utilizing an alternative approach by substitution of sounds for talk may overestimate a child's status and obscure a significant injury (Shapiro, 1985). In addition, any alterations in the application of the GCS for children need to be as well standardized as the GCS itself has been with adults, or it will be difficult to compare one group of injured children with another in any reliable way.

In order to assess loss of consciousness accurately in infants and children up to 3 years of age, Raimondi and Hirschauer (1984) developed the Children's Coma Scale (CCS) (Table 2-3). It utilizes behaviors and physiological indicators that can be observed but are not necessarily in response to stimulation. Although the items on the scale are appropriate for infants and young children, the scale is not certain to be as predictive as the GCS until it is widely used. One of its limitations is its reliance on physiological

Table 2-3 Children's Coma Scale

Ocular Response	
Pursuit	4
Extraocular muscles intact (EOM), reactive pupils	3
Fixed pupils or EOM impaired	2
Fixed pupils and EOM paralyzed	1
Verbal Response	
Cries	3
Spontaneous respirations	2
Apneic	1
Motor Response	
Flexes and extends	4
Withdraws from painful stimuli	3
Hypertonic	2
Flaccid	1

Source: From "Head Injury in the Infant and Toddler" by A.J. Raimondi and J. Hirschauer, 1984, *Child's Brain, 11,* pp. 12–35. Copyright 1984 by Springer-Verlag.

---

indicators, which may be less accurate as an overall measure of cognitive-related functioning after injury than the response to stimulation approach utilized by the GCS (Jennett & Teasdale, 1981).

Measurement of Post-Traumatic Amnesia

After the recovery of consciousness, there is usually a more prolonged period (estimated at approximately 4 times as long), during which recent events are not remembered reliably, consistently, or accurately. This phenomenon is called *post-traumatic amnesia* (PTA). In adults, the definition of post-traumatic amnesia consists of that period when an individual cannot store continuous memory of ongoing events, that is, when the patient cannot remember today what happened yesterday. It usually relies on the individual's own account of when the person regained memory or "woke up." Although there may be isolated islands of memory before resolution of PTA, the individual is usually quite clear about the difference between these snatches and ongoing memory. One of the classifications of injury severity based on the length of post-traumatic amnesia was proposed by Jennett (1976) (Table 2-4).

Assessment of post-traumatic amnesia in children poses even more significant difficulties than the assessment of unconsciousness. Young children are in a period of memory development and cannot be expected to remember events from day to day as reliably as adults. Nor are they nec-

Table 2-4 Severity of Injury through Assessment of Length of Post-Traumatic Amnesia

Length of PTA	Severity of Injury
Less than 5 minutes	Very mild
Less than 1 hour	Mild
1 to 24 hours	Moderate
1 to 7 days	Severe
More than 7 days	Very severe
More than 4 weeks	Extremely severe

Source: From "Assessment of the Severity of Head Injury" by B. Jennett, 1976, *Journal of Neurology, Neurosurgery, and Psychiatry, 39,* pp. 647–655. Copyright 1976 by British Medical Association.

essarily the most accurate reporters of information that adults believe is important but young children may not. For these reasons, attempts to standarize assessment of post-traumatic amnesia in children must consider the developmental level of the child in terms of both the developmental processes of normal memory and the accuracy of using the child as a reporter. The less frequently reported occurrence of post-traumatic amnesia in children younger than 9 years of age (Klonoff & Low, 1974) may in fact reflect these ambiguities in assessment and knowledge of memory development.

In an attempt to quantify the length and extent of PTA, similar to the assessment of unconsciousness utilizing the GCS, Levin, O'Donnell, and Grossman (1979) developed the Galveston Orientation and Amnesia Test (GOAT). This brief scale can be administered on a daily basis to the injured individual to obtain direct information about basic orientation, anterograde amnesia (recall of events before injury), and post-traumatic amnesia. Subsequently the GOAT was modified for use with children as the Children's Orientation and Amnesia Test (COAT), which has been normed and is being used in research studies (Ewing-Cobbs, Levin, Fletcher, Miner, & Eisenberg, 1989). The COAT assesses general orientation for name, age, school, family, place, and time. It also includes basic memory and attention questions.

Another approach for assessing post-traumatic amnesia in children has utilized structured parent interviews (Rutter, Chadwick, Shaffer, & Brown, 1980). Although the interviews developed for this purpose appear extensive and detailed, the information derived from them is likely to be considerably more accurate if it is obtained while the child is recovering from post-traumatic amnesia than if the interviews are administered long after the child has emerged from post-traumatic amnesia.

Assessment of Recovery after Traumatic Brain Injury

For individuals who are more severely injured and make progress slowly over an extended period, measures such as the GCS that are appropriate for assessment of acute periods of coma can be less useful. The GCS has a relatively low ceiling effect and cannot be used to assess patients who are consistently responsive to commands but are not oriented or ready for formal psychological evaluation. To bridge this gap and to describe the stages of cognitive improvement that moderate to severely injured individuals often progress through, the Levels of Cognitive Functioning Scale (known informally as the *Rancho Scale*) was developed (Hagan, Malkmus, & Durham, 1979) (see Table 2-5). Although the Rancho Scale was initially devised for use with adults, adaptations for children younger than 5 years have been developed.

The Rancho levels are divided into 8 stages, extending from deep coma through independent behavior (though not necessarily complete recovery to preinjury functional level). These levels are descriptive in nature and roughly attempt to capture the essence of behavior across a variety of areas at any one time. The Rancho Scale is therefore not a test but a method of organizing observations in a generalized way. Thus it cannot be used to quantify functional level or recovery for research purposes, but it can be useful clinically. The Rancho levels are utilized in this way as part of a description of the natural history of traumatic brain injury in the second part of this chapter.

Alexander (1982) has also proposed a descriptive schema for the traumatic brain-injury recovery process. His stages, though, not only emphasize the injured individual's behavior but also focus on management and treatment needs at each level (see Table 2-6).

Table 2-5 Levels of Cognitive Functioning Scale (Rancho Levels)

    I. No response to stimulation
    II. Generalized response to stimulation
    III. Localized response to stimulation
    IV. Confused, agitated behavior
    V. Confused, inappropriate, nonagitated behavior
    VI. Confused, appropriate behavior
    VII. Automatic, appropriate behavior
    VIII. Purposeful, appropriate behavior

Source: From *Rehabilitation of the Head Injured Adult: Comprehensive Physical Management,* 1979, Downey, CA: Professional Staff Association of Rancho Los Amigos Hospital, Inc. Copyright 1979 by Professional Staff Association of Rancho Los Amigos Hospital, Inc.

Table 2-6 Recovery from Severe Traumatic Brain Injury

Stage of Recovery	Focus of Treatment
1. Coma	1. Restoration of gross wakefulness
2. Unresponsive vigilance	2. Development of purposeful wakefulness
3. Mute responsiveness	3. Recovery of speech
4. Confusional state	4. Resolution of period of post-traumatic amnesia
5. Independent in daily self-care; adequate social interaction	5. Cognitive improvement
6. Independent intellectually	6. Develop normal goal-directed behavior
7. Complete social recovery	

Source: From *Psychiatric Aspects of Neurologic Disease,* Vol. II, by F. Benton and D. Blumer (Eds.), 1982, New York: Grune & Stratton, Inc. Copyright 1982 by Grune & Stratton, Inc.

Both the Rancho levels and the Alexander stages can be useful in helping to make a prolonged recovery process more explicable both to family members and to staff who are not familiar with the long-term process of improvement from more severe injuries. However, both scales have been criticized for the difficulty of using them in a reliable or quantifiable way (Gouvier, Blanton, LaPorte, & Nepomuceno, 1987). An alternative is the Disability Rating Scale (DRS) developed for use with head-injured patients (Rappaport, Hall, Hopkins, Belleza, & Cope, 1982). The DRS is a 30-point scale that rates 8 dimensions of behavior: (1) eye opening, (2) verbalization, (3) motor responsiveness, cognitive skills necessary for (4) feeding, (5) toileting, (6) grooming, and overall level of (7) dependence and (8) employability. Although it has been used reliably and validly with adults, it needs modifications for use with children and adolescents.

In conclusion, the assessment and measurement of traumatic brain-injury severity in children and adolescents is only beginning to be addressed in a systematic, developmentally appropriate manner. Considerable work needs to be done in this area before the classification of injury severity across the developmental period from infancy through adolescence can be both quantitatively measured and qualitatively described in a meaningful way.

NATURAL HISTORY OF PEDIATRIC HEAD INJURY RECOVERY

Recovery from coma after traumatic brain injury and resumption of daily activities and preinjury capacities follows a somewhat predictable course. In this section, the process of recovery is illustrated across stages in terms of the experience at each period for traumatically brain-injured children, their families, and the professional staff working with them. In order to demonstrate the progression of stages best, a hypothetical older child or adolescent who has had a good recovery from a severe head injury is described as that patient might change over time.

Since progress is slowed in the case of severe injury, each stage can be quite distinctive in terms of its characteristics and length of time. In contrast, recovery stages from mild or moderate injuries can follow in quick progression with several stages merging in the space of less than one day or over a period of a few days. Each stage is described in terms of its primary issues and the possible crises that can occur. Even though a complete recovery is used for illustration purposes, it is important to remember that for any one individual, the sequelae of traumatic brain injuries may be so severe in one or many areas as to limit improvement and functioning. There is certainly no guarantee that all head-injured children will recover to the point of independent capacities, that they will improve at the same rate, or even with the most adequate of recoveries that they will not continue to experience significant differences and impairments when compared with preinjury levels of performance.

Unlike recovery from physical injuries or sudden onset of illnesses that do not impair brain functioning, recovery from traumatic brain injuries involves discontinuities in the capacity of injured individuals to deal with the effects of impaired functioning, which is out of step with what their families or the staff working with them are experiencing. For example, if children sustain severe leg and hip fractures in pedestrian or automobile accidents, they are aware at the time of injury that they are hurt very badly. They may be able to tell emergency personnel where they are hurt, how much they can move, and possibly explain what happened. Physically injured children may also be aware of what people are doing to help and could tell others who they are and how to contact their families. Caretakers could explain what they are doing, what hospital they are going to, and what medical procedures will be done and why. From early on after injury, these physically injured children may be able to be active participants in their own care and recovery. Emotionally these children also can experience the fear and the worry surrounding issues of "will I be okay?" In addition, they can directly experience the guilt and the responsibility for injury, especially if their own behavior played a part in the injury.

With traumatic brain injuries involving loss of consciousness and coma, this process of involvement and awareness of the fact of injury and its impact is markedly altered. Figure 2-1 illustrates the different experiences that the head-injured child, the family, and the professionals working with them undergo.

The following is a discussion of the experiential differences for the children and adolescents, their families, and their therapists during the various stages of recovery from traumatic brain injury, with the Rancho levels used as illustration.

No Response or Generalized Response to Stimulation (Rancho Levels I and II)

At this stage, traumatically brain-injured children are in coma and not aware of what has happened. They are not aware of injury, hospitalization, or medical procedures. After severe injuries, children usually do not look at all like themselves since their physical appearance has been altered by the direct effects of injury (e.g., bruising), brain swelling, surgery (sometimes including shaved hair), and multiple tubes and machines to control breathing, feeding, urination, and monitoring of medical status. Their bodies may also be contorted by abnormal posturing and need to be managed carefully to prevent contractures and bedsores. Their level of response is markedly impaired. They either appear to be in deep sleep (Level I) or demonstrate vague, generalized reactions such as moving their bodies on the bed, making some sounds, or reacting with grimaces or generalized discomfort to pain (Level II).

In contrast, the family is in an acute period of crisis and grief, with the once normal, healthy child's life and future threatened. Family life is completely disrupted and revolves almost totally around the injured child, the hospital, and interactions with medical personnel. Parents often live at the hospital during this period as they literally wait and hope hour by hour. They may be told that it is not clear if their child will survive, and if so, whether the child will ever be the same. Parents are often overwhelmed by their inability to have protected their child from injury and to make him or her recover. This is intensified if they were directly involved in the accident; they may then be overcome by guilt. If they were not involved in the accident, they may be consumed by anger at whomever they hold responsible for their child's injury. This is especially the case when the child has been a victim of someone else's behavior, such as children who are hit by drunk drivers, injured in hit-and-run accidents, or supervised by other people. Parents often make psychological bargains either with God or themselves to ensure their child's survival.

The other children in the family are often cared for by relatives or family friends, with disruption in their lives as well. It is not unusual for other children in the family to have been involved in the accident, either as passengers in the car, as fellow pedestrians, or as observers. They can

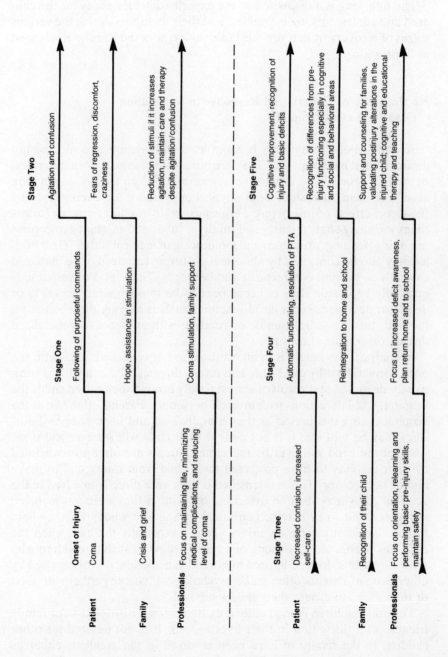

Stage One

Onset of Injury

Patient — Coma — Following of purposeful commands

Family — Crisis and grief — Hope, assistance in stimulation

Professionals — Focus on maintaining life, minimizing medical complications, and reducing level of coma — Coma stimulation, family support

Stage Two

Patient — Agitation and confusion

Family — Fears of regression, discomfort, craziness

Professionals — Reduction of stimuli if it increases agitation, maintain care and therapy despite agitation/confusion

Stage Three

Patient — Decreased confusion, increased self-care

Family — Recognition of their child

Professionals — Focus on orientation, relearning and performing basic pre-injury skills, maintain safety

Stage Four

Automatic functioning, resolution of PTA

Reintegration to home and school

Focus on increased deficit awareness, plan return home and to school

Stage Five

Cognitive improvement, recognition of injury and basic deficits

Recognition of differences from pre-injury functioning especially in cognitive and social and behavioral areas

Support and counseling for families, validating postinjury alterations in the injured child; cognitive and educational therapy and teaching

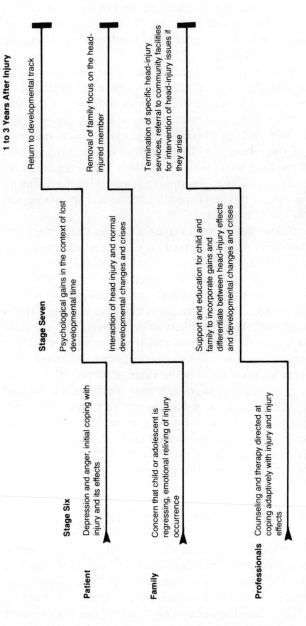

1 to 3 Years After Injury

Stage Seven

Patient — Return to developmental track

Psychological gains in the context of lost developmental time

Family — Removal of family focus on the head-injured member

Interaction of head injury and normal developmental changes and crises

Professionals — Termination of specific head-injury services, referral to community facilities for intervention of head-injury issues if they arise

Support and education for child and family to incorporate gains and differentiate between head-injury effects and developmental changes and crises

Stage Six

Patient — Depression and anger, initial coping with injury and its effects

Family — Concern that child or adolescent is regressing, emotional reliving of injury occurrence

Professionals — Counseling and therapy directed at coping adaptively with injury and injury effects

Figure 2-1 Recovery and coping process

experience extreme fear, guilt, and stress but do not have their parents to rely on to help them handle these feelings. At the same time, they are often expected to continue with their normal activities of going to school, doing their homework, and being with their friends. They may also not be able to visit their injured brother or sister and therefore may not really believe that their sibling is still alive.

Primary concerns for the medical personnel caring for the child are to maintain life, minimize complications of injury, carry out appropriate treatment, and reduce the level of coma. It is extremely difficult for medical personnel, especially in intensive care units, to manage both the complex medical needs of the child and the overwhelming psychological needs of the family. Because of this, there may be periods of strained interaction between parents and medical staff, with accusations and complaints on both sides. Involvement of psychosocial support personnel is critical during this period, whether provided by the hospital social worker, psychologist, chaplain, or the family's own minister.

If children remain in deep coma for a prolonged period after they are medically stable, they usually are transferred either to a regular pediatric unit or to a rehabilitation unit. At this time, ongoing therapies should be initiated, especially involving physical and occupational therapists and sometimes therapists who specialize in stimulation techniques to reduce the depth of coma. The longer the child remains in coma, the more strain these therapists are under since they are likely to be involved with the child and family on a daily basis. The therapists can feel very drained by the need to contain and respond to the family's fears of poor outcome. Both the family and the therapists may question the value of therapy if the child does not progress quickly, and the therapists may feel that this lack of recovery is somehow their fault. In a positive way, the family may experience considerable support from the daily contact and concern of their child's treating therapists. However, the shared grief may be particularly difficult for therapists to tolerate day in and day out if they are working with children who are demonstrating little change.

Localized Response to Stimulation (Rancho Level III)

During this period, children begin to react specifically, but very inconsistently, to stimuli in a predictable manner. That is to say, how they will respond is predictable, but they do not respond every time. They demonstrate this by turning their heads to sounds around them, focusing on objects presented to them, looking at people close to them, and visually following people around the room. If medical procedures involve pain and discomfort, such as insertion of needles for blood samples, only the affected arm or leg is pulled away (in contrast with the generalized, nonspecific response to pain at the previous level). Similarly restraints, nasogastric tubes, and catheters may be pulled at and sometimes pulled out. However, this is usually not done purposefully or with awareness of the outcome but more as a reaction to removing a source of discomfort. The emergence of consistent following of simple commands, even though in a delayed manner, is usually seen as the end of the period of deep coma. It is important, though, not to confuse reflexive movements with purposeful responses and to give commands in such a way that the child has the ability to respond. For example, if head-injured children are physically unable to control their arms, they are not able to squeeze someone's hand when told to, not because of inability to understand the command but because of their physical impairment. Giving commands that can be responded to through eye, mouth, or leg and foot movements may alleviate this difficulty. Children who are aphasic after injury and therefore cannot understand what has been said to them may not be able to respond to verbal commands and yet be beyond the period of deep coma. Purposeful imitation of actions may provide some indication of their abilities to respond to nonverbal stimuli despite their speech and language impairments.

For families, this is the beginning of hope that their children may indeed not only survive but recover. However, this is mixed with profound fears that their children may not progress further. Parents may begin to question whether they can live with their head-injured children if they never get any better. Since children at this level may respond and react more strongly and consistently for familiar people than for strangers, parents often see better and more consistent responses than do medical personnel.

As the children begin to show improvements, comparisons to preinjury appearance and functioning are often quite poignant for their therapists, physicians, and caretakers. Medical staff are often quite aware of how far the children need to progress before they will look like the photographs their parents have brought in and act as their parents have described them before injury. The therapists' role is that of a realistic pessimist, both to hope with the family but also to provide as objective as possible a picture of the child's progress and limitations. It is especially important for the family and the therapists to see the child together because of the differential response the child often has to familiar people. This can allay differences in perception of the child's responsiveness and reduce a sense of competitiveness between the family and staff as to who can stimulate the child more effectively.

Emergence of Agitation and Confusion (Rancho Level IV)

During this period, the level of the children's agitation increases markedly, with flailing around in bed, screaming, crying out, swearing, hitting out, attempting to remove restraints or tubes, and crawling out of bed in what appears to be a purposeful manner. Reactions may be out of proportion to what appears to cause them and may continue even after attempts have been made to make the children more comfortable. Because speech often re-emerges during this period, children's behavior may be seen as more purposeful than it is. However, the content of children's language usually makes it clear how confused they are. Since children often recover physically quite quickly, they also may be able to reach out, sit, and even walk at this stage without any awareness of where they are or what they are doing. In addition, they are not able to perform self-care activities reliably, even such routine tasks as eating independently, dressing, or toileting. Both their behaviors and verbalizations are often bizarre, often in reaction to internal confusion and not necessarily in response to what is going on around them.

If family members are not prepared to expect a period of agitation and confusion, they can interpret it as regression rather than progress. It can then be even more painful to see their children in such apparent distress with little success in being able to control or comfort them. Parents can also be fearful that their children have become crazy or psychotic because of their confused verbal ramblings and bizarre behavior. It is important for parents to be told that their children are not aware of what they are doing and are likely to remember little of this period afterward.

The child's agitation presents constant difficulties for medical and therapeutic management, as well as for maintenance of basic safety. Nasogastric tubes must be frequently replaced, only to be pulled out again. Diapers may be used instead of catheters in attempts to reduce stimulation that could exacerbate agitation. Stimulation of all kinds must be reduced, which can be a difficult thing to do in a noisy, brightly lit, busy hospital. Alternatives, such as a Craig bed (a mattress on the floor with high solid foam walls around it), may be used to restrain the child more safely than tying down and with no risk of falling out of bed. Because of the child's high agitation level and inability to cooperate, attend, or remember, the wear and tear on the medical staff and therapists can be extremely tiring and frustrating. After being hit or sworn at for days in a row, it can be difficult for therapists to remember that a child is not aware of those actions.

Continuing Confusion with Inappropriate but Non-Agitated Behavior (Rancho Level V)

Agitation usually does not diminish all at once but may continue to be present at specific times (especially during the evening or at night) or occur directly in response to external circumstances. However, in general, children at this level appear attentive and are able to respond to structured, simple requests fairly consistently. Even though attention is more adequate, children are easily distracted by irrelevant details and need to be continually redirected back to tasks. For example, head-injured children at this stage may focus on an adult's jewelry, shoes, or a picture on the wall, rather than on what they were asked. If requests are too complex for the children to handle or the situation is unstructured, nonpurposeful, random, and fragmented behavior reappears.

Children at this level function most adequately in response to their body needs, familiar people, places, and activities. They may be able to perform such self-care activities as toileting, feeding, and personal hygiene. However, their performance of self-care activities may not be consistent, and unusual behavior may occur with any change of setting. For example, children may use the bathroom appropriately on the nursing unit but urinate on the floor in a therapy room. Memory continues to be severely limited, both for previous life events and for what is occurring on a daily basis. Because of this, new learning and new information is usually not incorporated; this includes remembering what has happened to them, why they need to stay in the hospital, and sometimes even the fact that they are in the hospital. Children at this level are often able to talk quite well and do so frequently. The content of what they say may appear to be well oriented and appropriate but is usually only so for more stereotypic comments, such as over-learned social exchanges (greetings). Less-structured, prolonged conversations can be quite unusual, confused, perseverative, and even bizarre.

With the abating of agitation, parents' hopes that their children will be all right increase. If parents are alerted that confusion will begin to appear and that their children may not make sense or may disagree with what they say, parental fears of their children becoming crazy diminishes. During this period, parents usually first report that their children are beginning to act and behave like themselves. Often this does not mean that they are at the same level as before injury but that their general style of relating and reacting is typical of them. Parents may be quite struck by the similarity of their children's present behavior to that when they were considerably younger. Since behavior during confusion is often quite humorous (though unintentionally so) and the family is feeling so relieved, a tendency to reward or play into inappropriate behavior should be avoided.

Therapy at this time focuses on relearning and performing previously mastered activities. Because of severe memory limitations, children at this level are not able to master new learning, which may include remembering therapists' names and activities completed just minutes ago. Safety needs become critical, especially with children who are ambulatory and who on a surface level appear to be more oriented than they are. They may require 24-hour supervision because of the combination of their rapidly improving physical abilities and their significantly reduced memory and judgment. Even though children at this level can often state their needs, they may be confused and perserverative. For example, they may insist that they have not eaten when they have just finished a meal and that they have to go to the bathroom when they have gone every 10 minutes for the past hour. Due to their cognitive limitations, reasoning with children at this level of recovery is usually not successful, but redirection is often surprisingly easy and effective since they can be so easily distracted.

Therapists often have a dual role at this time. The first is to work with the child around reorientation and relearning of previously mastered activities. The second is to work with the family on recognizing their child's present limitations, as well as to teach them to redirect and supervise their child. At this time, conflicts between staff and family can escalate around issues of management and understanding the children's level of functioning. Therapists often perceive the parents as underestimating the children's deficits and overestimating their capacities, with the fear that parents will not adequately supervise their children. Parents may feel that the therapists are being overly cautious and are trying to tell them how to raise their children. Being able to share both the pleasure of having the children continue to improve and strategies to manage their unusual behavior at this stage usually helps to limit the polarization of family and staff that can begin to emerge. It is also the time to initiate discussion about discharge planning and home management, with frequent visits home for those children in rehabilitation programs. Gradually the primary care for the children again returns to their parents, with reduction in the comprehensive responsibility the staff and therapists have temporarily assumed.

If head-injured children have been cared for solely in an acute-care hospital, they may be sent home at this level since primary medical care is often no longer necessary. There may be the feeling among acute-care staff that the children will do better at home than in the hospital. Although this may be accurate, it can also be extremely overwhelming for the family to take traumatically brain-injured children home during this period, especially if they do not understand what is happening and how to manage their children's confused, unusual behavior. Even rehabilitation hospitals, which may be more oriented to physical disabilities, may have difficulty justifying continued hospitalization. However, children at this level are often unsafe and certainly unable to resume their activities at home and at school.

Continuing Confusion but Emergence of Appropriate Behavior (Rancho Level VI)

Until this period, improvements in all areas have often been extremely rapid with changes evident on a daily or weekly basis in many children, even those who have been relatively severely injured and are experiencing good recoveries. However, from this stage on, improvements are usually more subtle and prolonged, though they continue to be more rapid than the pace of normal development if progress persists.

With continuing improvement, children begin to behave in a more appropriate manner. They are more consistently aware of their basic needs and can attend to them more reliably. Preinjury memories begin to reemerge, though they are usually somewhat patchy. Reminders from family members about past events are often effective in reviving old memories. Recent memory also begins to improve, as the children consistently recognize familiar staff and remember the kinds of activities in different therapies. However, children may deny that they have been in the hospital for very long and may state that they have only been receiving therapy for a few days rather than the actual period of weeks or longer. Explanations of what happened to them and why they are in the hospital begin to be incorporated and can be remembered from day to day. Often, recall of the specifics of the accident and injury is limited to factual information with little emotional impact or reaction. Short-term memory impairments continue to be very apparent, especially in learning situations. New information can be mastered with significant repetition and specific focusing of attention. However, learning usually does not generalize to new situations or people and deteriorates quickly in unstructured settings. Because children are beginning to take control of their own behavior but have severe difficulties anticipating consequences, learning from errors, and monitoring their effect on others, approaches to teaching and behavior management must be limited to immediate contingencies.

Although parents continue to be pleased with their children's progress, they may also begin to be more aware of the impairments and differences from preinjury functioning and behavior. They have usually been able to see differences in how their children function at home, with their friends, and in public. However, their children or adolescents are usually very unaware of their own deficits and the need for increased parental supervision. Head-injured children and adolescents during this stage are often quite adamant that nothing is wrong and that they can go home and resume their usual activities. Because of this, it may be increasingly difficult to convince them to continue in therapy, to remain in a rehabilitation program, and in general to reason with them. Redirection, which had been surprisingly effective before, now becomes less so, and arguments can become more frequent and prolonged. Since the children are not able to reason clearly, somewhat unlikely rationales may make sense to them. For example, one adolescent was convinced to remain in a rehabilitation program when told that if he did not return to the hospital after a weekend pass, his parents would have to pay for his hospitalization rather than the insurance company. Parents may also be surprised and possibly even relieved at the usually unemotional way that their children react to learning about their injuries and accidents. It is very important that parents know that this matter-of-fact reaction is actually part of their children's inability to understand the implications of their injuries and to be aware of cognitive and behavioral changes, and that it is directly related to their stage of traumatic brain injury recovery.

For therapists this is a difficult period to keep children and adolescents involved in therapeutic activities. Confrontation often needs to be utilized with the children or adolescents since they insist that they are just fine and are quite unaware of even the immediate effects of their injuries. Since children and adolescents at this stage do not realize why they continue to need services and are often quite resistant, therapists usually need to take the responsibility for continued intervention. Therapists have the tricky role of confronting the children with their deficits and yet at the same time allying with the children against the deficits, of having the children directly experience their deficits and yet not overwhelming them by frustration and failure. It is important that the children and adolescents understand that the head-injury effects are the enemy, not the therapists or their parents. This is the time to establish a close personal relationship with the children and recognize their emerging strengths and personalities without overlooking deficits. Emotional lability and confusion may need to be dealt with directly.

Automatic, Appropriate Behavior (Rancho Level VII)

As overt confusion abates, head-injured children and adolescents are increasingly more oriented in all settings and in general behave appropriately. Their daily routine is performed with little difficulty, and they can care for most if not all of their self-care needs independently. Interest in preinjury activities re-emerges and can be self-initiated. For example, children and adolescents can again become excited about planning to go to a party, decide which movie they would like to see, remember their favorite music performers, and prefer some friends over others. However, deficits are noticeable in more complex cognitive and social areas. Learning is usually slow and tedious, though the children themselves may continue to have little awareness of this. Understanding of rapid social interchanges or jokes may be significantly limited, with misinterpretations of other's behavior and conversation. Insight, planning, and handling of unexpected situations are impaired, though not recognized as such by the children.

Almost all children and adolescents at this level are at home and are returning to some kind of school setting. However, their teachers and community-based therapists are often ill-prepared for managing the complex cognitive, behavioral, social, and emotional needs of those in the acute phases of recovery after traumatic brain injury. Head-injured children's and adolescent's specific impairments in information processing, memory, fatigue, behavioral control, and social interaction are frequently apparent in school and community settings. Even if these deficits are transitory, as in mild head injuries, they are often misperceived as intentional and characteristic of the individual, rather than as expected impairments subsequent to injury. This is especially confusing for school teachers since these invisible and subtle sequelae often coexist with surprisingly good physical recovery and often better-preserved overlearned academic skills. Therefore, intervention at this stage must involve school and community personnel, especially focused on educating them about the effects and management of children and adolescents after head injuries.

For the families of the children and adolescents, this may start as a relatively placid period with the feeling that life is beginning to resemble normality. Their children are living at home, interacting with their friends, and attending school. However, parents may gradually or quickly realize that things are not going so well. Their children may not be doing well in school, with teacher reports of behavioral and learning difficulties. Friends may begin to drift away, even if they have persisted up to this point, as they are confused by changes in the head-injured children and adolescents. The need for continued close supervision for safety reasons is apparent as judgment difficulties are enacted in everyday life. This can become extremely important with adolescents who recently began to drive before injury or become eligible for their licenses shortly after injury. Because their children and adolescents are usually still somewhat unaware of their deficits, parents can become frustrated with attempting to control their child's behavior and trying to counteract their child's arguments that "there's nothing wrong with me." Support for families is critical during this period, as is preparation for the emotional stresses that usually follow.

Purposeful, Appropriate Behavior (Rancho Level VIII)

At this level, many of the overt cognitive deficits have improved significantly and allow the children and adolescents for the first time since injury to understand fully and therefore react emotionally to the impact of injury on their lives, both present and future. At this point, the Rancho levels end. However, there are several extremely important areas of change in social and emotional areas that are not covered in the Rancho levels since they focus primarily on stages of cognitive improvement.

Postacute Period (beyond Rancho)

This period is actually an extremely critical one, especially for older children and adolescents, since during this time they begin to understand, grieve, and cope with the experience of traumatic brain injury. This delay in the emotional reaction to injury and the ability to deal with its effects is one of the primary differences between traumatic brain injuries and other traumatic injuries and illnesses. Even though head-injured children and adolescents have usually made striking improvements in all areas of functioning, usually only at this point do they have the capacity to understand and react to the possible sequelae, the changes in their lives, and the developmental time they have lost because of their traumatic brain injuries. Although they are functioning better than they have at any time since injury, they also are often more aware, angry, and depressed about having been injured and altered.

It is possible to conceive of this process as consisting of a series of phases of its own, similar to the Rancho levels for cognitive recovery. Initially a period of acute emotional distress occurs with the emerging ability to self-monitor postinjury changes. This distress is multidimensional and affects many areas of functioning. It is often in reaction to the awareness of persisting subtle cognitive processing and memory impairments with resulting frustration that learning and performance cannot be completed as effortlessly and successfully as before injury. A sense of not being oneself pervades, not only in cognitive areas but also in social and personality areas, with a loss of self-confidence and increased dependence on others.

Even though these changes are more easily recognized at this stage, they are usually heartily resented.

Gradually children and adolescents confront the reality of injury and its impact on their lives, daily functioning, and their future. If they can tolerate this confrontation, are able to adjust to postinjury changes, and constructively handle them, then they are better able to adapt in ways that further their development and compensation for persisting impairments. If not, their development may be stymied, with continued difficulties in personal adjustment, school and vocational participation, and interpersonal relationships. Because of the nature of development in childhood and adolescence, the process of working through the emotional reaction to injury and adapting to injury sequelae may be more prolonged than in adults and may re-emerge during developmental transitions.

Parents of children and adolescents who have had head injuries are often quite aware of the changes that they have undergone. Although they rarely report that their children's personalities have altered, parents are likely to perceive that their children's behavior and other people's reactions to them have altered subsequent to injury. Both parents and siblings are usually aware of the impact of injury before the head-injured children or adolescents themselves. This may reawaken fears that the injured child may never quite be the same, as well as stimulate strong feelings of grief to re-emerge. There is the sense that subtle deficits continue to surface and a fear that the negative changes will never end. In addition to handling their own feelings, during this period the children and adolescents themselves begin to experience fully the integration of cognitive understanding of postinjury changes and the subsequent emotional reaction. If family members are not prepared for both the changes in their own emotional reactions and the emergence of their children's emotional reactions, they can perceive this period as a time of crisis and regression. The focus of therapeutic work with the family is to increase the family's sense of control, both by giving an understanding of what is occurring and specific guidelines for managing their children's behavior and emotional reaction. The eventual goal is to reconstitute the family gradually without having the head-injured children or adolescents be the focus forever.

Unfortunately few professional resources or programs are designed for head-injured children, adolescents, and their families at this stage. This contrasts with resources available for head-injured adults. A relatively large network of such postacute services and programs has expanded rapidly in recent years; they are geared specifically for intervention of the longer-term cognitive, social, vocational, and emotional needs. Children and their families usually must rely on existing educational and mental health services whose staff may not be aware of the unique characteristics of children and adolescents after traumatic brain injuries.

In summary, the measurement of injury severity for traumatic brain injuries occurring in the developmental period is a more complex endeavor than for adults. All current measurement approaches have significant limitations, especially when they are applied to the youngest age groups. However, there is considerable clinical experience available to guide the development of useful, reliable approaches for assessing injury severity in infants, children, and adolescents. Clinical experience is also essential in helping to make the process of traumatic brain injury recovery and improvement more understandable for the head-injured children and adolescents, their families, and the medical and community professionals who work with them. Awareness of this process can reduce the level of stress and perceived crisis that often complicates work with these children and their families.

REFERENCES

Alexander, M.P. (1982). Traumatic brain injury. In F. Benton & D. Blumer (Eds.), *Psychiatric aspects of neurologic disease, Vol. II.* New York: Grune & Stratton.

Annegers, J.F. (1983). The epidemiology of head trauma in children. In K. Shapiro (Ed.), *Pediatric head trauma.* Mt. Kisco, NY: Futura Publishing Co.

Brink, J.D., Garrett, A.L., Hale, W.R., Woo-Sam, J., & Nickel, V.L. (1970). Recovery of motor and intellectual function in children sustaining severe head injuries. *Developmental Medicine and Child Neurology, 12*(5), 565–571.

Ewing-Cobbs, L., Levin, H.S., Fletcher, J.M., Miner, M.E., & Eisenberg, H.M. (1989). Posttraumatic amnesia in head-injured children: Assessment and outcome. *Journal of Clinical and Experimental Neuropsychology, 11,* 58.

Goethe, K.E., & Levin, H.S. (1984). Neuropsychological consequences of head injury in children. In R. Tarter & G. Goldstein (Eds.), *Advances in clinical neuropsychology.* New York: Plenum Press.

Gouvier, W.D., Blanton, P.D., LaPorte, K.K., & Nepomuceno, C. (1987). Reliability and validity of the Disability Rating Scale and the Levels of Cognitive Functioning Scale in monitoring recovery from severe head injury. *Archives of Physical Medicine and Rehabilitation, 68,* 94–97.

Hagan, C., Malkmus, D., & Durham, P. (1979). Levels of cognitive functioning. *Rehabilitation of the head injured adult: Comprehensive physical management.* Downey, CA: Professional Staff Association of Rancho Los Amigos Hospital, Inc.

Hendrick, E.B., Harwood-Hash, D.C.F., & Hudson, A.R. (1964). Head injuries in children: A survey of 4465 consecutive cases at the Hospital for Sick Children, Toronto, Canada. *Clinical Neurosurgery, 11,* 46–65.

Jane, J.A., & Rimel, R.W. (1982). Prognosis in head injury. *Clinical Neurosurgery, 29,* 516–124.

Jennett, B. (1976). Assessment of the severity of head injury. *Journal of Neurology, Neurosurgery, and Psychiatry, 39,* 647–655.

Jennett, B., and Teasdale, G. (1981). *Management of head injuries.* Philadelphia: F.A. Davis Co.

Klonoff, H. (1971). Head injuries in children: Predisposing factors, accident conditions, accident proneness, and sequelae. *American Journal of Public Health, 61*(12), 2405–2417.

Klonoff, H., & Low, M. (1974). Disordered brain function in young children and early adolescents: Neuropsychological and electroencephalographic correlates. In R.M. Reitan & L.A. Davison (Eds.), *Clinical neuropsychology: Current status and applications* (pp. 121–178). New York: John Wiley & Sons.

Levin, H.S., & Eisenberg, H.N. (1979). Neuropsychological outcome of closed head injury in children and adolescents. *Child's Brain, 5,* 281–289.

Levin, H.S., O'Donnell, V.M., & Grossman, R.G. (1979). The Galveston Orientation and Amnesia Test: A practical scale to assess cognition after head injury. *Journal of Nervous and Mental Disorders, 167,* 675–684.

Raimondi, A.J., & Hirschauer, J. (1984). Head injury in the infant and toddler. *Child's Brain, 11,* 12–35.

Rappaport, M., Hall, K.M., Hopkins, K., Belleza, T., & Cope, D.N. (1982). Disability Rating Scale for severe head trauma: Coma to community. *Archives of Physical Medicine and Rehabilitation, 63,* 118–123.

Rutter, M., Chadwick, O., Shaffer, D., & Brown, G. (1980). A prospective study of children with head injuries: I. Design and methods. *Psychological Medicine, 10,* 633–645.

Shapiro, K. (1985). Head injury in children. In D.P. Becker & J.T. Povlishock (Eds.), *Central nervous system status report, 1985.* Bethesda, MD: National Institute of Neurological and Communicative Disorders and Stroke, National Institutes of Health.

Teasdale, G., Knill-Jones, R., & Van Der Sande, J. (1978). Observer variability in assessing impaired consciousness and coma. *Journal of Neurology, Neurosurgery, and Psychiatry, 41,* 603–610.

Teasdale, G., & Jennett, B. (1974). Assessment of coma and impaired consciousness: A practical scale. *Lancet, 2,* 81–84.

Zimmerman, R.A., & Bilanuik, L.T. (1981). Computed tomography in pediatric head trauma. *Journal of Neuroradiology, 6,* 257–271.

Chapter 3

A Developmental Perspective

Ellen Lehr

INTRODUCTION

In Chapter 2, recovery or improvement from traumatic brain injury in children and adolescents is described not as a static event but as a process that occurs over an extended period lasting at least several months and sometimes as long as several years. Head injury in children can actually be conceptualized as one process imposed on another process. That is, the process of recovery or improvement is imposed on the ongoing process of development. This chapter focuses on the process of development as it is affected by traumatic brain injury in infants, children, and adolescents.

Surprisingly little research and even clinical work with head-injured children and adolescents proceeds from a developmental base. Part of this is understandable in that the information from developmental and clinical child psychology has not been integrated with the effects of acquired neurological injury. Since most of the research and clinical experience in the area of traumatic brain injury has dealt with adults, it is difficult not to rely heavily on this accumulation of knowledge when dealing with children and adolescents. However, the findings from work with adults cannot necessarily be directly applied to children and adolescents. Not only are children qualitatively unlike adults, their brain organization, structure, and function are known to be quantitatively different. The effects of head injury in children, whose brains are at varying stages of development, cannot be assumed to be the same as in the adult, nor indeed of children at different periods of development. Even the mechanisms of injury and the effects of injury on the developing brain have been shown to be both similar and different than in the adult brain (Boll & Barth, 1981). These effects, though, are not necessarily well understood, especially for infants and young children.

Interestingly, age effects of traumatic head injuries have rarely been the focus of study during the rapid developmental periods of infancy through adolescence. To clarify the effects of age, not only does the age at injury need to be considered but also the relationship of age to speed of recovery, to patterns of deficits, and to the ultimate extent of impairments in all areas of functioning including cognitive and learning aspects, as well as behavioral, psychosocial, and emotional aspects.

This chapter attempts to integrate developmental knowledge from a variety of perspectives including developmental neurology and neurophysiology, developmental psychology, and clinical child psychology in order to understand more fully the children who have been injured, the effect on them at the time of injury, and the possible disruption of their further development. To keep the children and adolescents at the forefront, case presentations are incorporated, utilizing a longitudinal focus as much as possible. Drawings by children and adolescents who have sustained head injuries are used to illustrate how they perceive themselves and understand what has happened to them.

GENERAL CONCEPTS

Differences between Adult and Child Injuries

The comparability of injuries in adults and children has been questioned, even when using somewhat objective measures like the Glasgow Coma Scale (Levin, Ewing-Coggs, & Benton, 1984). Much of the work with adults has involved focal, open-head injuries, especially those sustained by soldiers in combat. However, even with closed-head injuries related to acceleration and deceleration effects, adults and children may react differently. The presentation of head injury in the emergency room setting can be quite different with children. They are more likely to be conscious, even after severe injury. In one study, only 3% of children showed alteration in consciousness, but 8% had historical, physical, or x-ray evidence of significant head injury (Shapiro, 1983). Children may initially show little change in neurological functioning despite severe injury, such as bleeding in their brain, only to deteriorate quickly to the point of a medical emergency.

The response of the brain to traumatic injury in children also has some unique characteristics. Cerebral swelling is more frequent, and bleeding within the brain (intracranial hematomas) is less frequent in pediatric than adult injuries (Zimmerman & Bilaniuk, 1981). The mechanism of brain swelling appears to be related to increased blood volume, rather than to tissue swelling or edema (Bruce, Alavi, Bilaniuk, Dolinskas, Obrist, Zimmerman, & Uzzell, 1981). The young child's more flexible skull bones may enhance the capacity of the skull to absorb traumatic forces and reduce the likelihood of focal bleeding (Craft, Shaw, & Cartlidge, 1972; Gurdjian & Webster, 1958). In general, traumatic brain injuries in children have more diffuse effects, especially on the white matter or nerve fibers, and less focal effects subsequent to bleeding in the brain than injuries in adults. There is growing evidence that children exhibit more severe acute neurological dysfunction after injury and may need less impact at the time of injury to cause similar neurological effects as in adults (Bruce, Schut, Bruno, Wood, & Sutton, 1978). However, despite the possibility of a grave acute neurological condition after injury, children also have a relatively favorable prognosis for survival. This may be attributed to diffuse injury sparing some parts of many systems allowing for the residual parts to mediate greater recovery (Kolb & Whishaw, 1985).

Medical effects may also show developmental variation across the pediatric age range. Most of these are not well delineated and may only be suspected. The data available on differential age effects in seizures after injury can be useful as an illustration (Black, Shepard, & Walker, 1975). Only about 5% of children after head injuries experience seizures, most commonly after a relatively severe injury. The overall incidence of early seizures in children appears to be considerably higher than in adults, but the late occurrence of seizures in children appears to be lower than in adults. However, this pattern does not hold throughout the entire developmental period. Instead infants (up to 2 years of age) show a low incidence of early seizures but a relatively high incidence of late onset seizures. This is the reverse of the pattern in older children (2 to 15 years of age) but is quite similar to the adult pattern. Children younger than 5 years of age seem to require only a relatively mild injury to be at risk for post-traumatic seizures, which often develop into persistent epilepsy (Boll, 1984). This example makes it clear that the effects of head injury in children should not be assumed to be the same across the entire developmental age span. It also illustrates the complexity of trying to compare the effects of head injuries in adults with head injuries in children.

Brain Development

The immature brain continually demonstrates both structural and biochemical changes throughout the developmental age span (Bolter & Long, 1985). The actual formation of brain cells stops early, probably before the end of the second year of life. However, the brain increases in weight by about 25% after that age (Friede, 1975). This increase in weight is related to several processes that aid in increases in the efficient, more complex neurological functioning during development. Axons and dendrites, the projections that connect nerve cells together, extend and branch into more complex configurations that bridge each other more efficiently across synapses (Jacobson, 1978). This increases the ability of nerve cells to communicate more directly with each other, as well as to integrate functioning within different areas of the brain. The axons, or "wires" of the brain cells, gradually become more efficient at carrying messages as they become myelinated or covered with a fatty insulation. The process of myelinization begins before birth and continues in different parts of the brain during specific periods of development at least through the late adolescent and early adult years. The developing brain generally increases in energy and materials brought through increased blood supply from the heart. All of these processes contribute to the greater complexity and speed of connections between nerve cells, leading to more complex and reliable neural networks and more efficient brain functioning.

In general, cortical maturation processes correlate well with overall functional changes and parallel the gradual emergence and refinement of cognitive and motor capabilities (Bronson, 1982). However, despite what is known about continuing brain development during childhood, it is difficult if not impossible to draw a direct relationship between complex behaviors and changes in neural functioning. The maturational pattern is complex, occurs at different levels within the brain, and varies both within and across the right and left hemispheres. The whole concept becomes more complex when the mutual interaction between the development of brain structures and behavior is recognized. That is, brain development does not simply occur in an internally driven way but is reliant on the experience of learning and environmental stimulation (Gottlieb, 1976).

Luria (1966, 1980), a Russian neuropsychologist, was instrumental in conceptualizing stages of brain development and the ways in which injuries sustained at different times might result in different patterns of functional deficits. His theory proposes 5 stages of neuropsychological development that correspond to the emergence of functioning in different areas of the brain. The first stage normally occurs before and shortly after birth and involves the maturation of those areas of the brain that regulate arousal and attention. The brain is most vulnerable to damage during the perinatal period, when it is being formed. The second stage occurs concurrently with the first and involves basic sensory (visual, tactile, and auditory perception) and motor functioning. These areas are highly specific for the tasks they perform, and behaviors mediated by them appear to have had some survival function. Stage 3 begins early in life and continues through the preschool period. It involves the development of the unimodal association areas and the secondary areas of the cortex and allows for such capacities as coordinated movement, visual and auditory recognition and discrimination, and the association of spoken words as symbols for objects.

During Stage 4 the posterior area of the brain that links basic perception of visual, auditory, and tactile sensations develops. This does not occur until approximately 5 to 8 years of age and is responsible for the integration of information allowing for activities involved in learning such as reading, arithmetic, understanding of complex grammatical structures, reasoning with analogies, and categorizing. Damage to this area limits academic learning and much of what we traditionally perceive as intelligence. The fifth stage of development involves maturation and elaboration of the prefrontal area of the brain, or what is commonly known as the *frontal lobes*. This area is the last to develop, probably not beginning until late childhood or adolescence, and is the most vulnerable to damage. It has rich and complex connections to the rest of the brain and is involved in activities related to the development of mature adult functioning such as intention, planning, evaluation of behavior, impulse control, and cognitive flexibility.

Luria proposed that the brain is organized into functional systems and that these systems vary and alter as brain development proceeds. A particular activity is completed in different ways, possibly utilizing different neural areas at different stages of development, even though the resulting behavior may appear to be the same.

Also, brain injuries in adults and children can be both different and similar. For example, similar patterns of deficits can arise in children and adults with different injuries, as well as the converse: different patterns of deficits can occur after similar injuries in children and adults (Luria, 1965). An illustration of this comes from research with monkeys (Goldman, 1974, 1978). In studies of how monkeys learn to complete delayed response tasks, two different age-related patterns emerged. Infant monkeys rely on subcortical parts of their brain in order to respond after a delay. After cortical structures mature, though, the involvement of subcortical structures diminishes. Therefore, the infant monkeys have more difficulty completing the delayed learning task after subcortical injuries, but the adult monkeys have more difficulty after cortical injuries.

Plasticity

Central to the understanding of the effects of injury on the developing brain and therefore the developing child is the concept of plasticity. Plasticity refers to the resilience of the brain and behavior and is conceived of as the ability to reorganize after injury or damage. However, this is a difficult and complex issue, not as simple as previously assumed (Rutter, 1982). According to the Kennard principle proposed from research findings with monkeys (Kennard, 1936, 1938, 1940, 1942), younger organisms recover better than older ones. That is, the earlier injury is sustained, the greater the sparing of abilities and the better the functional recovery. However, subsequent research and clinical work shows that the limits and role of plasticity in early brain damage are less clear and more contradictory than after the pioneering work of Kennard in the 1930s and 1940s (St. James Roberts, 1979; Satz & Fletcher, 1981).

Recent research has compiled evidence that a degree of plasticity does exist in the developing brain to a greater extent than in adults, but it has also shown the limits of this plasticity. The concept of plasticity relies on the theory that the developing brain is less committed to specific functions than the adult brain. That is, if an area of the brain is functionally immature, it is more plastic than an area that is already mature and committed to a specific function (Goldman, 1971; Hecaen & Albert, 1978). An area that is plastic is assumed to be able to take over from a damaged or destroyed area. However, of primary importance is the finding that even in infants, certain areas of the brain may already be committed to specific functions and that not all areas of the brain are able to do all things. Kinsbourne (1974) has proposed an additional limitation: sometimes partial damage can be more deleterious than complete destruction in terms of other brain areas being able to take over function. He has theorized that the genetically dominant hemisphere for a particular function cannot assert itself in the presence of competition from the hemisphere originally slated to control that function, even if that hemisphere is partially damaged (Boll & Barth, 1981).

The amount of sparing or plasticity depends on a variety of factors, including the age of the child at injury, the age at which the function appears in the normal course of development (critical periods), injury size and location, and prior and subsequent experience. There are usually qualifications about the level and degree of functional ability after injury even in young children who appear to have had sparing of function after damage. The original research done by Kennard with monkeys found that on follow-up those who received brain lesions as infants never acquired the expected motor precision of fingers and toes, even though they recovered gross motor abilities (Kennard, 1936). It is likely that early injuries may tend to leave elementary functions relatively intact while impairing the development of more complex aspects of performance. In general, this has been upheld by research findings with sparing least in evidence the more complex the function expected (Goldman, 1971; Hecaen & Albert, 1978). For example, young children experience sensory sparing after injury to a greater degree than adults (Rudel, 1978; Rudel, Teuber, & Twitchell, 1966). In fact, very young children may become hypersensitive to sensory input. However, the development and refinement of perceptual capacities that rely on sensory input and intactness are not spared (Rudel, Teuber, & Twitchell, 1974). Deficits gradually become more apparent as these abilities do not develop as expected. Similarly the capacity to speak appears to be spared to a great degree in children, but it cannot be assumed from this that these children's language abilities are equally spared (Kolb & Whishaw, 1985). (The work on recovery of language abilities after injury in children is further discussed in Chapter 5.)

Sparing also depends on the location and size of injury. There is less sparing of function after injuries affecting subcortical areas of the brain, that is, those areas that develop the earliest, than with injury to cortical or later maturing areas. With cortical injuries, the size of injury location may need to be larger in children to have similar effects after injury in adult years (Rutter, 1982). This is probably related to the developing brain being somewhat less localized in function than the mature adult brain. However, with large lesions the effects of injury are likely to be similar in children and adults.

From consideration of these factors, it makes sense that damage to the developing brain may result less in specific, circumscribed sensory or motor deficits as in adults but rather in global cognitive limitations (Pirozzolo & Papanicolaou, 1986). The long-term effects of injury at very young ages may be more, rather than less, severe, especially in more complex areas of functioning (Levin et al., 1984). The abilities needed for the development of intelligence in childhood are likely to be different from those needed for the retention of intelligence in adults. For this reason also, early injuries may have a less selective, more widespread and profound effect than injuries in adults (Hebb, 1942).

Interestingly there are contradictory findings from the work on effects of deprivation and neurological diseases in infants and young children with the research on recovery from injuries sustained at early ages (Rutter, 1982). Deprivation and illness effects have usually been found to be profound, leading to prolonged deficits with the youngest children affected the most severely. That deprivation alone, without evidence of damage, can lead to severe functional impairments stresses the sensitivity of the brain to environmental inadequacies and its limitations in terms of recovery (Rudel, 1978).

Depending on the nature of the injury and the age at which it was sustained, there are three possible patterns for the occurrence of functional deficits (Teuber & Rudel, 1962). First, deficits may be apparent soon after injury and then later disappear. This is attributed to one part of the brain that is not yet committed to the function it usually performs being able to take over for a damaged part. The drawback of this form of recovery is that it may lead to atypical neural connections, poor survival mechanisms, and deficits in a different area as parts of the brain are subsequently not available for the function they eventually should perform. Second, there may be deficits related to general effects of injury that are apparent at all ages. These have not been well explored but may consist of deficits such as slowing of reaction time, less efficient processing of language and other information, fatigue, and less adequate storage of information. This may be the price paid for takeover of function by a less direct, less competent neural substrate than the one genetically specified. Third, deficits may not appear after injury but gradually become apparent after a delay. This can occur in a variety of ways. The damaged structure itself may not be functionally mature and not utilized at the time injury occurs. However, when it is expected to be viable but is not able to support complex functioning, deficits are readily apparent. Other structures may also be able to mediate the function of the damaged area at least to a degree, but when functional requirements become more complex and demanding, their limitations may become noticeable.

Delayed Effects

The delayed appearance of cognitive, psychosocial, and emotional sequelae is unique to childhood. This is not only a component of recovery as it can be in adults but is an integral aspect of development. The effects of injury on higher problem-solving functioning in academic and psychosocial areas do not become apparent until the child is old enough for their expected appearance. However, it is not clear if any of these delayed effects can be avoided or ameliorated through early intervention. Since these delayed effects can sometimes become apparent long after the onset of injury, the psychological rehabilitation management of the head-injured child can be a long-term process extending over many years. From work with animals, the experience or training that an injured young individual receives may affect the level and degree of capacities that emerge as the brain matures (Goldman, 1976; Rudel, 1978). This has been demonstrated even though the young animals did not appear to be benefiting from training while it was occurring. However, those that did receive the training were able to develop higher-level abilities, while those animals that were similarly injured but did not receive training were not able to. This has obvious implications for the long-term management and education of children after head injuries at early ages.

SPECIFIC PERIODS OF DEVELOPMENT

The rest of this chapter focuses on specific periods of development divided into infancy and toddler years—birth to 3 years of age; preschool and kindergarten years—3 to 6 years of age; childhood—6 to 12 years of age; and adolescence—12 to 18 years of age. The neuroanatomical and neurodevelopmental aspects of normal development and how they are affected by injury are discussed for each developmental period. Normal developmental processes and emphases in the areas of learning, social, emotional, and behavioral functioning are briefly presented, especially in terms of how injury is understood by the child and how injury can either disrupt or alter development during each period. To illustrate each period, case studies are incorporated into each section.

The ability of the child to face and surmount various developmental tasks depends on such factors as physical maturation and functioning, cognitive and communicative capacities, behavioral mastery, and changing social and affective needs. In addition to these, the temperament or personality of the child as well as the characteristics and presence of the parents and family affects the attitudes and responses to injury.

Infants and Toddlers

Over the past 10 to 15 years, the perception of infants has undergone vast changes. Babies are no longer seen as completely helpless, noninteractive beings but as competent infants with more sophisticated visual, sensory, and discrimination abilities than previously believed (Stone, Smith, & Murphy, 1973). The interaction of infants and their parents is seen as much more of a two-way relationship from the beginning. There is considerably more respect for the specific characteristics that the infant brings to the relationship rather than a focus solely on what parents do with their babies.

The rapid growth and development in the first years of life in all areas have never ceased to amaze both parents and professionals. Over a relatively brief period, babies develop the ability to perceive, move, talk, think, and feel, and then actually do these things independently in their own unique way, literally at a pace that appears to lead to changes each day. Early development also appears to be especially closely integrated with sensory, motor, social, language, and emotional areas heavily dependent on each other.

But what if the infant suffers a traumatic brain injury? The causes of injury in infants and toddlers were covered in Chapter 1. To review briefly, the primary etiologies include falls, injuries to unrestrained children in motor vehicle accidents, and injuries related to child abuse.

Despite the widely held belief that the younger the child, the better the possibility of good recovery after traumatic head injury, infants and toddlers appear to be at exceptionally high risk both in terms of dying (mortality) and becoming disabled (morbidity) (Kaiser, Rudeberg, Fankhauser, & Zumbuhl, 1986). In fact, the prognosis for infants and toddlers younger than 2 years is less favorable than for children injured during the school-age years. This has been postulated to be related to the increased vulnerability of the brain during this period of rapid growth (Dobbing & Smart, 1974) when the skull sutures are open. It is particularly striking for infants injured before their first birthday—13.4% experience a poor recovery, compared with 4.9% of 2- and 3-year-olds (Raimondi & Hirschauer, 1984). Infants and toddlers also have a significantly higher risk of developing persistent, post-traumatic epilepsy than do older children (Black et al., 1975; Jennett, 1975). In a follow-up study of 120 infants after head injury, one-third had major sequelae and two-thirds were described as experiencing full recovery (Hoffman & Taecholarn, 1986). However, these were the only two classifications included, and the possibility of subtle or late emerging deficits does not appear to have been considered.

Why are infants and toddlers possibly more vulnerable to the effects of traumatic brain injury? From a developmental point of view, the infant is learning to perceive the environment through the senses (vision, hearing, touch), to act upon it (motor and language), to understand and learn to communicate with language, to understand the basic nature of relationships (both cognitive and emotional), to learn to act and interact within these relationships, and to develop a basic sense of self, as well as a sense of trust in caretakers. A traumatic brain injury can alter the basic ability of an infant to master any and all of these tasks. After a severe injury, the infant's sensory and motor capabilities may be significantly altered subsequent to impairments in vision, hearing, touch, and fine and gross motor functioning. Even after less-severe injuries, the infant's ability to attend to and comprehend the cognitive and emotional relationships that much of learning is dependent on may be altered and less efficient. These alterations may be quite subtle but apparent, especially to parents who may state that their baby does not react in the same way as before injury. At present, these alterations are better known clinically and do not appear to have been studied in a formal way, despite available research methods.

In comparison with infants with chronic illnesses, who often react with distress to discomfort and separation from their parents and familiar environments, infants after more significant brain injuries may appear somewhat impervious to changes or they react with distress on a generalized basis. This is especially so in the period shortly after onset of injury when the infants' level of consciousness has been altered and in the period of emergence from coma. The effects of separation at this time may be much more acutely felt by parents and family than by the infants. Because of the parents' often overwhelming feelings of guilt surrounding their babies' injury, maintaining their perception of competence in being able to care for and nurture their infant while recovering is essential.

The toddler period presents some special concerns and unique characteristics. There is probably no parent or caretaker who has not been seriously concerned about the potential or actual danger of injury to his or her toddler. Surviving the toddler years is literally surviving the ever-present threat of injury. It can be a period of great satisfaction in seeing a dependent infant become an independent mover, talker, and thinker, usually with a definite mind of one's own. However, it can also be a period of worry and constant supervision, with the lurking sense that no matter how carefully a toddler is watched, the possibility of injury is always present. This is not only a period of striving for autonomy but also a period of beginning constraints. A toddler continually tests capacities, indefatigably explores the world, and whole-heartedly tries out his or her ability to control and manipulate it (Kleinberg, 1982). At the same time, parents not only provide the safety for all of this to occur but also begin to place constraints on the toddler in terms of how to behave and what is allowed.

Traumatic brain injuries during the toddler period can interfere markedly with this process of developing individual competence and complying with beginning social constraints. After injury, toddlers may not have the energy, either physical or mental, to pursue the learning and exploration on all fronts characteristic of this period. Because of the effects of injury, toddlers may not be able to engage in active interaction with their environment and experience their previously emerging sense of control. They may not be able to run, climb, play with toys, go to the toilet, or feed themselves, either because of motor impairments or deficits in attention or cognition. Only after trying to encourage and create the energy and initiative, taken for granted and sometimes lamented during this period, can its significance in terms of developmental importance be appreciated. Toddlers often experience extreme distress when separated from their parents. While this is often painful for parents, it is also expected as an indication of their mutual special attachment. Parents are also most likely to be able to console their toddlers by being able to relate and talk in the way familiar to their own child, as well as being able to understand and interpret their child's needs and communications.

After a head injury, a toddler may demonstrate changes in behavior and functioning. The more predominant of these, such as alterations in the ability to walk, talk, or engage in play, may be particularly difficult for parents to tolerate since the appearance of these developmental milestones has been so anticipated and so satisfying. The more subtle changes in attention, activity level, and relating, even though they may be difficult to quantify, may be especially upsetting for parents and give rise to concern about the toddler's capacity to continue to learn and develop as they were before injury. For toddlers who recover remarkably well, significant alterations in their functioning may not be apparent, even after severe injuries. However, this cannot necessarily be assumed to mean that their development has not and will not undergo significant changes related to their traumatic brain injury.

Little is known about the long-term psychological effects in terms of cognitive abilities, behavioral control, social relatedness, or personality development after head injuries are sustained in the very early years of life. Severe damage to either the right or left hemisphere has been shown to interfere equally with speech, with usually only a temporary disruption of function (Alajouanine & Lhermitte, 1965). However, the long-term effect of injury on language development is not as positive (Dennis & Whitaker, 1976; Woods & Carey, 1979). If what is most vulnerable to traumatic brain injury is the capacity to learn rather than the loss of what has already been mastered, then very young children would be at the highest risk for extensive interference in their ability to proceed with learning and development. Even with those infants and toddlers who appear to recover well from significant head injuries, there may be generalized lowering of ability, rather than specific deficits. The long-term impact of mild injuries in young children is basically unknown at this time.

CASE STUDIES

In order to protect the privacy of the children and their families, the case study material presented in this chapter has been altered.

Andrew

Andy was 1 year old when he was injured as an unrestrained passenger in a motor vehicle accident. He sustained bruising to the brain stem, or lower part of the brain that controls many life sustaining functions, and mild brain swelling shortly after injury. As he began to move spontaneously, it became evident that he was less able to control the right side than the left side of his body. Five days after he was injured, Andy began to open his eyes and became agitated. At this time, the breathing tube was removed. Two weeks later he was admitted to the rehabilitation hospital. Although he was alert, Andy did not respond to his parents any differently than he did to hospital staff. He cried when he was uncomfortable and continued to have periods of agitation, but he was able to be calmed by being held and rocked. He did not respond to what he saw or heard and did not smile or babble.

Before his injury, Andy was described as a happy, bubbly child who was easy to care for. He had been able to walk, was learning to swim, responded to his name, and was beginning to say a few words ("ma-ma," "da-da," "bye-bye," "car").

During his rehabilitation admission, Andy gradually became more responsive. By the time of formal evaluation 3 months after injury, he was delightful and engaging. He frequently smiled and laughed, obviously enjoying interaction with his parents, staff, and other children on the unit. Andy especially enjoyed playing peek-a-boo and singing and clapping games. He enjoyed exploring and manipulating toys and had begun to babble and imitate a few words ("da-da" and "bye-bye"). Physically he was regaining function of his right arm and leg, which were more affected from his injury. He was able to hold toys in his right hand and was starting to creep while holding onto furniture or someone's hand.

On evaluation, with the Bayley Scales of Infant Development, Andy functioned overall at the 12-month level when he was 15 months of age. Even though he was beginning to jabber and imitate some words, this appeared to occur less spontaneously and less frequently than before his injury. However, he seemed to understand much of what was said to him and eagerly pointed to what he wanted. Andy especially enjoyed playing with and exploring toys. He liked putting small objects into containers and taking them out again but had difficulty persisting if he was expected to put in more than two or three and leave them in the container. His major areas of deficit were his reduced speech and reduced use of the right side of his body. However, he was making rapid gains, seemingly on a daily basis. He would clearly be able to continue to grow and learn, but his injury had obviously affected his present level of development and function. The overall effect of injury on his long-term development could not be determined at this time. In psychosocial areas, he appeared to have undergone remarkably little change and was an engaging, active child.

Christina

According to her parents, Christina was a bright, verbal child who before she was 2 years old could talk in full sentences, recite the alphabet, sing several nursery songs, and loved to have stories read to her. She was a cuddly child who often asked for hugs but who was also physically active and had a mind of her own. By the time of her injury when she was almost 2 years of age, she and her parents had developed a very loving relationship.

When she was 23 months old, she was admitted to a local hospital emergency room comatose with severe traumatic brain injuries after a fall backward off of a porch onto a cement sidewalk. She had multiple fractures of the skull bones in the back of her head and massive bleeding in her brain. The pressure from the bleeding was pushing her brain over toward the left side. Because brain swelling was so severe, she underwent surgery; most of the right side of her brain needed to be removed. When she came to the rehabilitation hospital, Christina was not able to sit by herself, could not move the left side of her body, was fed by a tube in her nose, and made sounds if she was uncomfortable. She did not appear to recognize her parents, but she would look at objects and people around her.

Christina was hospitalized for 6 months at the rehabilitation hospital and changed considerably over this period. She began to talk but usually what she said was imitative and repetitive. For example, she would continually say, "What time is it?" when she saw people's watches, or she would repeat parts of what people said to her. She could not use her language to express her needs or to communicate. Much of her time was spent in repetitive and continual mouthing and biting of the strap on her helmet, her clothes, and other objects within her reach. This could rarely be interrupted for more than a few minutes without causing her to become very upset and agitated.

During therapy she would easily become overstimulated, even by someone touching her, or moving her or by staff talking around her. She would then become highly distraught with loud crying and yelling while biting, pinching, and pulling the therapist's hair. The same behavior was seen with her parents when they attempted to work with her. The best time of day became mealtime. Eating was very prolonged, but she began to enjoy finger-feeding herself, even though she refused to drink from a cup or bottle. However, she was easily distracted by the sights and sounds around her and continually needed to be reminded to continue eating or chewing. Playing with toys was usually limited to mouthing, biting, and throwing. Although she could put toys in and take them out of containers, she did this only when directly asked to and then only for brief periods before resorting to mouthing or throwing them.

When she was tested before discharge from the rehabilitation hospital, Christina was 2 years 5 months old. She was able to complete verbal and language parts of testing activities, such as pointing to pictures when they were named, occasionally saying what an object was used for, and identifying pictures by name. However, she often hesitated a long time before naming things and often called them by the wrong name. Even though she was able to use only her right hand to do testing tasks that involved materials such as puzzles and small toys, her difficulty attending to these tasks and her difficulty in figuring them out seemed to interfere the most in completing them. She was able to scribble with a crayon but had to be watched closely so she did not put it into her mouth and bite it. She was able to express more emotions, smiling more frequently and expressing both anger and annoyance. However, she did not appear to be aware of or react to the daily separations from her parents until shortly before discharge home. The overall impression from formal testing was similar to that of an adult who had sustained a severe traumatic injury with the right side of the brain significantly more damaged than the left. The exception was the kind of alteration in behavioral areas, especially the perseverative mouthing and biting, as well as severe deficits in attention, characterized by both extreme distractability and perseveration.

Christina was re-evaluated when she was almost 3 years old, approximately 1 year after she was injured. She had had surgery to replace the bone in her skull and no longer needed to wear a helmet. Although she was able to crawl, she was not able to walk and usually got around outside of her house by being pushed in a large stroller. During testing, she was able to sit on a chair at a small table and work on activities presented to her for longer periods of time, up to several minutes on a task if it interested her. However, she continued to take pieces out of a puzzle or pegs out of a pegboard before she had finished and was easily distracted by sounds and sights around her. Christina mouthed toys much less and was sometimes able to inhibit when told not to bite. At times she was even able to remind herself not to bite things and inhibit her own response. However, this could not be sustained when she was tired or when too many things were going on around her.

Her language continued to improve more rapidly than her ability to use her eyes, hands, and perceptual abilities. When asked to point to a small toy object according to function (e.g., pointing to a hat in response to "Which one do we wear on our heads?"), Christina listened to the question, answered it verbally, and only then looked to find the object that she had named. She could name pictures and objects more quickly than before and her mistakes were more understandable (calling a knife *scissors* and a coat *blouse*). However, she could not describe story pictures in even the simplest way. Activities that she needed to use perceptual and motor abilities to complete, such as building a tower, imitating lines with a crayon, or completing simple puzzles, continued to be very difficult for her.

In language areas she tested about 8 months behind her age level, but her spontaneous language for daily use and play was not as functional as this would indicate. She continued to have difficulty expressing her needs or using language for imaginative play. She simply talked much less frequently than would be expected at even the level she tested, and much of what she said continued to be repetitive. Although she was able to say what she was doing and could tell what was happening around her, she was not able to tell about events that had occurred several hours before, even after being reminded. Christina continued to be easily overstimulated even by conversation around her. When her mother and her therapists talked to each other in her presence, Christina would initially talk as well but then would escalate until she was screaming and pulling hair.

She needed extremely close supervision since she was moving around more on her own and was attracted to all sorts of things but had no sense of danger. For example, she would put her fingers into car hubcaps when being wheeled through a parking lot in her stroller and put anything and everything in her mouth. Christina clearly knew her parents and reacted to strangers. She was usually friendly, smiling in a lopsided way and saying "What's your name?" to whomever she met. She could listen to stories for up to 10 minutes on a good day but not at all on a bad day. Although she used a spoon and a fork, it was difficult for her to remember not to use her fingers, even with foods like mashed potatoes. Toilet-training had been attempted but was not yet successful.

Christina was involved in both a preschool program and in private therapy. However, planning for an appropriate school program created difficulties. She could be with children who were more handicapped than she was, none of whom could talk, and she would receive physical, occupational, and speech therapy. Or she could be with children who were closer to her psychological functional level with whom she could talk, play, and socialize, but she would not have access to therapy services since these children did not have physical handicaps. Her therapists also had difficulty with the specific nature of her deficits since her behavior was so different from that of the children with congenital handicaps such as cerebral palsy and spina bifida, who comprised most of the children in the early intervention programs.

Christina continued to be followed and was again re-evaluated at 4 years of age, approximately 2 years after injury. In the intervening year, she made significant gains in physical areas and was able to walk with short leg braces, although her balance was somewhat unsteady when she changed direction or position. Her increased ability to move independently made it more difficult to keep her involved in sitting at a table and in fact made her attention deficits more apparent. Her mother stated that she rarely mouthed or bit objects anymore, but this was still seen during testing as a reaction to being in a demand setting and in response to frustration. Christina was able both to experience and to state her frustration and difficulty completing tasks, saying "hard one" or "I don't want to." She spoke quicker, without long pauses while she searched for the words she wanted, and was better able to tune out distractions around her. However, her social language and response to more complex tasks like describing pictures continued to be significantly impaired.

Interestingly she was much more involved and accurate in completing perceptual-motor activities, and the difference between her performance in these areas and in language was beginning to dissipate. However, she was only able to scribble with a pencil and could not imitate either a line or a circle. She enjoyed the responsibility of setting the table for dinner and asked questions for which she expected an answer, such as "Where is Daddy?" She also enjoyed relaying messages from one person to another at home. Although she had been bowel trained, she was still not bladder trained. Many of the gains she had made in the year since the previous evaluation were more evident qualitatively than quantitatively. At 4 years old, Christina was functioning on testing like a 2 1/2- to 3-year-old child. However, she performed better on testing than she was able to consistently in real-life activities such as keeping herself occupied, playing with other children, and displaying the spontaneous curiosity and learning typical of toddlers and preschool children.

By the time she was 4 years old, Christina was much easier to live with and did not require the constant, close supervision that she did a year previously. Her parents continued to remember clearly what she had been like, what she had been able to do before her injury, and felt considerable guilt about her accident. Her 8-year-old brother was beginning to ask more questions about Christina, about why she was not able to do many things he could do at 4 and whether she would ever get better. He was also beginning to be teased at school for having a sister who was "retarded" and became less comfortable about inviting friends to play at his house. Though Christina not only had survived an injury that was definitely life-threatening and had done so much better than anyone, including her neurosurgeons, would have predicted, clearly she would never be normal again. She would grow up with persistent physical disabilities despite being able to walk and use her left hand to some extent. Even though she was capable of learning new things, she was also likely to always function significantly below age level in all areas and would probably never be able to live entirely on her own.

Preschool Age Children

The preschool period continues to be one of high risk for traumatic head injuries. In fact, it has been reported as the second highest period in terms of incidence, next only after adolescence (Hendrick, Harwood-Hash, & Hudson, 1964; Klonoff, 1971; Mannheimer, Dewey, & Melinger, 1966). The primary cause of injury continues to be predominantly related to falls, but an increasing number of severe injuries are due to pedestrian accidents (Moyes, 1980). Also at this time behavioral characteristics of the child, such as hyperactivity, attention deficits, and decreased compliance, are described as being increasingly related to a greater propensity for injury risk (Golding, 1986). However, at this age, parents usually assume primary responsibility for their childrens' accidents and injuries (Klonoff, 1971).

Despite the importance of injury on subsequent development and the relatively high incidence during the preschool years, no research studies have focused specifically on the outcome after head injuries in this age range. In fact, preschool children have rarely been included either in research on infants and toddlers after injury or in research with older children.

Lateralization for hand preference is basically established by the beginning of the preschool period, with an increase in consistency afterward (Bryden & Saxby, 1986). Even though the child's brain is close to adult size in terms of weight, its metabolic activity rate is increased markedly, using twice as much energy as the adult brain by ages 3 and 4 (Chugani, Phelps, & Mazziotta, 1987). It also has significantly more synapses or connections in the cortical thinking parts of the brain than the adult brain does (Huttenlocher, 1984; Huttenlocher, de Courten, Garey, & Van Der Loos, 1982). The child spends much more time in deep sleep than adolescents or adults (Feinberg, 1982–83), possibly as a way of maintaining this supercharged brain. The higher activity level and larger number of synapses in the brain during childhood have been postulated as possible explanations as to why children might do better after injury than adults. However, with severe injuries, a major disruption in the brain while it is in high gear could also be helpful in understanding why severe injuries can be so devastating in young children.

The preschool years can be characterized as the first real immersion of children into the larger social world as competent beings in their own right. Preschool children are able to do so in part because of their emerging understanding of how the world works, what makes them tick, and how others interact. They do this through an explosion in conceptualization and can now begin to grapple with understanding concepts of time, quantity, size, interpersonal relationships ("I'm going to marry you, Mommy."), personal awareness ("I'm tired."), and emotion ("I hate you."). Even though they are amazingly egocentric to adults, preschoolers are equally surprising in the degree to which they associate their knowledge and apply it from one area to another. They become truly thinking humans, though much of their learning is at a concrete level and is gained through active play, imagination, and fantasy. Preschoolers also begin to take some of their competency for granted and become very upset when it is jeopardized. They are much more realistic about what they can or cannot do, ask spontaneously for help, can recognize whether they have performed the way they wanted, and can clearly become frustrated when they are not able to succeed. Social learning is critical during this period, with its emphasis on sharing, recognition of other people's feelings and rights, and an emerging sense of empathy. Preschool children are becoming increasingly aware of their bodies, sexuality, and vulnerability to pain and mutilation and readily express fears that can be both very individualized as well as fantasy-based.

Head injuries in preschool-age children can interfere in all areas of their functioning. Head-injured preschoolers may not have the energy to play nor have the same cognitive drive to engage in and learn from play. They may not therefore be able to use their play either as a reassuringly normal activity or as a way to deal with the emotional effects of injury, as many sick children at this age can and readily do. This is especially true in the early postinjury period, but it can be prolonged in preschoolers with severe injuries. Initially after injury, preschool-age children may be apathetic and unaware of their changes in capabilities. Helping them to regain an appropriate level of independence and desire for self-control can be a major issue after injury. For some of the children, this can involve encouragement to try to do things by themselves as they become able. For others, it involves curbing their activities to restrain them from the consequences of acting impulsively with reduced judgment. Gradually preschool-age children may become aware of their injuries and express the feeling that being hurt was a punishment for being bad. They may become extremely fearful of the settings in which injury occurred, such as being afraid to cross the street even with an adult, becoming anxious while riding in a car, and refusing to ride their bicycles. Not only the injured children themselves experience these fears, but also their preschool-age brothers, sisters, and playmates.

Direct behavioral effects of injury are often described in the preschool years. This can include difficulties with attention, distractability, perseveration, and hyperactivity. However, not all preschoolers show these difficulties to the same degree, and some of these problems can be exacerbations of preinjury behavior. Young children, though, do not appear to be as aware of the changes in their behavior, their learning abilities, or their personalities as do older children. However, they can be quite aware of generalized frustration and of physical changes that limit their sense of competence. Toward the end of the preschool period, they are often capable of expressing how they feel about these changes, referring to themselves as stupid, or, as one boy stated, "I hate my brain." They often respond well if their home and school environments are carefully structured and managed, but it is not clear what the long-term effects may be in all areas of functioning. Although many of these children have demonstrated that they are able to master basic preacademic and academic skills, even while they are in the immediate period of recovery after injury, it is not clear that they will be able to make the transition to the more abstract, independent learning expected of them later.

Two case studies are presented to illustrate some of the characteristics of injury during the preschool period. One is of a boy who presented with primary behavioral difficulties after injury, the other of a girl with language difficulties subsequent to injury. Both children sustained severe injuries but recovered physical functioning very rapidly.

CASE STUDIES

Jonathan

Jonathan was 3 1/2 when he fell from a second-floor window through a screen that was not securely fastened. On admission to the emergency room, he was reportedly semicomatose and a fracture involving the base of his skull was diagnosed. He also had a large collection of blood in the right front part of his brain (right temporal hematoma), which had to be removed surgically 3 days after his injury. He improved markedly after surgery, was able to move his arms and legs 8 days after injury, and was able to follow verbal commands 10 days after injury. When he was admitted to the rehabilitation hospital, he was able to talk but only sparsely, was beginning to feed himself, was taking a few steps by himself, but had not regained bowel and bladder control. By the time of discharge from the rehabilitation hospital, Jonathan was able to talk fluently, would go to the bathroom with reminders, and was able to walk with monitoring for impulsiveness and balance.

Before his injury, Jonathan was described as an angel, who had clearly been a favorite child, not only of his mother and older brother but also of his entire extended family. He and his 10-year-old brother were extremely close and were continually together, sharing a bedroom and toys. After school, they would play with two older boys and their little brothers, building forts and riding their bikes. The accident had occurred while Jonathan was playing with his older brother in their room. His brother was devastated by the accident and blamed himself for it. He refused to sleep in their room and rarely could tolerate visiting Jonathan in the hospital. Because his mother spent much of her time in the hospital with Jonathan, his brother was left alone for long periods.

As Jonathan improved, his mother began to notice changes in his behavior. He was no longer able to wait but wanted things immediately. If he did not get them, he would yell or cry. If not watched carefully, he would impulsively take toys from other children or hit them if they bothered him. He had considerable energy and could easily engage in a full 6-hour day of therapy, but had difficulty channeling his energy in less-structured playtime. When asked to do specific tasks, Jonathan demonstrated difficulty in being able to stay with them longer than 5 minutes without being distracted onto something else. If pushed, he would then refuse to try again. However, he was able to play with toys during supervised play sessions for up to 30 minutes. Jonathan especially liked playing with a dollhouse and repeatedly had the people fall from the roof onto their heads. After they broke their heads, he then had them go the hospital to get better.

On formal testing 2 months after injury, Jonathan was functioning about 10 months below his chronological age level. Although he was able to talk fluently in conversation, he had difficulty naming and describing pictures during testing. His verbal responses were slowed, and he substituted closely related words (*shoe* for *foot* and *lock* for *key*). He was not able to copy a circle, and his way of holding a pencil was noticeably awkward. Jonathan especially enjoyed putting puzzles together but could only maintain his attention for puzzles with 4 or 5 pieces.

After he returned home, Jonathan continued to need close supervision. Once when he was hungry, he put a piece of leftover pizza directly on top of a stove burner to heat it. His brother continued to feel very guilty about the accident but began to deal with it by watching out for Jonathan and playing with him again. However, he also was very aware that Jonathan was not as much fun to be with as before injury and that he had to be carefully watched so that he did not get hurt again.

Heather
Heather was 5 1/2 years old when she was hit by a car while crossing the street on her way to visit a friend. According to her parents, Heather was usually careful when crossing the street, but she was particularly excited because she was going to a birthday party. Even though she was accompanied by her mother, Heather darted out so quickly that she could not be stopped fast enough to avoid injury. She was unconscious shortly after being hit and immediately was taken to the hospital. CT scan indicated contusion and brain swelling. After a 5-week stay in the acute-care hospital, Heather was sent home because she would do better there. At discharge, she could walk, but was not able to talk or use her right arm and hand well. Initially she received outpatient physical therapy, occupational therapy, and speech/language therapy, but she soon returned to her full-day, academically oriented kindergarten program. At 6 months after injury, Heather was referred for evaluation because she was getting up in the early hours of the morning when it was still dark, dressing herself, and getting ready for school. When she was told that it was still time to sleep, she became confused, upset, and cried inconsolably.

During her initial evaluation, Heather was a friendly, delightful child, who did not overtly appear to have had a severe injury only

7 months previously. She was able to work on testing activities for long periods, showing fatigue only after several hours. Her language, though, was markedly impaired. She spoke very hesitatingly, in single words or very brief phrases, and only after long pauses. During these pauses, she sometimes appeared to be in a daze, but this seemed to be related to the enormous amount of energy and concentration that it took for her to understand what was expected of her, to put together her response, and then to execute it. Heather appeared to understand what was said to her better than she was able to talk. Her attempts to express herself verbally in response to testing questions were characterized by attempts at compensation. For example, when asked what a hat was, Heather responded by singing, "My hat it has three corners," and only then was able to say, "Wear on your head." Despite her obvious language impairment, Heather performed on verbal testing tasks at an average level for her age because she was able to convey content sufficiently well through her compensation strategies. However, from her parents' and teacher's reports, Heather was probably functioning well above average before injury.

At this time, Heather continued to have fine tremors in her right hand that interfered with but did not keep her from writing and drawing. Her drawing of her family, though, reflected her narrowed perception of her world and some of her difficulty with spontaneity (see Figure 3-1). Despite being directly asked, Heather could not draw complete figures, only stick ones. Interestingly she was able to perform quite well on academic activities despite the onset of letter and two-digit number reversals since her injury. In fact, she reportedly had been learning new academic skills in kindergarten in both basic number and letter areas since her injury. When her school day was reduced to a half-day program, Heather no longer woke in the middle of the night.

Heather was seen for a re-evaluation 1 year after injury, when she was 6 1/2 years old. She was then in a full-day first-grade classroom in an academically rigorous school program. She initially became very tired when going to school all day after her summer break; when a rest period was instituted in the middle of the day, she did better. Heather had begun to talk more about what had happened to her and was more frustrated with her areas of deficit. She made comments such as "I can't do it," "I hate my mind," and "I hate myself." She did not want any special treatment at school and very much wanted to attend all day like the rest of the children. Her language was more spontaneous and

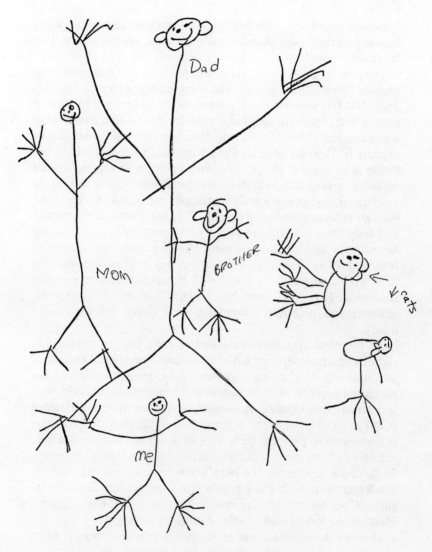

Figure 3-1 Drawing of her Family by a 6-year-old Girl 7 Months after Injury

fluent but continued to be reduced in terms of amount. As her parents described, she was not yet able to chatter again. She continued to make more grammatical errors, especially with verb tenses, that made her sound like a younger child.

Even though Heather continued to enjoy testing tasks and did well on them, her performance appeared to be somewhat disorganized. She would sometimes begin a task and then start talking, losing her place in what she had been doing. However, she was usually able to pick it up again and clearly recognized when it was complete. She could also sometimes become stuck while working on a task, repeating the same mistakes, and not being able to figure out other ways of trying to attempt it. When this occurred, Heather could appear to be stubborn and was likely to feel that she had failed. Interestingly her functioning on intelligence testing decreased in terms of her scores, especially on timed tasks such as puzzles or block designs. This decrease occurred even though she was clearly more competent than she had been on the first evaluation and had mastered the basics of reading in the intervening period. Letter reversals were no longer apparent, but Heather continued to have difficulty with reversing two-digit numbers and paying attention to math operation signs, usually adding when she was supposed to subtract.

Heather was able to engage in pretend play with her dolls for long periods and also enjoyed drawing pictures. She was again able to express her feelings and needs through her drawings. When asked to draw a picture of her family, Heather asked to use markers instead of a pencil and completed the drawing in Figure 3-2. She not only could complete whole figures in contrast to her stick figures 6 months previously, but she could use her drawing to express her feelings of being displaced in her family. After completing the figure of her father, mother, and younger brother, Heather appeared to be upset and confused about where to place herself. She finally squeezed herself between her parents. At this time, her parents were concerned about the increased tension between the two children, who were only a year apart in age. After Heather's accident, her brother was the more competent of the two children and began to take over the role of the older child. By the time Heather was a year postinjury, she became very aware of this and resented not being treated as the older child (see her drawing of her brother, Figure 3-3). Her brother, though, was equally clear about how jealous he was because of the amount of attention Heather had been receiving, especially from their parents. Arguments and fighting increased at this time, even though they had been able to play well together both before and initially after Heather's accident. Heather also began to express her feelings of being rejected by other children; she stated that they were mean to her and would not let her play, to which she reacted by being sad or angry. Although she was

Figure 3-2 Drawing of her Family by a 6 1/2-year-old Girl 1 Year after Injury

very pleased about her academic success, especially in reading, Heather was puzzled and confused about her relationships with other children. At this time, play therapy for Heather and family therapy with the 4 of them was recommended.

Heather was seen again for evaluation 2 years after injury when she was 7 1/2 years old. She was now able to chatter in conversation, and previous significant language deficits were hardly noticeable. However, she became confused with quick, verbal shifts during conversation, especially if several people were talking around her. Heather was capable of keeping herself occupied with writing notes to her friends and playing with her Barbie dolls. She had a brief period of occupational therapy to reduce hand fatigue and

Figure 3-3 Drawing of her Brother by a 6 1/2-year-old Girl 1 Year after Injury

improve her handwriting. She and her brother were able to play together again for longer periods without arguing. Heather, though, seemed to be able to play with one friend at a time more successfully than she could interact in a group of children. She had become quite sensitive to what she perceived as criticism and made comments such as "You're mad at me" and "I'm no good." However, she was also able to describe what she liked about herself. She considered that her primary problems were in finding it difficult to make friends and feel accepted and feeling nervous about performing on tests in school. Heather had considerably more energy than a year ago and could engage in testing activities for several hours, with energy left for playing and talking with friends.

Her scores on formal intelligence testing continued to decline but remained in the average range. At the same time, her academic skills continued to increase. By the end of second grade in an academically challenging school, she was reading and spelling between the fourth- and fifth-grade levels. Math continued to be more difficult for her, but she had improved a grade level during the past year and was approximately at the middle to end of second grade. Her drawings of a boy and a girl were completed at a level expected for her age (see Figures 3-4 and 3-5).

Figure 3-4 Drawing of a Boy by a 7 1/2-year-old Girl 2 Years after Injury

School-Age Children

When compared with the rates in infancy, preschool, adolescence, and adult years, the school-age years are one of the lowest periods in terms of incidence and one of the highest in terms of survival from head injuries. Motor vehicle accidents are the cause of most severe injuries, including those in which children are either a passenger or a pedestrian. Sports-related injuries increase during this period, with accidents involving bicycles, skateboards, and baseball bats among others. At this time, parents begin to take less direct responsibility and begin to attribute the cause of injury to the children themselves (Klonoff, 1971).

Figure 3-5 Drawing of a Girl by a 7 1/2-year-old Girl 2 Years after Injury

Neuroanatomically, myelination of the corpus callosum, the major nerve fiber bundle connecting the two cerebral hemispheres, nears completion by 6 years of age and then continues slowly until about 10 (Hewitt, 1962). The more efficient connection of the two hemispheres of the brain and the myelinization of the tertiary association area connecting the sensory-perceptual areas together have a major impact on how children are able to understand themselves and their world. The association area is responsible for efficient performance of academic skills including reading, spelling, writing, and arithmetic, as well as reasoning skills since it allows for integration across the modalities of auditory, visual, sensory, and tactile information processing. The child's brain continues to be supercharged throughout this period of development, utilizing more energy, comprised of more connections, and requiring more sleep than the adolescent or adult (Chugani et al., 1987; Feinberg, 1982–83; Huttenlocher, 1984).

School-age children are immersed in learning about themselves, their families, other children, and the world around them. They are engaged in acquiring mastery of those skills and knowledge that their society, both the adult and the child components, deems important. Learning in school is only one aspect of this, but it is a particularly important one. School performance involves mastery of basic academic skills, the application of these in school and community, and social skills such as making friends and being able to interact as a member of a group. Children are also very involved in mastery of their bodies through activities such as bicycle riding, sports, and other recreational pursuits. They often engage in these activities informally with their friends, as well as in formally organized classes and teams. It is a time when the concepts of self-esteem, self-concept, and self-confidence take on a special meaning as the child challenges the self in order to build and understand his/her own capacities in relationship to others. Children are expected to begin to learn to delay and to gain beginning control of their impulses and behavior. Not to do so usually results in loss of both adult and peer approval. Children in turn attempt to establish control of their world by understanding as much as they can about it.

During this period, children are progressively moving away from their immediate families. Time spent with other children increases, not only at school but also in free time. Children begin to plan their own activities and schedules, which may conflict with their parents' plans. There is a separate subculture among the children themselves, with a unique set of rules governing behavior, clothes, and activities that is not necessarily shared with adults. In this way, children learn to create a place for themselves on their own merits both in dealing with their families and with other children.

How does a traumatic brain injury sustained during childhood interfere with the unique characteristics of development during this period? It has been relatively well-documented that after a loss of consciousness exceeding 24 hours, intellectual deficits are frequent, serious, and persistent (Levin & Eisenberg, 1979; Klonoff & Paris, 1974). Less is known about the intellectual effects of milder injuries in children. However, because of the critical importance of learning and mastery of information and skills during this period, any alteration or diminution of cognitive abilities must be taken very seriously. What is at stake is not only whether a child will be able to master specific skills, such as learning to read, but also the effect of a learning reduction on the sense of self and on relationships with both adults and other children. Sustaining a traumatic brain injury during this period threatens the very core of childhood; that is, learning to be in control of one's self, being able to function as part of a group, and being able to master the skills and information that are important to the child and those in one's world.

In contrast with how children cope with other injuries and illnesses during this period, traumatic brain injuries directly interfere with children's ability to use their developing cognitive abilities in understanding and subsequently feeling more in control of what is happening to them. Because the brain itself is injured, children are not able to mobilize and utilize their emerging abilities to understand either the nature of their brain injury or the procedures and therapy necessary to manage and treat it. However, they may be very aware of their losses in terms of physical prowess, ability to learn, and separation from family and friends. They are more aware of their bodies, and older children begin to complain of somatic symptoms similar to adults, including complaints of fatigue and headaches. They may also be very angry about disruptions of their usual, and especially of anticipated, activities including loss of vacation time because of being in the hospital if injury occurred in the summer. Children usually resent the greater restrictions placed on them after injury, for example, having closer supervision at home than they have been used to, not being able to go with their friends without an adult, and not being able to ride their bicycles.

Whereas cognitive effects of head injury are often directly related to injury severity, there is a less direct relationship of severity to behavioral and psychosocial/emotional sequelae. Although hyperactivity has not been found to be a universal behavioral sequelae of traumatic head injury, younger children have demonstrated an increased frequency of temper tantrums, as well as impulsive, aggressive, and destructive behavior (Brink, Garrett, Hale, Woo-Sam, & Nickel, 1970). However, hypoactivity or a reduction in initiative is also common after head injury in children. The primary behavioral characteristic directly related to injury severity in children is marked social disinhibition, which has been compared with the frontal lobe syndrome in adults (Rutter, Chadwick, & Shaffer, 1983).

Other children may be curious and wary of a child after head injury. They are often aware of the circumstances and the severity of injury in at least general terms. When a child after head injury is not able to engage in the same activities as before injury, looks different, and behaves with less control, other children may have little tolerance for these changes. The head-injured child may then be teased, feel left out, and experience of loss of preinjury friendships. Reductions in competence in physical activities and learning in school only enforces this sense of being different, not only from their preinjury self but also from other children. Necessary changes in school programming, including tutoring, therapy, and special education services make cognitive and learning difficulties real to both the child with a head injury and to the other children. A child who requires special education services may be called brain-damaged or retarded after return to school. Even without overt changes in school programming, children of school age are very aware of the standing of each child in the class and can readily recognize when a child can no longer maintain preinjury learning capacity. The changes in behavior, which interfere with understanding and joining in the child culture, as well as reduced behavioral control may cause a child to be called weird. Especially if the child physically appears to be normal after head injury, it can be very difficult for other children and adults to understand that behavioral and learning changes are a direct result of injury. The head-injured child may then gradually retreat and become shy, depressed, and angry in reaction to changes in functioning and feeling of not being accepted by other children and adults.

CASE STUDIES

Alexander

Alex was 6 1/2 years old when he and his family were involved in a motor vehicle accident. Alex was thrown from the car and sustained an open head injury and depressed fracture of the frontal part of his skull. Approximately 8 days after injury, he was able to respond to yes/no questions by a hand squeeze but was not able to talk. On admission to the rehabilitation hospital a month after injury, Alex was alert and confused. He told anyone who asked what had happened that he had been in a fire and had needed to jump out the window of his house to escape. Even though Alex was clearly confused about where he was and what had happened to him, he was able to perform most self-care tasks, was very mobile in getting around in his wheelchair, soon was able to walk, and readily engaged both adults and children in conversation.

Before injury, Alex had completed the first grade. Because of his birth date, he had undergone screening to assess readiness for kindergarten and first grade. Screening results reportedly suggested age-appropriate fine-motor and language abilities, and he began school as one of the youngest members of his class. However, both his parents and teachers described Alex as hyperactive, with a shorter attention span than expected for his age, and as being less socially competent than his classmates at the beginning of first grade. By the end of the year, though, they felt he had adjusted well and was achieving at an expected level.

At evaluation before discharge from the rehabilitation hospital, Alex functioned in the average range on verbal tasks and in the low-average range on visual-perceptual-motor tasks. Although he was able to respond to verbal questions at an age-appropriate level, he had more difficulty as questions became longer and more complex. Alex needed longer questions repeated before he could answer them adequately. When asked to draw a picture of a person, he drew a boy (Figure 3-6) including a heart "to make him breathe" and a stomach because "if you swallow food and you didn't have a stomach it would just come out of your mouth." Even though he was able to express concern about his body and its functioning through his drawing, Alex's concern did not focus on his injured brain. He was impulsive and demonstrated a shortened attention span, but he was able to be involved in testing activities for about 20 minutes. However, after about an hour of alternating work and play periods, he needed an extended break in order to avoid behavioral expressions of fatigue and frustration. Much of his fatigue appeared to be mental, as he continued to have abundant physical energy at the end of a day of therapy.

Toward the end of his hospitalization, Alex could engage in independent play activities in an organized way for up to a half hour. His play and drawings were utilized in helping him to be able to understand, express his reactions, and begin to cope with his accident, injury, and hospitalization. During one of his play therapy sessions, Alex drew a picture of his sister who had been in the accident but had not been injured (Figure 3-7). Alex said that the "red cross" in the picture was there "to protect my sister" and "to remember that no one can kill you and break into your house and hurt you and have to go to the hospital."

Before discharge, Alex was tried on Ritalin, with improvements in both behavioral control, attention, and concentration. He was

Figure 3-6 Drawing of a Boy by a 6 1/2-year-old Boy 3 Months after Injury

placed in a self-contained class for children with learning disabilities on his return to school. Although he was quite successful in academic areas, Alex had considerable difficulties in maintaining behavioral control in less-structured school settings, such as in the lunchroom and on the playground. He was often involved in pushing and shoving, yelling, and going where he was not supposed to be. His impulsivity, disinhibition, and frustration were seen as emotional problems by school personnel, and he was referred to the school social worker for therapy sessions.

When he was seen a month after discharge, Alex was very difficult to keep in the room. He charged the door to go out and get a drink. However, when he was asked to draw, Alex was able to sit. His initial drawings were of a tree and airplanes bombing and were completed rapidly with crossing out when he was not satisfied with the quality of one of the planes (Figures 3-8 and

Figure 3-7 Drawing of his Sister by a 6 1/2-year-old Boy 3 Months after Injury

3-9). When verbal structuring was used by telling him to draw slowly and carefully, doing the best he could, Alex completed the drawings in Figure 3-10, spontaneously writing the words to label his drawings.

A reward system using stars was initiated at home and in an after school day-care program with successful management when it was used consistently. Alex became more aware of other children's reaction to him and complained about having "no friends" and that "nobody likes me." He stated that children teased him because of the scars on his forehead, calling him Frankenstein. He talked persistently about the accident in the following months and began to look forward to plastic surgery to minimize his facial scarring. At school, he was mainstreamed into a regular class for reading and math but continued to need the small, structured class to maintain behavioral control for the majority of the school day. At home his younger sister had become quite protective of Alex. When his parents attempted to discipline him, Alex's sister would become very upset and angry and tell them that they could not hurt her brother.

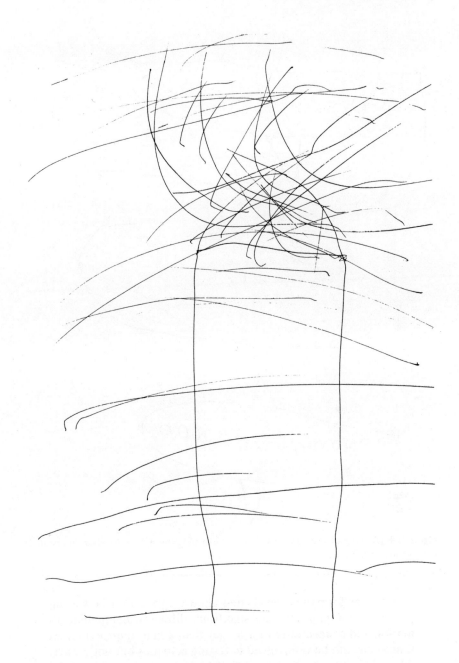

Figure 3-8 Drawing of a Tree by a 6 1/2-year-old Boy 4 Months after Injury under Unstructured Conditions

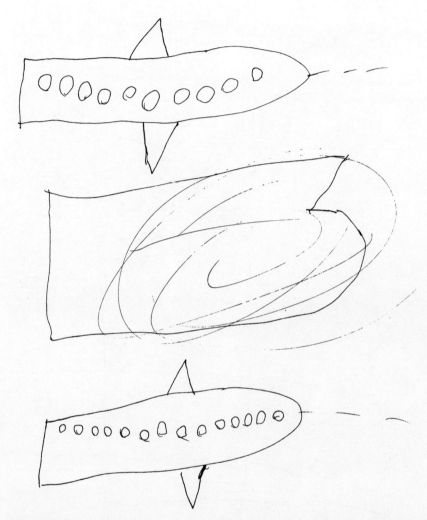

Figure 3-9 Drawing of Airplanes by a 6 1/2-year-old Boy 4 Months after Injury under Unstructured Conditions

Alex was formally re-evaluated almost a year after he was injured. He continued to have significant difficulty maintaining attention and concentration for longer than a half-hour period. At times he could be re-involved in testing activities but not always. Alex did not try to run out of the room, nor did he appear to be deliberately provoking the examiner. Rather he seemed to have marked difficulty containing his need for physical movement and

Figure 3-10 Drawings Completed by a 6 1/2-year-old Boy 4 Months after Injury under Structured Conditions

trying to maintain attention on tasks. During particularly difficult periods, Alex would slide off his chair, lie on the floor, and open and close nearby desk drawers. He was easier to engage in activities that involved materials, such as puzzles or drawings, than on those requiring only a verbal response to questions. Alex performed many tasks quickly but not always accurately with variable monitoring of his performance for errors. Transitions between tasks were especially difficult for him.

On cognitive testing, Alex continued to function in the average range on verbal tasks and in the low-average range on visual-perceptual-motor tasks, with little change since the previous evaluation. Overall academic skills were at grade level. However, his performance could be quite variable and was significantly reduced on activities that required concentration for longer than a few minutes. When asked to draw a picture of a person, Alex drew a girl (Figure 3-11) who would be "mad if her brother beats her up." During informal conversation, Alex talked about his feelings of being "a dummy." When talking about the accident and his injury, Alex said, "I'm really not dead."

Difficulties with behavioral control continued; several years after injury Alex was still primarily reliant on external management, including reward systems and adult monitoring. This persistent difficulty finally resulted in placement in a self-contained school program for children with behavioral disorders. As other children his age began to demonstrate increasing control of their behavior, judgment, and independent learning, Alex behaviorally was falling further and further behind what was expected.

Kim

Kim was 8 years old when she was injured in a pedestrian and motor vehicle accident. She was comatose and had seizures at the scene of the accident. At the acute-care hospital, bleeding in the left side of her brain was diagnosed (subdural hematoma); this

Figure 3-11 Drawing of a Girl by a 7 1/2-year-old Boy 1 Year after Injury

gradually was resolved by 3 weeks after injury but resulted in weakness of the right side of her body. She had severe swelling of her brain after injury. Deep coma reportedly lasted about 2 weeks. When she was admitted to the rehabilitation hospital 5 weeks post injury, Kim was able to feed herself, could sit but not walk, was alert to what was going on around her, had periods of agitation, but was not able to talk.

Before injury, Kim had completed the second grade at a private school. She reportedly had difficulty learning to read and read aloud slowly. Scores on achievement testing completed at school shortly before her injury indicated that she was about 4 to 5 months behind her class placement. However, because she was a bilingual child, this was not considered unusual.

By the time she had been in the rehabilitation hospital for a month, Kim had begun to talk and spontaneously greeted people. However, her speech was very limited, and she appeared to be quite confused about what had happened to her. A month later she was aware that she was in the hospital and did not want to return after a short visit home. On the unit, Kim was quite social and enjoyed being an older sister for the younger children. She also was very appropriate with adults, who enjoyed talking and interacting with her. Behavior control was not an issue during hospitalization, and she enjoyed being able to go to therapy sessions on her own.

Formal testing was completed before discharge. At this time Kim was 4 months postinjury. She talked slowly, softly, and deliberately, with obvious difficulty finding the exact words she wanted to say. Understanding verbal directions and questions also was impaired, and she did best when the instructions were brief and repetitive. She frequently misunderstood questions. For example, when asked what she should do if she cut her finger, Kim initially responded, "It will grow back." She was beginning to be aware of her performance and at times was able to correct her errors or appropriately ask for help. Fatigue and listlessness began to interfere with her performance after about an hour of working. Fine-motor tremors limited her ability to write or draw (Figure 3-12) but interfered less when she was playing with toys or puzzles. Cognitively Kim functioned in the impaired range at the educably mentally handicapped level on both verbal and visual-perceptual-motor tasks with no significant difference between the two. Academic skills were inconsistent and ranged from the end of kindergarten to the end of second grade, depending on the nature

Figure 3-12 Drawings of a Girl by an 8-year-old Girl 4 Months after Injury

of the task. With the exception of being able to recognize correct spelling of words, her academic skills were approximately at the first-grade level. She was able to write her name, could recognize some sight words and spell them, but had difficulty paying attention to operation signs when attempting arithmetic problems.

After discharge, Kim was placed in a self-contained class for children with physical disabilities because of her need for continued physical and occupational therapy as a part of her school program. She was able to walk short distances by herself, with only a short leg brace on her right leg. Her placement in the physically handicapped program was designed to be temporary, especially since this program was less able to provide the services for children with learning problems that she also needed.

Kim was re-evaluated almost 2 years after injury when she was 10 years old. She was physically ready to leave the school program for children with physical disabilities and was evaluated for placement in a self-contained class for children with severe learning disabilities. During the testing, Kim was motivated to do well since she wanted to return to a regular school. She was able to walk independently but continued to use a light brace on her right leg for support and stability. Although she used her right hand for writing and drawing, she used her left hand for any activity requiring strength. Kim talked easily and fluently about her family and friends. In fact, she needed to be redirected from conversation back to testing activities. Kim was aware that some tasks were hard for her, but she usually could not improve her performance. At this time, she demonstrated little overt frustration, even when tasks were difficult.

Cognitively she had made very little improvement in functioning since previous evaluation in terms of the rapid recovery usually seen after head injury. She continued to perform in the impaired range at the educably mentally handicapped level on verbal tasks and in the borderline range on visual-perceptual-motor tasks, with no significant gains overall over the past 1 1/2 years. Instead she appeared to be continuing to learn at a significantly reduced rate. Her drawings reflected both her improved fine-motor control and also her reduced cognitive functioning (Figures 3-13 and 3-14). Academic learning was similar in that she was performing overall beween the mid-first- and mid-second-grade levels. Two years after injury, she was beginning to perform at the level before her accident. Despite her fluent speech, Kim continued to show significant impairment in language on formal testing. Because of the lack of progress in learning areas, significant changes in her school program and re-initiation of speech and language therapy was recommended. Socially, though, Kim was doing much better. She was very popular with other children in her neighborhood, even though she did not go to school with them. She was able to go to the store by herself and enjoyed being responsible for spending her own money. Recently she had become interested in early adolescent concerns such as dieting to lose weight, clothes, and boyfriends and was described as constantly on the phone.

Within the next year, Kim began to experience mood swings, especially becoming more angry, yelling, and swearing if she did not get her way at home. She began to talk back to her parents and physically scratched and hit out if they restricted her privileges. Although this appeared to be related to onset of puberty, it also seemed to be more extreme than normally expected. She became more frustrated and angry with her difficulties learning in school, having become more aware that she was not able to read well despite tutoring and her own hard work. Her behavior gradually improved over the next 6 months with clear expectations being enforced both at home and at school. With a change in

Figure 3-13 Drawing of a Girl by a 10-year-old Girl 2 Years after Injury

teachers the following year, Kim's behavior deteriorated at school. It became clearer how dependent she was on the external structure and expectations of the adults around her. Concern about if and how she would be able to become more independent without jeopardizing her behavioral control or safety increased especially since she was very attractive and definitely becoming a young adolescent.

Adolescents

The incidence of head injuries, which remains relatively stable throughout childhood, increases dramatically in adolescence. The number of severe

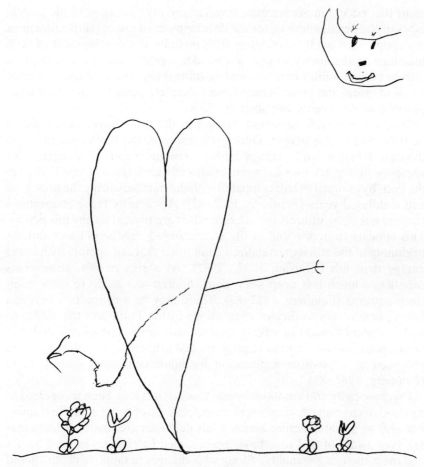

Figure 3-14 Drawing of a Heart by a 10-year-old Girl 2 Years after Injury

injuries in the 15- to 19-year age range equals that of all the previous 14 years combined (Gross, Wolf, Kunitz, & Jane, 1985). Since most injuries in adolescence are related to motor vehicle accidents, it is not surprising that this increase occurs when adolescents are getting their driver's licenses and spending much time driving around, as well as experimenting with alcohol and drugs. However, it cannot necessarily be assumed that all accidents are related directly to adolescent behavior; they are also vulnerable to injuries related to adults' behavior on the road.

Physiologically adolescence is seen as a period of rapid growth, development of secondary sex characteristics, and hormonal changes. However, until recently less neurophysiological or neuroanatomical changes were postulated to be occurring. The primary change in neurological development that occurs in adolescence involves the myelinization of the frontal lobes of the brain, allowing for the development of the executive functions associated with adult functioning. This includes the development of such functions as the ability to plan ahead, delay gratification, evaluate one's own behavior, inhibit impulses and emotional expression, exercise higher levels of moral and ethical control, and complete more sophisticated analysis of complex events and abstract ideas.

In recent research, profound changes in the brain have been found to be occurring in this period. During adolescence, the brain appears to go through a major, and perhaps its last, reorganization. The number of synapses or connections between brain cells undergoes a significant reduction, by as much as half compared with the number during the preschool and childhood years (Feinberg, 1982–83). Apparently those connections that are not being utilized and are redundant are pruned during this period. This appears to be the end of the supercharged childhood brain and the beginning of the efficient, stabilized adult brain that can operate with lower energy demands (Chugani et al., 1987). As a sign of this, adolescents experience much less deep sleep than children and begin to show adult sleep patterns (Feinberg, 1982–83). There may be a connection between having fewer, more efficient connections in the brain and the ability to sustain logical thought in solving abstract and complex problems. A defect in this maturational process of programmed synapse elimination has been proposed as a possible explanation for adolescent-onset schizophrenia (Feinberg, 1982–83).

Psychosocially and emotionally adolescence has long been recognized as a period of changing demands with an expectation of being adults in training but also as a hiatus before actual adult demands are made. Adolescents are very aware of and sometimes preoccupied by changes in their bodies and their emerging sexuality. Along with changes in thinking come altered perceptions of self, overt emphasis on identity formulation both in terms of "who am I" and "what is my place in the world," striving for independence from family, and an immersion in friendships with members of both sexes developing into intimacy with one person. Adolescents are in the process of defining themselves in their own right, according to what they look like, what their goals and ambitions are, what they hope their future will be, and who they want to be with. They do this with a burgeoning sense of energy, independence, self-sufficiency, and self-confidence. The invulnerability that is part of adolescence is counterbalanced by the ability to appreciate more fully the fragility of life and the reality of death.

How is this affected by traumatic brain injury? Despite the high incidence of injury during this period, adolescents have rarely been studied as a distinct group. They are usually combined with children in pediatric studies or grouped with adults, with little appreciation for the unique character- istics of adolescent development and characteristics. From the few studies that have focused on adolescents, it appears that intellectual deficits after injury may be less pronounced than in children (Brink, Garrett, Hale, Woo-Sam, & Nickel, 1970; Levin, Eisenberg, Wigg, & Kobayashi, 1982). The effect on development of executive functions has not been addressed specifically, even though it is essential in the transition from adolescence to adulthood.

Psychosocial and emotional aspects of injury have been less adequately studied and may be particularly difficult for adolescents. Physical changes, such as loss of hair, tracheostomy and other scars, and decreased physical abilities—even if they are transient—can interfere with the adolescent's perception of attractiveness and be resented more than less visible deficits such as cognitive changes. Identity development and independence striving can be significantly threatened or interrupted by injury. From clinical ex- perience, adolescents after head injuries often perceive a significant loss of self-confidence and invulnerability, with an increase in depression and suicidal ideation even after good recoveries. In reaction, they may want to ignore their head injuries. However, they are keenly aware that they cannot just be one of the crowd because of the notoriety their accidents and injuries have often given them. Usually few people in their schools and communities are not aware of the fact that they have been injured, especially if their injuries were severe. Although they may enjoy this at- tention, at the same time it can be resented since it emphasizes their differentness from other adolescents.

Adolescents can also struggle with trying to figure out why they were injured and why they survived. This can be done through heightened feel- ings of religiosity, both of a positive (saved for a purpose) or negative (punishment for their activities, often sexual or substance abuse–related) character. They can also resent the pressure put on them if others regard their survival as a miracle or a second chance. They often become socially isolated from their peers and experience difficulty making up for lost de- velopmental time subsequent to injury. The high school years are partic- ularly difficult to interrupt, even for brief periods, without major academic and psychosocial effects. Because head injury involves not only the im- mediate loss of time due of hospitalization but also an often prolonged recovery period, this is especially crucial for adolescents.

In the latter part of adolescence, the threat of being derailed from a planned transition to adulthood is especially critical. The last 2 years of high school are a period of concentrated planning involving getting ready for jobs, vocational training, or continued schooling through college pro- grams. This planning can be stressful enough without the added pressure of a head injury throwing into question when and whether the adolescent will be able to handle high school work, much less the greater independence expected from jobs and college. There is considerable anxiety normally about life after high school, without having to question basic skills, abilities, and personal characteristics that were taken for granted before injury. When the reality about the implications of their head injury for their plans sinks in, the resultant depression is a grief reaction related to lost plans and dreams. These may involve the loss of friends if they cannot graduate with their class, major alterations in career plans such as not being acceptable for the military or not being able to work in the occupation they had planned, changes in school plans if they are not able to succeed at college-level work or are not able to go away to college, loss of independence if they are not allowed or able to drive, and altered intimacy plans if the effects of injury affect their relationships with boyfriends or girlfriends. In an attempt to blunt the emotional impact of this grief, older adolescents may resort to alcohol or drug use. However, substance use after head injury can not only further impair functioning but also can lead to repeated injury.

CASE STUDIES

Shawn

Shawn was 12 1/2 years old when he was hit by a car while riding his bicycle with his friend. He was hospitalized for approximately 1 month, with a coma lasting about 5 to 6 days. By 2 1/2 weeks after injury, he was able to talk but demonstrated confusion about where he was and what had happened to him. He continued to have difficulties coordinating his vision at 2 months after injury, which primarily interfered with being able to read comfortably. Before injury, he was in gifted classes and had completed the seventh grade. Because his injury occurred in early summer, Shawn had almost 3 months to recover before returning to school in fall. During the summer, he was involved in both outpatient therapy and tutoring.

He was initially evaluated in mid-August to help plan for his school programming. Shawn was quite anxious about testing and was very aware of the purpose of the evaluation. He was interested in finding out how well he was doing and was very interested in doing his best on testing activities. After a couple of hours of working he became noticeably fatigued. Even though he expressed his willingness to continue, his performance was not as accurate or as efficient as it had been. Despite the severity of his injury, he had no visible sequelae, apart from mildly reduced physical coordination. Before injury, Shawn was described as very quiet, shy, and reserved. He expressed pleasure with the mild disinhibition he had been experiencing since injury, expressing his pleasure in the greater ease he had in talking with people and presenting his ideas. In fact, this was a part of being injured that he wanted to continue, and he did not see it as a deficit at all.

On cognitive testing, Shawn functioned in the superior range on verbal tasks and in the average range on visual-perceptual-motor tasks, with a highly significant 25-point difference between the two. This was markedly reduced from findings from preinjury testing completed for gifted placement in school. Verbal testing was consistent in the superior range, but his previous functioning on visual-perceptual-motor tasks had been significantly higher, in the very superior range. After injury he especially had difficulty completing timed paper-and-pencil tasks quickly, although his drawing continued at an advanced level (see Figure 3-15). He also had significant difficulty with complex problem-solving and memory tasks. Sustained performance on academic testing was reduced from what would have been expected of a gifted eighth-grader (40th percentile for reading, 4th percentile for math) but was also lowered by fatigue and time restrictions.

Shawn returned to school with a reduced course load and the addition of study periods at the end of the day. He continued in one of his gifted classes and did well with it. School personnel noticed that he was more outgoing and talked more easily, but his disinhibition did not appear to interfere with his relationships with adults or peers at school. At home, though, he was seen as becoming more resistant and stubborn about doing his homework. His disinhibition was described by his parents as becoming pushy, rude, interrupting other people, and needing constant attention.

As a summary of the school year after his head injury, Shawn had an okay beginning, a very good middle, and sloughed off at the end of the year. He did not make the honor roll and blamed his teachers for this rather than his own performance. He had just recently begun to read books again for pleasure and was able to complete them in a couple of days, in contrast with the very long time it took him to read a book shortly after injury. He had also begun to write creative stories and had won a school prize for one. However, he appeared to have more difficulty in math

Figure 3-15 Drawing of a Boy by a 12 1/2-year-old Boy 2 1/2 Months after Injury

than preinjury, especially in more spatial areas such as understanding diagrams and performing calculations.

On reevaluation a little over 1 year after injury, Shawn remembered all of the tests and continued to be anxious about his performance. However, he noticeably relaxed when it became apparent to him that he was doing better than before. He asked for direct feedback about how he was doing. When this was given to him at the end of testing, he had a tendency to overestimate how well he had done. On cognitive testing, he continued to perform in the superior range on verbal tasks with little change from testing a year previously. His performance increased on visual-perceptual-motor tasks to the high-average range but continued to be significantly reduced from preinjury levels. Performance on a timed paper-and-pencil task and on complex problem-solving continued to be reduced at a mildly impaired level.

During an interview session, he appeared to be quite sad except when talking about the stories he had been writing. He also continued to enjoy drawing and completed a figure of "a male in his early 20s who is standing on a pile of rocks near a mountain," who will be happy "when he gets to the top" (see Figure 3-16). He expressed concerns about his own competence through talking about his drawing, saying that the man in the drawing would be angry and sad if "he fell down and had to start all over again" and that he would be jealous "if somebody does better than him." He was quite aware of his own abilities, especially his strengths in drawing and his difficulties with math. His memories and the experience of hospitalization and therapy after injury appeared basically positive. However, he now worried about "things that might happen to my brother."

Jennifer

Jennifer was 16 1/2 years old when she and a group of her friends were involved in a motor vehicle accident when returning from a party. She was the only one of the group who was severely injured; the others were either treated in the emergency room or required no medical intervention. Jennifer was intubated and on a ventilator, with a deep coma lasting approximately 5 days. She

Figure 3-16 Drawing of a Man by a 13 1/2-year-old Boy 1 Year after Injury

had several seizures in the days immediately following the accident. Duration of posttraumatic amnesia was reportedly about 3 weeks. When she was admitted to the rehabilitation hospital a month after injury, Jennifer was able to walk, talk, and care for herself. Despite her relatively high level of functioning, her parents were very concerned about personality changes. Before injury, she was described as a very mature, responsible adolescent, who was trusted with the care of her two younger sisters after school.

Primary changes in her functioning included memory deficits and immature behavior, including inappropriate smiling and giggling. She remembered waking up in the acute-care hospital but relied on her mother to fill in many of the details for her. In general, Jennifer appeared to be uncertain and hesitant, rather than disoriented or confused. She was especially interested in talking about the minimal effect of the accident on her physical appearance. While in the acute-care hospital, Jennifer had learned to do needlepoint and continued to complete a pillow cover with little assistance while in the rehabilitation hospital. She also enjoyed helping out with the younger children on the unit during evening recreation programs.

At the time of the accident in March, Jennifer was in the latter part of her junior year of high school. She was reportedly a B and C student, taking a regular academic course load including biology and geometry. Because of the accident and subsequent hospitalizations, Jennifer had been absent from school for about 2 months.

During the initial evaluation completed while she was an inpatient at the rehabilitation hospital, Jennifer was readily involved in testing activities. She complained about being bored and not being able to think of the specific words she wanted to say. Although she often performed tasks quickly, she was sometimes able to catch and correct her errors. On intelligence testing, she functioned in the low-average range on verbal tasks and in the average range on visual-perceptual-motor tasks, but the difference between the two was not significant. Her performance was somewhat uneven, as she was either able to catch on quickly to what was expected or she had great difficulty figuring out what to do, with little evidence of active problem solving. Academic skills were at the fifth- to seventh-grade levels, well reduced from what would be expected of a high school junior. Her drawing of a girl strikingly echoed her usual facial expression (Figure 3-17).

Figure 3-17 Drawing of a Girl by a 16 1/2-year-old Girl 1 1/2 Months after Injury

Jennifer stated that the girl was "going to a dance, but first before she goes, she has to ask her mother, right?" She was willing at this point to let adults make major decisions for her as long as they were fair and the reasons were explained to her.

She went home after a 3-week stay in the rehabilitation hospital and returned to her regular high school program with learning disability resource room support. During the summer, she received tutoring in academic subjects. Jennifer was able to maintain passing grades, but school work was more difficult for her than before injury. She expressed considerable frustration in returning to her high school classes related to her sense of having studied the material before but not being able to remember the specific information or skills. Her group of friends remained very close. They felt quite responsible and protective of her and appeared to be more aware than Jennifer of the severity of the accident and the subtle changes in her behavior and capacity. Her parents continued to be concerned about her altered level of maturity and reduced independence. Jennifer had difficulty tolerating her younger sisters, becoming irritable and yelling at them frequently. Because of this, both she and her sisters were relieved when their parents made other arrangements for the younger sisters' care after school. Jennifer also became more rigid with her friends and criticized their driving, their behavior, and social drinking. In general, she could easily become argumentative and persist with the same points over and over.

At almost a year after injury, Jennifer was readmitted to the rehabilitation hospital for a more thorough evaluation of persistent headaches and probable temporal lobe seizures. She began experiencing visual hallucinations several months before this admission, which initially terrified her and led to psychiatric evaluation. She did not experience loss of consciousness with her seizures but rather an alteration in perception and sensations of which she was aware but not in control. Jennifer described her perceptions during these episodes as feeling that people were "watching her," and seeing people's faces distorting into "scary Halloween masks," "sidewalks floating up at her," and "seeing fish dancing in an aquarium." She also reported feeling hot and cold sensations and appeared sometimes to be able to predict them. Afterward she described feeling very lethargic and having more difficulty with both physical coordination and finding the words she wanted to say. Her group of friends gradually drifted apart, and Jennifer had become quite desperate about trying to replace them. She had begun involvement in psychotherapy after the seizures started, in part to help her cope with them and her feelings of going crazy but also to help her to deal with the long-term effects of her traumatic brain injury in general.

During formal testing at this point, Jennifer's performance on verbal tasks had improved to the average level (a gain of 5 points) and her performance on visual, perceptual, and motor tasks had significantly increased to the high-average level (a gain of 27 points). Recall of verbal information both immediately and after a 30-minute delay continued to be impaired. Her basic academic skill level had increased to between the eighth and eleventh grades, but math was less adequate at the sixth- to seventh-grade level. Her memory deficits continued to interfere with her performance in school and heightened her anxiety about not being able to do well on tests. Although she was significantly depressed at this time, her depression was not sustained and alternated with periods of unrealistic optimism (Figure 3-18). She continued to be socially immature, with periods of disinhibition and difficulty in accurately perceiving social interaction. She was not able to graduate with her class but was allowed to participate in the senior prom and

Figure 3-18 Drawing of a Woman by a 17 1/2-year-old girl 1 Year after Injury

---

graduation exercises. High school coursework was not completed until January of the following year.

Jennifer was evaluated again 2 years after injury and shortly after completing high school courses (Figure 3-19). Her seizures were adequately managed by medication, but she was very upset about the limitations placed on her by not being able to drive. She had been able to maintain a relatively low-level job as a hospital transporter, with very good reliability when working full-time during the previous summer and part-time during the fall. Her employer wanted her to continue after graduation on a full-time basis, but Jennifer wanted to attempt to go to college while living at home. Cognitive improvement seemed to have stabilized, but memory deficits persisted, especially with short-term recall of verbal information. Emotionally she appeared to be under significantly more tension than previously. She complained of widely fluctuating moods, with considerably more awareness of the long-term implications of her injury and seizure limitations. She was significantly depressed, to the point of raising concern about possible thoughts of suicide. Even though she had not had

Figure 3-19 Drawing of a Woman by an 18 1/2-year-old Girl 2 Years after Injury

any seizures for months and was aware that she had to be seizure-free for a year before being allowed to drive, Jennifer questioned the effectiveness of her medication and threatened to stop taking it. She expressed her strong desire to just be cured and not to have to cope on a daily basis with the effects of head-injury sequelae and seizure management.

Three years after injury, Jennifer had a close relationship with a man and several women friends. She had attempted to attend college on a part-time basis but was not able to succeed with college-level work. Instead she returned to her previous job. She and her boy friend had plans for marriage, but until then she felt appreciated but somewhat limited by her work. Her seizure management continued to be effective, and she had been allowed to return to driving in the past year. Both she and her friends appeared to be more tolerant of her behavior, but the characteristics described after injury persisted.

Summary

In conclusion, the effects of traumatic brain injuries in childhood depend intimately on the specific nature of neurological development at the time of injury, as well as on the general characteristics of development at each stage from infancy through adolescence. Both research studies and clinical work with individual children need to proceed from a comprehensive developmental perspective in order to comprehend fully the effects of head injury.

REFERENCES

Alajouanine, T., & Lhermitte, F. (1965). Acquired aphasia in children. *Brain, 88*, 653–662.

Black, P., Shepard, R.H., & Walker, A.L. (1975). Outcome of head trauma: Age and post-traumatic seizures. In R. Porter & D. FitzSimmons (Eds.), *Outcome of severe damage to the central nervous system.* Ciba Foundation Symposium 34. North Holland, Amsterdam: Elsevier, Excerpta Medica.

Boll, T.J. (1984). *Assessment of psychological consequences of head injury in children. Advances in the behavioral measurement of children, Vol. 1.* Greenwich, CT: JAI Press.

Boll, T.J., & Barth, J.T. (1981). Neuropsychology of brain damage in children. In S.B. Filskov & T.J. Boll (Eds.), *Handbook of clinical neuropsychology.* New York: John Wiley & Sons.

Bolter, J.F., & Long, C.J. (1985). Methodological issues in research in developmental neuropsychology. In L.C. Hartlage & C.F. Telzrow (Eds.), *The neuropsychology of individual differences: A developmental perspective.* New York: Plenum Press.

Brink, J.D., Garrett, A.L., Hale, W.R., Woo-Sam, J., & Nickel, V.L. (1970). Physical recovery after severe closed head trauma in children and adolescents. *Journal of Pediatrics, 97*, 721–727.

Bronson, G.W. (1982). Structure, status and characteristics of the central nervous system at birth. In P. Stratton (Ed.), *Psychobiology of the human newborn.* New York: John Wiley & Sons.

Bruce, D.A., Alavi, A., Bilaniuk, L.T., Dolinskas, C., Obrist, W.A., Zimmerman, R.A., & Uzzell, B. (1981). Diffuse cerebral swelling following head injuries in children: The syndrome of "malignant brain edema." *Journal of Neurosurgery, 54*, 170–178.

Bruce, D.A., Schut, L., Bruno, L.A., Wood, H.H., & Sutton, L.N. (1978). Outcome following severe head injury in children. *Journal of Neurosurgery, 48*, 679–688.

Bryden, M.P., & Saxby, L. (1986). Developmental aspects of cerebral lateralization. In J.E. Obrzut & G.W. Hynd (Eds.), *Child neuropsychology: Theory and research. Vol. 1.* San Diego: Academic Press.

Chugani, H.T., Phelps, M.E., & Mazziotta, J.C. (1987). Positron emission tomography study of human brain functional development. *Annals of Neurology, 22*, 487–497.

Craft, A.W., Shaw, T.A., & Cartlidge, M.E.F. (1972). Head injuries in children. *British Medical Journal, 3*, 200–203.

Dennis, M., & Whitaker, H.A. (1976). Language acquisition following hemidecortication: Linguistic superiority of the left over the right hemisphere. *Brain and Language, 3*, 404–433.

Dobbing, J., & Smart, J.L. (1974). Vulnerability of developing brain and behavior. *British Medical Bulletin, 30*, 164–168.

Feinberg, I. (1982–83). Schizophrenia: Caused by a fault in programmed synaptic elimination during adolescence. *Journal of Psychiatric Research, 17*, 319–334.

Friede, R.L. (1975). *Developmental neuropathology.* New York: Springer-Verlag.

Golding, J. (1986). Accidents. In N.R. Butler & J. Golding (Eds.), *From birth to five: A study of the health and behavior of Britain's 5-year-olds.* New York: Pergamon Press.

Goldman, P.A. (1971). Functional development of the prefrontal cortex in early life and the problem of plasticity. *Experimental Neurology, 32*, 366–387.

Goldman, P.S. (1974). An alternative to developmental plasticity: Heterology of CNS structures in infants and adults. In D. Stein, J. Rosen, & N. Butters (Eds.), *Plasticity and recovery of function in the central nervous system*. New York: Academic Press.

Goldman, P.S. (1976). The role of experience in recovery of function following orbital prefrontal lesions in infant monkeys. *Neuropsychologia, 14*, 401–411.

Goldman, P.S. (1978). Development of frontal association cortex in the infrahuman primate. [Monograph No. 22]. *The neurological basis of language disorders in children: Methods and directions for research*. Bethesda, MD: National Institute of Neurological and Communicative Disorders and Stroke, National Institutes of Health.

Gottlieb, G. (1976). Conceptions of prenatal development: Behavioral embryology. *Psychology Review, 83*, 215–234.

Gross, C.R., Wolf, C., Kunitz, S.C., & Jane, J.A. (1985). Pilot Traumatic Coma Data Bank: A profile of head injuries in children. In R.G. Dacey, R. Winn, & R. Rimel (Eds.), *Trauma of the central nervous system*. New York: Raven Press.

Gurdjian, E.S., & Webster, J.E. (1958). *Head injuries: Mechanisms, diagnosis, and management*. Boston: Little, Brown.

Hebb, D.O. (1942). The effect of early and late brain injury upon test scores, and the nature of normal adult intelligence. *Proceedings of the American Philosophical Society, 85*, 275–292.

Hecaen, H., & Albert, M.L. (1978). *Human neuropsychology*. New York: John Wiley & Sons.

Hendrick, E.B., Harwood-Hash, D.C.F., & Hudson, A.R. (1964). Head injuries in children: A survey of 4,465 consecutive cases at the Hospital for Sick Children, Toronto, Canada. *Clinical Neurosurgery, 11*, 46–65.

Hewitt, W. (1962). The development of the human corpus callosum. *Journal of Anatomy, 96*, 355–364.

Hoffman, H.J., & Taecholarn, C. (1986). Outcomes of craniocerebral trauma in infants. In A.J. Raimondi, M. Choux, & C. DiRocco (Eds.), *Head injuries in the newborn and infant*. New York: Springer-Verlag.

Huttenlocher, P.R. (1984). Synapse elimination and plasticity in developing human cerebral cortex. *American Journal of Mental Deficiency, 88*, 488–496.

Huttenlocher, P.R., de Courten, C., Garey, L.J., & Van Der Loos, H. (1982). Synaptogenesis in human visual cortex—Evidence for synapse elimination during normal development. *Neuroscience Letters, 33*, 247–252.

Jacobson, M. (1978). *Developmental neurobiology* (2nd ed.). New York: Plenum Press.

Jennett, B. (1975). *Epilepsy after non-missile head injuries*. Chicago: Wm. Heinemann.

Kaiser, G., Rudeberg, A., Fankhauser, I., & Zumbuhl, C. (1986). Rehabilitation medicine following severe head injury in infants and children. In A.J. Raimondi, M. Choux, & C. DiRocco (Eds.), *Head injuries in the newborn and infant*. New York: Springer-Verlag.

Kennard, M.A. (1936). Age and other factors in motor recovery from precentral lesions in monkeys. *American Journal of Physiology, 115*, 138–146.

Kennard, M.A. (1938). Reorganization of motor functions in the cerebral cortex of monkeys deprived of motor and pre-motor areas in infancy. *Journal of Neurophysiology, 1*, 477–496.

Kennard, M.A. (1940). Relation of age to motor impairment in man and in subhuman primates. *Archives of Neurology and Psychiatry, 44,* 377–397.

Kennard, M.A. (1942). Cortical reorganization of motor function: Studies on a series of monkeys of various ages from infancy to maturity. *Archives of Neurology and Psychiatry, 48,* 227–240.

Kinsbourne, M. (1974). *Mechanisms of hemispheric disconnection and cerebral function.* Springfield, IL: Charles C Thomas.

Kleinberg, S.B. (1982). *Educating the chronically ill child.* Rockville, MD: Aspen Publishers.

Klonoff, H. (1971). Head injuries in children: Predisposing factors, accident conditions, accident proneness, and sequelae. *American Journal of Public Health, 61*(12), 2405–2417.

Klonoff, H., & Paris, R. (1974). Immediate, short-term and residual effects of acute head injuries in children: Neuropsychological and neurological correlates. In R. Reitan & L. Davison (Eds.), *Clinical neuropsychology: Current status and applications.* New York: Halstead Press.

Kolb, B., & Whishaw, I.Q. (1985). *Fundamentals of human neuropsychology* (2nd ed.). New York: W.H. Freeman & Co.

Levin, H.S., & Eisenberg, H.N. (1979). Neuropsychological outcome of closed head injury in children and adolescents. *Child's Brain, 5,* 281–289.

Levin, H.S., Eisenberg, H.N., Wigg, M.D., & Kobayashi, K. (1982). Memory and intellectual ability after head injury in children and adolescents. *Neurosurgery, 11,* 668–673.

Levin, H.S., Ewing-Coggs, L., & Benton, A.L. (1984). Age and recovery from brain damage: A review of clinical studies. In S.W. Scheff (Ed.), *Aging and recovery of function in the central nervous system.* New York: Plenum Press.

Luria, A.R. (1965). Vygotsky and the problem of localization of functions. *Neuropsychologia, 3,* 387–392.

Luria, A.R. (1966). *Human brain and psychological processes.* New York: Harper & Row.

Luria, A.R. (1980). *Higher cortical functions in man.* New York: Basic Books.

Mannheimer, D.I., Dewey, J., & Melinger, G.D. (1966). Fifty thousand child-years of accidental injuries. *Public Health Reports, 81,* 519.

Moyes, C.D. (1980). Epidemiology of serious head injuries in childhood. *Child Care, Health and Development, 6,* 1–9.

Pirozzolo, F.J., & Papanicolaou, A.C. (1986). Plasticity and recovery of function in the central nervous system. In J.E. Obrzut & G.W. Hynd (Eds.), *Child neuropsychology: Theory and research, Vol. 1.* San Diego: Academic Press.

Raimondi, A.J., & Hirschauer, J. (1984). Head injury in the infant and toddler. *Child's Brain, 11,* 12–35.

Rudel, R.G. (1978). Neuroplasticity: Implications for development and education. In J.S. Chall & A.F. Mirsky (Eds.), *Education and the brain.* Chicago: University of Chicago Press.

Rudel, R.G., Teuber, H.L., & Twitchell, T.E. (1966). A note on hyperesthesia in children with early brain damage. *Neuropsychologia, 4,* 351–366.

Rudel, R.G., Teuber, H.L., & Twitchell, T.E. (1974). Levels of impairment of sensori-motor functions in children with early brain damage. *Neuropsychologia, 12,* 95–108.

Rutter, M. (1982). Developmental neuropsychiatry: Concepts, issues, and prospects. *Journal of Clinical Neuropsychology, 4,* 91–115.

Rutter, M., Chadwick, O., & Shaffer, D. (1983). Head injury. In M. Rutter (Ed.), *Developmental neuropsychiatry*. New York: Guilford Press.

St. James Roberts, I. (1979). Neurological plasticity, recovery from brain insult and child development. In H.W. Reese & L.P. Lipsitt (Eds.), *Advances in child development and behavior, Vol. 14*. New York: Academic Press.

Satz, P., & Fletcher, J.M. (1981). Emergent trends in neuropsychology: An overview. *Journal of Consulting and Clinical Psychology, 49*, 851–865.

Shapiro, K. (1983). Care and evaluation of the conscious head injured child. In K. Shapiro (Ed.), *Pediatric head injury*. Mt. Kisco, NY: Futura Publishing.

Stone, L.J., Smith, H.T., & Murphy, L.B. (Eds.) (1973). *The competent infant*. New York: Basic Books.

Teuber, H.L., & Rudel, R.G. (1962). Behavior after cerebral lesions in children and adults. *Developmental Medicine and Child Neurology, 4*, 3–20.

Woods, B.T., & Carey, S. (1979). Language deficits after apparent clinical recovery from childhood aphasia. *Annals of Neurology, 6*, 405–409.

Zimmerman, R.A., & Bilaniuk, L.T. (1981). Computed tomography in pediatric head trauma. *Journal of Neuroradiology, 6*, 257–271.

Chapter 4

Cognitive Aspects

Ellen Lehr

INTRODUCTION

There is a direct relationship between injury severity and cognitive deficits, with more severe injuries related to more severe cognitive deficits. However, the degree and nature of cognitive changes can vary considerably among children and adolescents after traumatic brain injury. Some children and adolescents may have no appreciable alterations in cognitive functioning, while others are profoundly impaired for the rest of their lives. This chapter focuses on the nature of cognitive deficits after head injury, the evaluation of these deficits, and intervention approaches for remediation of cognitive deficits in children and adolescents.

No one questions the importance of the development of cognitive abilities during the formative years. This has been a very active area of research for many years in terms of the nature of cognitive development in normal children, the processes by which it proceeds, and how it can be both enhanced and altered (Carey, 1984). Little of the research with normal children has been applied to children and adolescents after head injury. As discussed in Chapter 3, little is known about the effects of alterations in cognitive development subsequent to traumatic brain injury. This is especially true in infants and preschool-age children, whose injuries have the potential of interfering most significantly over the longest period of development. In general, the premise that traumatic brain injury has the potential for impairing the capacity for learning, and consolidation of new information appears as applicable to children and adolescents as it is to adults. The sheer amount of learning that infants, children, and adolescents are undertaking emphasizes the importance of this premise when it is applied to head injuries sustained during the developmental period.

There are limitations in our current state of knowledge about the cognitive effects of head injury in children and adolescents. Very few studies have utilized control groups of noninjured children for comparison or have followed children after injury for any extensive period. The research by Rutter's group (Chadwick, Rutter, Brown, Shaffer, & Traub, 1981; Chadwick, Rutter, Shaffer, & Shrout, 1981; Rutter, Chadwick, & Shaffer, 1983; Rutter, Chadwick, Shaffer, & Brown, 1980) continued for a little over 2 years postinjury, and that by Klonoff's group (Klonoff, Crockett, & Clark, 1984; Klonoff, Low, & Clark, 1977; Klonoff & Paris, 1974) for 5 years after injury. Much of what we know about the longer-term effects of head injury in children comes from the efforts of these two research groups. Other research problems that tend to make findings difficult to interpret consist of inadequate documentation of head-injury severity with mild to severe injuries combined into one head-injured group, groups tested at different periods postinjury or tested only once, and lack of information about preinjury cognitive functioning (Levin, Benton, & Grossman, 1982). The latter is especially important in attempting to differentiate cognitive effects in children and adolescents who may have had learning problems before injury and in adolescents who may have been involved in drug or alcohol use or abuse before injury.

Although all head injuries do not necessarily cause cognitive deficits (Chadwick, Rutter, Brown, Shaffer, & Traub, 1981), some degree of cognitive impairment is common in children who were comatose for longer than 24 hours (Klonoff & Paris, 1974; Levin & Eisenberg, 1979) or who were in posttraumatic amnesia (PTA) for 2 weeks or more (Chadwick, Rutter, Brown, Shaffer, & Traub, 1981). The extent of reductions in cognitive abilities after head injuries is difficult to estimate due to frequent lack of information about preinjury functioning levels for comparison. Estimated declines in performance on intelligence testing shortly after injury have been from 10 to 30 points (Klonoff & Low, 1974; Richardson, 1963). Although many children and adolescents continue to function in the low-average and average ranges of intelligence after injury, this is less likely after severe injuries (Brink, Garrett, Hale, Woo-Sam, & Nickel, 1970). During the first year or 2 after injury (Black, Blumer, Wellner, & Walker, 1971; Chadwick, Rutter, Shaffer, & Shrout, 1981) and possibly up to 5 years after injury (Klonoff, Low, & Clark, 1977), performance on intelligence testing and other neuropsychological test measures increases. The initial rate of recovery of cognitive functioning appears to be quicker, with slowing over time. However, the recovery and improvement process may continue longer for children with more severe injuries than in those with milder injuries. Changes are more apparent on timed perceptual-motor tasks than on overlearned verbal tasks, at least in older children and adolescents. The time course of recovery and improvement and the degree of persistent deficits are not well known in infants and young children after head injuries. Although the problem of delayed cognitive effects is much more critical in these young head-injured children, this has not yet been studied.

Before the recent increase in research on the cognitive effects of head injury in children, it was widely believed that children sustain fewer and less severe impairments in this area than adults. This belief has not been upheld by research findings. There is no support for the viewpoint that children are spared residual cognitive deficits following traumatic brain injury. Children not only exhibit intellectual sequelae, but there is evidence that their recovery is no better than that of adults (Fletcher, Ewing-Cobbs, McLaughlin, & Levin, 1985). After severe injuries, younger children (under 8 years of age) tend to do worse cognitively than do older children (Brink et al., 1970), and older children tend to do worse than adolescents (Levin, Eisenberg, Wigg, & Kobayashi, 1982). When diffuse injury occurs at an early age, there is evidence of more severe intellectual impairment (Goethe & Levin, 1984).

Simple comparisons of the cognitive effects of head injury in children and adults have led to two different fallacies that do not take into account the developmental nature of cognitive effects of head injury in children. When children and adults are compared directly, the impact of cognitive deficits on development is often underestimated. This is usually related to not fully considering and respecting the importance of learning during childhood, rather than the products of learning as reflected in adult capacities in areas such as employment. However, an overestimation of deficit also can occur if all children are expected to have cognitive impairments after head injury and if all learning difficulties are seen as related to acquired deficits. Neither of these generalizations is accurate, and the tendency to reduce complex observations and data to either one of them should be avoided.

The complexity and functional impact of cognitive effects of head injury in children are only beginning to be understood. Both obvious and subtle deficits must be considered. However, to capture fully the developmental nature of effects after injury in children, deficits cannot be seen as static. Rather the focus must be on processes of change. That is, we need to study the ways in which traumatic brain injury in childhood disrupts the normal processes of cognitive change that we call *development* (Fletcher & Taylor, 1984). The order in which skills are acquired, the rate of development, and the alterations in transitions from one stage to another must be examined to understand the implications of cognitive deficits after head injury in children. This comparison needs to be made not only with some standard of normal cognitive development but also with the individual child's preinjury development. A child who was learning well above average before injury and who functions at an average level with reductions in efficiency after injury, has sustained significant impairment in cognitive functioning despite normal performance. Efforts to estimate preinjury intellectual functioning using statistical approaches have so far not been very successful with children (Kleges & Sanchez, 1981), and attempts to capture the quality or course of development after injury have not yet been made.

SPECIFIC DEFICIT AREAS

Cognitive abilities comprise a variety of component areas, each of which can be differentially involved after traumatic brain injury and each of which can affect cognitive processing capacities. The information from the following sections relies primarily on developmental psychology research and research with head-injured adults. Studies with children and adolescents after head injury have rarely reached this level of specificity. However, better information about how head injury in children and adolescents affects attention and concentration, memory, language, and visual-perceptual-motor aspects of cognitive processes is essential in attempting to design intervention approaches to increase learning and remediate cognitive deficits after injury.

Attention and Concentration

Clinically, alterations in the maintenance of attention and concentration have been hallmarks of deficits after head injury. However, there has been little formal research in this area, either with adults or with children. The neuroanatomy of attention is not well understood and has limited the development of a clear theory of attentional processes. Local areas of the brain at a cortical and a subcortical level, as well as widespread systems that facilitate the processing of attended information, appear to be involved. Attentional processes have been difficult to define but consist of at least the following three aspects (van Zomeren, Brouwer, & Deelman, 1984). First, selectivity is the mechanism we use to sort out what to attend to and what to ignore among the multitude of stimuli around us. Head injury appears to interfere especially with selective attention in controlled as contrasted with automatic processing of information. Although head-injured individuals often complain about the ability to divide attention, there is no research evidence for focused attention deficits after injury in adults. Second, speed of information processing partly determines what we notice and how much is unnoticed. The slowing of controlled cognitive processes has been well documented after head injury especially at the level of mental transformations, decision making, and response selection. This slowing of information processing means that "the head injured patient has less attention to pay than the healthy individual" (van Zomeren, Brouwer, & Deelman, 1984). Third, alertness involves shifts in the efficiency or quality of behavior that affects general receptivity to stimulation. After severe head injuries, deficts in prepared alertness have been documented in research, but this does not necessarily include deficits in overall vigilance. In summary, attentional deficits in head-injured adults who are beyond posttraumatic amnesia appear mainly the result of slowing down in the execution of consciously controlled strategies, which also interfere with performance on timed tasks and limit memory.

Even though attention has rarely been studied directly in children and adolescents after head injury, there is a basis for research in this area from developmental psychology and educational research. In children, differences in the ability to control attention have been clearly associated with age (Hagen & Hale, 1973; Miller & Weiss, 1981), hyperactivity (Douglas & Peters, 1979; Rosenthal & Allen, 1980), intelligence (Stankov, 1983), and learning disabilities (Douglas & Peters, 1979; Samuels & Edwall, 1981; Santostefano, Rutledge & Randall, 1965). Children with a variety of learning disabilities have been consistently observed to perform more poorly than noninvolved peers on tasks of sustained attention, but they have not been shown to have difficulty in selective attention (Grabe, 1986). Difficulties in selective attention were found to be task-specific and possibly more related to cognitive aspects of the task than to attentional aspects (Krupski, 1986).

Lack of consensus about the definition and theory of attention has made it difficult to develop widely accepted measures to assess attention. An observational rating scale to assess disorders of attention and arousal has been developed to aid in assessing changes after head injury, as well as the possible effects of medications (Carper, Cohen, & Mapou, 1987). Although this scale has been developed for use with adults after head injury, it has potential for being utilized with children and adolescents as well. The Continuous Performance Test has been used to assess attention in children with epilepsy. Alteration of this technique by varying the level of environmental lighting increased the attentional stress and aided in differentiating brain injured from normal children's performance (Campanelli, 1970). Picton, Stuss, and Marshall (1986) highlighted the need for a new battery of tests designed to measure attention at the sensory, motor, and cognitive levels. This battery needs to be adjustable for difficulty so that it can be applied across different levels of development and utilized across a wide range of clinical disorders. Attentional measures also need to be applicable to learning in educational settings and not merely confined to laboratory settings.

Memory

As with attention, memory is not a unitary trait or skill. There is more than one kind of memory (Squires, 1986), and the different aspects of memory are not necessarily related to each other. In other words, if a child's recall of designs is accurate, then the recall of stories could be either poor or adequate. Although there are wide variations of memory abilities across normal children, there are also developmental changes in memory abilities. As children grow older, they remember more effectively. Not all components of memory develop at the same rate. Some components of memory are present during early infancy. Simple recognition recall is surprisingly sophisticated in babies and appears to undergo little change over time (Kail, 1979). In fact, developmental changes in some memory components and efficiency are most closely related to increasing cognitive abilities. Older children are able to scan complex stimuli more effectively and use meaningful relationships as strategies for storage of information. The development and use of such strategies develops throughout childhood. For developmental psychologists, memory is not an independent intellectual faculty but instead a process intimately related to all cognitive processes (Flavell, 1971). Memory can be considered as a shorthand term for an assortment of cognitive processes including encoding, retrieval, rehearsal, search, clustering, elaboration, and schemas (Kail, 1979).

Memory has also been divided according to the time involved. Working memory is the temporary storage of information necessary for the performance of cognitive tasks such as reasoning, comprehending, and learning. Long-term memory involves the storage of information for longer than a relatively brief period. The storage of information or knowledge is referred to as *semantic memory*, the storage of personally experienced events as *episodic memory*, and the recall of personal information as *autobiographical memory*. Procedural learning or memory is the ability to perform a .task more efficiently after exposure to it, even though the individual may not be able to recall having done it before. And last, a little-studied area consists of *prospective memory*, or the ability to remember to do a particular thing at a particular time in the future.

Delineation of different aspects or components of memory is important in examining the possible sequelae of head injury since the aspects of memory that are vulnerable to traumatic brain injury can be quite discrete.

In adults, memory deficits are common after resolution of the posttraumatic amnesia period and are related to injury severity. Immediate recall of short sequences of information, such as on forward digit span tasks, and recall of overlearned material before injury appears to be comparatively resistant to the effects of head injury (Levin, Benton, & Grossman, 1982). However, disturbances in long-term storage and retrieval of information acquired since injury are common. These deficits are observed during testing in difficulty recalling stories, word associations, visual designs, and backward digit sequences (Brooks, 1976). The effects of memory deficits on everyday living appear to be significant for many head-injured adults, but they are only recently being studied in any formal way. The development of the Rivermead Behavioral Memory Test is one attempt to measure the impact of memory deficits in real-life settings (Baddeley, Harris, Sunderland, Watts, & Wilson, 1987).

There has been surprisingly little research on memory effects of traumatic brain injury in children and adolescents. As with adults, severe injury is associated with residual impairment in retrieval skills in both children and adolescents, with children doing worse. Long-term storage and retrieval of words on a selective reminding task were especially impaired with nearly half of the children and adolescents having difficulty in this area (Levin, Eisenberg, Wigg, & Kobayashi, 1982). In a 10-year follow-up study of head-injured children, 25% of them had persisting memory deficits with verbal deficits more common than memory impairment for spatial location (Gaidolfi & Vignolo, 1980).

Both clinical and research efforts to understand the effect of head injuries in children and adolescents on memory have been hindered by the lack of single measures and batteries of tests designed to assess components of memory functioning in the developmental period. Despite their limitations, there are no equivalents to the Wechsler Memory Scales and other measures of memory for use with children and adolescents. Instead there are only a few scattered single tests, each of which assesses only partial aspects of memory, all of which are poorly normed and rarely related to research findings on memory development. The measures that do exist consist of limited adolescent norms (15 and older) for the Wechsler Memory Scale (Hulicka, 1966) and for the Wechsler Memory Scale-Revised (16 years and older) (Wechsler, 1987), the Denman Neuropsychology Memory Scale (10 years and older) (Denman, 1984), adaptations of the Wechsler Memory Scale stories for children younger than 10 years of age (Kimura & McGlone, 1979), the children's version of the Selective Reminding Test (Buschke, 1974), the Rey Complex Figure children's scoring and norms (Kirk & Kelly, 1986), the Benton Visual Retention Test with norms for children 8 to 14 years of age (Benton, 1974), the Sentence Repetition Subtest from the Wechsler Preschool and Primary Scale of Intelligence (Wechsler, 1967), memory for block shape and design from the children's form of the Tactual Performance Test (Reitan & Davison, 1974), and the subtests from the Memory Scale of the McCarthy Scales of Children's Ability (McCarthy, 1972). An experimental measure that shows promise in terms of format was developed by Cull and Wyke (1984). Their memory test includes components that assess meaningful and nonmeaningful verbal and figural information recall over a variety of periods: over three learning trails, after an intervening subtest, after 24 hours, and finally after a reacquisition trial.

Language

There is little question that infants, children, and even adolescents usually demonstrate less severe language deficits and recover and improve more rapidly and to a greater extent after traumatic brain damage than do adults (Satz & Bullard-Bates, 1981). However, the mechanisms for this more adequate recovery are not well understood. During the acute phase of recovery from traumatic brain injury, spontaneous mutism (not talking), expressive aphasia (reduced initiation of speech), and anomia (difficulty in word finding) are common in children (Hecaen, 1976; Levin & Eisenberg, 1979). However, classic aphasic syndromes appear to be less frequent long-term sequelae of head injury in children and adolescents than after vascular diseases in children or adults (van Dongen & Loonen, 1977). When classic acquired language impairments do occur, they are likely to be related to specific focal injury of language centers of the brain (Satz & Bullard-Bates, 1981). After such focal injuries, the incidence of aphasia in children is basically the same as in adults with similar injuries.

The characteristics of language deficits after traumatic injury in children consist of decreases in spontaneous speech, hesitant speech, dysarthria (articulation difficulty), and subtle language deficits, especially in complex areas such as writing to dictation (Levin, 1981). Even though such deficits may not be characterized as aphasic, they still have the potential of interfering significantly with learning and academic performance (Satz & Bullard-Bates, 1981). In complex areas that are most likely to be related to academic learning, such as written language, children have been found to perform less adequately than adolescents (Ewing-Cobbs, Fletcher, Landry, & Levin, 1985). Although spontaneous recovery occurs in many children after head injury, it by no means occurs in all. Language deficits especially in reduction of spontaneous speech and complex language frequently persist for a year after injury and can continue up to 10 years after injury (Satz & Bullard-Bates, 1981; Gaidolfi & Vignolo, 1980). Those children who were initially dysfluent and anomic did better than those with mixed expressive and receptive deficits (Levin & Eisenberg, 1979).

Visual-Perceptual-Motor

As discussed, pure motor deficits, such as hemiparesis (one-sided weakness of the body) often improve faster and better in children and adolescents than in adults. However, posttraumatic deficits are often apparent on tasks requiring rapid motor responses, especially after severe injuries but less so after mild to moderate head injuries (Bawden, Knights, & Winogron, 1985; Chadwick, Rutter, Shaffer, & Shrout, 1981). The severity of these performance deficits is related to length of coma and often persist for at least 1 to 2 years after injury, if not longer (Klonoff & Low, 1974; Klonoff, Low, & Clark, 1977). Impaired functioning, usually related to slowed speed on timed tasks, has been consistently reported on trailmaking tests, pencil-and-paper symbol-coding tasks, measures of finger- and foot-tapping speed, formboard assembly, and mazes. However, it is not clear if deficits are primarily related to slowed reaction time or to slowed information processing or a combination of the two (Bawden et al., 1985). The degree of deficit increases with the complexity of the task so that simple motor measures such as finger-tapping speed are less likely to be impaired than more complex perceptual-motor tasks such as completing formboards with eyes blindfolded. Deficits in speeded performance of perceptual-motor tasks also can exist in the presence of more adequate and apparently normal cognitive functioning in children after head injuries (Levin, Eisenberg, Wigg, & Kobayashi, 1982).

In summary, cognitive deficits after head injury are as common in children and adolescents as they are in adults and have the potential of interfering with development over an extended period. There are many ways of characterizing possible cognitive deficits after head injury. This section focused on attention and concentration, memory, language, and perceptual-motor areas primarily because of the research available in these areas as well as their pervasive impact on learning. Learning, though, involves the integration of these basic processes into complex processes such as comprehension, organization, flexibility, problem solving, abstraction, and generalization. These complex processes are important to children's and adolescents' learning after head injury and are discussed in terms of clinical evaluation and intervention approaches.

EVALUATION

This section focuses on evaluation of cognitive and learning aspects of head injuries in children and adolescents in terms of the rationale of evaluation, some of the measures that can be utilized, guidelines for interpretation of evaluation findings, and the process of evaluation. Case study presentations of cognitive functioning implications during different developmental periods have been incorporated into the case illustrations in Chapter 3.

Evaluation Rationale

In clinical practice, the evaluation of cognitive aspects of head injury cannot be easily separated from behavioral and psychosocial functioning in children and adolescents. In a comprehensive evaluation, the interaction of all three components are integrated in order to comprehend more fully the impact of traumatic brain injury for any individual child or adolescent. However, it is difficult to reach this level of integration without initially considering the cognitive and learning, behavioral, and psychosocial aspects of head injury separately. Clinical evaluation with children and adolescents after head injury necessarily involves an individualized approach. No characteristic pattern at any one point in time after injury can capture the range and variety of strengths and deficits of this heterogeneous group.

The evaluation of children and adolescents after head injury usually goes beyond traditional psychological assessment approaches, incorporating neuropsychological evaluation approaches. The difference between psychological and neuropsychological evaluation lies primarily not in the tests that are utilized but in the application of a knowledge base about brain functioning and the ways in which brain alterations can be expressed in behavior in the broadest sense. Therefore the difference resides not in the measures but in the training of the professional who is guiding the evaluation process and interpreting evaluation findings.

Neuropsychological evaluation is usually closely related to empirically derived medical data (Gaddes, 1985), especially when there is reason to suspect alterations in brain functioning, as in significant traumatic brain injury. Through a variety of tests measuring the integrity of both global brain functioning and the presence of deficits in specific areas, neuropsychological evaluation attempts to investigate the functional status of the brain through the analysis of behavioral responses (Teeter, 1986). The investigation of the functional status of the brain is conducted through the analysis of behavioral responses on a variety of tests, both of global brain functioning and those designed to assess the presence of deficits in specific focal areas of the brain. However, it also legitimately involves the study of behavioral interrelationships (and how these relationships change over the developmental period) without necessarily making a direct inference about brain functioning or dysfunction (Fletcher & Taylor, 1984). The neuropsychological evaluation of head-injured children and adolescents is concerned with more than diagnosis of the extent of deficits and the presence of preserved abilities. Equally important aspects of evaluation are the child's ability to adjust to and fulfill successfully daily responsibilities, potential for recovery, and recommendations for treatment and education (Cicerone & Tupper, 1986; Herbert, 1964; Teeter, 1986). Because of the nature of development during childhood, neuropsychological evaluation must also be able to address the process of and potential for expected change (Tindal & Marston, 1986).

Evaluation Measures

The neuropsychological evaluation of children and adolescents after head injury necessarily consists of a comprehensive approach to assess the areas of functioning that are involved in cognition and learning, as well as possible interferents and deficits. The specific areas of functioning usually included are intelligence; sensory, motor, and perceptual abilities; and language, memory, learning, reasoning, and academic skills. The tasks utilized need to vary according to difficulty level (including both simple and complex tasks), according to novelty (including both routinized and novel tasks), with and without motor components, utilizing both linguistic and figural materials, and under timed and nontimed conditions (Rourke & Adams, 1984). Preferably all measures should be well standardized and normed for noninjured children and adolescents. The evaluation data are then analyzed to delineate strengths, weaknesses, deficit areas, changes from preinjury levels, and comparison with normal children of the same age and ability level.

The measures available for neuropsychological evaluation of children and adolescents often fall short of this ideal. In contrast with the extensive history and development of intelligence testing, neuropsychological evaluation measures for children and adolescents have existed for less than 20 years. Because of less well-advanced neurodevelopmental theory and research, the development of tests that are solidly based on theory and research has been limited. The current neuropsychological batteries for the most part are downward extensions of adult measures that have been shortened or simplified for use with children and adolescents. These changes, though, do not necessarily mean that the tasks are age or developmentally appropriate. Because of developmental differences, the interpretations of adult measures may not be accurate when they are applied to children and adolescents. The test format may be the same or similar, but the brain functioning and development of the test taker cannot be assumed to be similar (Hartlage & Telzrow, 1986). Current measures are also, for the most part, inadequately normed (Hynd & Obrzut, 1986). The standardization and norming of tests for children and adolescents, though, are considerably more difficult and complex than with adults, usually involving age groups separated by no less than 1-year intervals. Probably one of the most striking limitations of existing tests, though, is their lack of continuity across ages and developmental periods. It is difficult if not impossible to assess any specific area of cognitive functioning in a continuous way as it develops over time with the existing neuropsychological measures.

Neuropsychological Batteries

There has been divided opinion about whether to use a consistent battery of tests with all children and adolescents after head injury or to choose specific tests to use with each individual, dependent on unique needs and deficit areas. In practice, the approach utilized often depends on the training of the clinician and the time constraints of the evaluation.

Current neuropsychological batteries always include measures of intelligence, most often the Wechsler scale, which is appropriate for the child's or adolescent's age. The Wechsler Intelligence Scale for Children-Revised (WISC-R) (Wechsler, 1974) has been found to be more sensitive to the kinds of deficits produced by neurological dysfunction in children than the adult form of the test in adults (Boll, 1983). In fact, the usefulness of the WISC-R has led some researchers and clinicians to question the utility of neuropsychological measures; they argue that they do not add significant information to justify their time and expense (Rutter, Chadwick, & Shaffer, 1983). There has been found to be a significant effect of IQ on 6 of the 14 tests of the Halstead-Reitan Neuropsychological Test Battery for Children (Seidenberg, Giordani, Berent, & Boll, 1983) as well as with the Luria-Nebraska Neuropsychological Battery-Children's Revision (Tramontana, Klee, & Boyd, 1984). As discussed in this chapter, neuropsychological measures can also be more sensitive to cognitive deficits in children and adolescents that are not identified on the WISC-R, especially on long-term follow-up.

Two batteries have been designed for use with children and adolescents from the Halstead-Reitan tradition: the Halstead-Reitan Neuropsychological Test Battery for Children for use with children 9 to 14 years of age and the Reitan-Indiana Neuropsychological Test Battery for Children 5 to 8 years of age. Adolescents 15 years and older are tested with the adult version of the battery, though limited norms are available (Fromm-Auch & Yeudall, 1984). The tests in this battery are designed to be given in such a way to elicit the child's optimal performance rather than typical performance. Tests in the battery include relatively complex measures of rhythm patterns, speech sound recognition, categories concept formation, and tactual performance. Additional measures usually consist of a Wechsler IQ test, aphasia screening, trailmaking, hand strength, sensory and perceptual exam, tactile form recognition, tactile finger localization, fingertip writing, lateral dominance, the Wide Range Achievement Test (Jastak & Wilkinson, 1984), and other academic measures. Few alterations were made from the adult version of the battery for administration to older children; however, significant changes were required to make the battery applicable to younger children, including development of new tests. The full battery can require 4 to 6 hours of testing time, depending on the age of the child and functioning level. (Refer to Reitan & Davison, 1974, for a complete description of the Halstead-Reitan test batteries.) Normative data are available for both batteries but should be used with some caution because they are not necessarily representative of the U.S. population (Klonoff & Low, 1974; Knights, 1970; Spreen & Gaddes, 1969).

The Luria-Nebraska Neuropsychological Battery was revised for use with children 8 to 12 years of age (Plaisted, Gustavson, Wilkening, & Golden, 1983) and an adaptation for use with younger children is under development. For adolescents, the adult version of the battery is utilized. The children's revision is a shortened form of the original adult version of the battery. It is composed of 11 scales consisting of motor skills, acoustico-motor organization (rhythm), higher cutaneous and kinesthetic functions (tactile), visual functions, receptive speech, expressive speech, writing, reading, arithmetic, memory, and intellectual processes. The battery takes about 2 1/2 hours to administer and has been normed on 125 children with 25 individuals at each age level. Because of its recent development, less research and clinical experience is available in the application of the Luria-Nebraska to the evaluation of children and adolescents after head injury.

Severe deficits, though, may limit and sometimes prohibit the use of either of the two neuropsychological batteries. Many of the tests comprising the Halstead-Reitan batteries require relatively intact fine-motor functioning of both hands to use a pencil, place blocks in a puzzle board, or push buttons. Although some of these tasks can be adapted, others cannot and require the use of alternative measures. Significant language deficits can also interfere with understanding of test instructions and limit the use of the existing neuropsychological batteries. If motoric limitations are severe, alternative measures of intellectual functioning such as the Pictorial Test of Intelligence (French, 1964) or the Columbia Mental Maturity Test (Burgemeister, Blum, & Lorge, 1962) may be useful in assessing cognitive abilities. Tests that can be administered through gesture and that do not require spoken responses such as the Leiter International Performance Scale (Leiter, 1948) and the Hiskey-Nebraska Test of Learning Aptitude (Hiskey, 1966) can be utilized to assess cognitive abilities in children and adolescents who are significantly speech- and language-impaired after head injury. Current neuropsychological batteries are limited to evaluating children who function no younger than approximately a 5-year developmental level. For infants and younger or more impaired children, measures that have been designed to assess cognitive abilities appropriate for these ages are usually utilized. Tests that may be utilized include the Bayley Scales of Infant Development (Bayley, 1969), the Stanford-Binet Intelligence Scale, Form L-M and the Fourth Edition (Terman & Merrill, 1960; Thorndike, Hagen, & Sattler, 1986), the Wechsler Pre-School and Primary Test of Intelligence (Wechsler, 1967), the McCarthy Scales of Children's Abilities (McCarthy, 1972), and the Kaufman Assessment Battery for Children (Kaufman & Kaufman, 1983). Even though these are not neuropsychological tests, they can often be interpreted in the light of neuropsychological knowledge by a well-trained clinician with experience with younger head-injured children.

Interpretation of Evaluation Findings

In order to understand fully the findings of neuropsychological evaluations with head-injured children and adolescents, both quantitative and qualitative approaches must be utilized. The quantitative sources of data provide a basis for severity of deficits and a comparison with nonimpaired children and adolescents. Qualitative approaches, though, help in the formulation of hypotheses about how functioning is impaired, as well as which compensatory and treatment techniques might be attempted. In recent years, with the development and increasing sophistication of neuroimaging techniques, there has been less interest in using neuropsychological evaluation findings to aid in localization of brain injury. Rather the emphasis has centered on functional, behavioral, and learning implications of neurological impairment—in other words, how brain impairment affects the child's or adolescent's cognitive functioning in the broadest sense, in learning, thinking, understanding, problem solving, and efficiency and speed of performance.

In the traditional approach to interpretation, neuropsychological evaluation data are analyzed in four ways: (1) level of performance, or the extent of severity of impairment: (2) differential patterns of ability, which can lead to possible diagnostic classifications, syndromes, and subtypes (Rourke & Adams, 1984); (3) comparisons of the functional efficiency of the two sides of the body with reference to brain functioning; and (4) specific deficits of pathognomic significance, that is, responses that are unquestionably associated with central nervous system impairment (Selz & Reitan, 1979). In the evaluation of children and adolescents after head injury, it is also important to include comparisons of preinjury and postinjury functioning (Rourke, 1981).

One of the patterns of test findings from evaluations of head-injured children and adolescents has been that of initial reduction in the performance IQ score on the Wechsler scales in comparison with the verbal IQ score. Within a year after injury, this difference is often no longer apparent with improvement in performance IQ scores. However, functioning on the coding subtest may continue to be significantly reduced for more than a year after injury (Rutter et al., 1983). This pattern has been found in older children, adolescents, and adults (Klonoff et al., 1977; Chadwick, Rutter, Brown, Shaffer, & Traub, 1981; Levin, Benton, & Grossman, 1982). However, it is not universal and cannot be considered prototypic of all head-injured individuals. It can be affected by variables such as focal deficits, especially those that interfere with language functioning and therefore depress verbal IQ scores, as well as preinjury strengths and weaknesses. For example, if a child has preinjury strengths in performance IQ areas, after injury the IQ scores could be equivalent on the verbal and performance subtests, even though for that child the Performance IQ is actually substantially reduced from preinjury levels. From clinical experience, younger children may not demonstrate this pattern after severe injuries as consistently as older children and adolescents. Rather they have been observed to have more equivalent performance on both IQ scales, with a possible decrease in measured cognitive abilities over time, even though they may be making academic and developmental progress. (See case studies in Chapter 3 for examples.) This needs further investigation to understand more clearly the implications of head injury on the subsequent cognitive development of individuals who were injured in infancy and early childhood.

Several qualifications need to be considered in the interpretations of test findings after head injury in children and adolescents.

- Old learning and well-established skills and abilities are most resistant to brain impairment. Especially in older children and adolescents, care should be taken not to overestimate learning ability and underestimate deficits.

- The focus of neuropsychological evaluation is often on obtaining the best possible performance, not a typical performance. This is done to determine the best performance that the child's brain can produce under optimal conditions so that deficits can be clearly identified and intervention approaches indicated (Rourke, Bakker, Fisk, & Strang, 1983). However, it can limit the generalization of test findings.

- On initial postinjury testing, head-injured children and adolescents can benefit less than normal children in terms of practice effects due to their cognitive deficits, especially in attention and memory areas (Brooks, 1987). However, on subsequent testing they may show greater practice effects than noninjured children and adolescents who have experienced testing the same two times.

- Testing occurs in a quiet, controlled, one-to-one setting with tasks that are often short in length and usually interesting in format. However, performance and learning in a school or even in a therapy setting are often quite different. Real-life settings tend to be more distracting and involve functioning within a group, with less consideration to slow speed, fatigue, and other deficits that can impair performance after head injury. Performance in a testing environment is also different from that required in independent learning and study, when a child or adolescent is expected to be able to focus on reading, writing, and math for extended periods with little available assistance. For example, reading a book chapter and taking a quiz the next day involves longer-term memory than usually assessed in evaluations. Schoolwork also often makes greater demands on comprehension and interpretation, especially through completion of longer assignments such as writing research papers and book reviews. Interpretation of test findings to real-life demands must be done carefully and take into consideration both the characteristics of the evaluation and the nature of the expectations across different settings.

Evaluation Process

Ideally children and adolescents are closely monitored and evaluated frequently to assess the cognitive implications of traumatic brain injury from the time of injury and continuing for as long as cognitive effects interfere with their learning and functioning. Even though informal mental status evaluations and observations can be conducted throughout recovery, formal testing can be validly completed only after the child or adolescent has emerged from posttraumatic amnesia and confusion. This initial testing, which gives a baseline measure against which further recovery and improvement can be compared, is important in estimating current and future cognitive functioning. One of the measures frequently utilized in baseline evaluation is the Wechsler intelligence scale that is appropriate for the child's age. The full-scale IQ score from these tests has been found to be the best predictor of long-term cognitive sequelae in children, more accurate than the period of unconsciousness (Klonoff et al., 1984). Depending upon the child's or adolescent's capacity for engaging in testing, a full neuropsychological battery may be completed at baseline evaluation. However, more severely impaired children and adolescents may not have the capacity or the stamina to undergo 5 or 6 hours of testing, especially not in 1 day. They may need short testing sessions of 30 to 60 minutes, with completion of testing over several days or a reduced battery of tests.

When children are involved in an ongoing rehabilitation, comprehensive evaluation can often be completed as part of their program. However, if the child or adolescent has received only acute-care hospitalization and management, evaluation may not be recommended until difficulties are encountered after return to school or when other attempts to assume preinjury activities are unsuccessful. These children and adolescents also would benefit from, at the minimum, a shortened, focused evaluation either to identify their postinjury needs or to document clearly that they are not experiencing impairments after injury.

Reevaluation is usually recommended at 6 months and 12 months after injury and then at 1-year intervals for the next several years, depending on the severity of injury and persisting deficits. Those children and adolescents who have sustained severe injuries often require evaluations over a longer period than those who have had mild or moderate injuries. The purpose of reevaluations is not only to assess the rate and degree of recovery or improvement in cognitive areas after injury but also to aid in ongoing decisions about the child's or adolescent's care and management. Evaluation findings can be utilized in planning and adapting school and therapy programs on a routine basis. Reevaluations are often requested when children and adolescents encounter difficulties in mastering basic academic skills and in making the transition to more independent learning and when they encounter failure. Evaluations are often useful in helping to plan for expected life transitions such as the beginning of formal education and changes in schools at any time from kindergarten through college and vocational programs, competency to drive a car, competency to manage possible financial settlements, and competency to be one's own guardian after 18 years of age.

For evaluations to be most useful, the findings need to be interpreted in a way that they can be understood and utilized in the child's or adolescent's management. However, there can be many audiences whose needs must be individually and specifically addressed. Evaluations are often seen as important markers for the parents of head-injured children and adolescents. It is a time to reexamine, sometimes painfully, how their child or adolescent is progressing in the context of preinjury and postinjury functioning. For the head-injured children or adolescents, evaluations can confront them with deficits that they would prefer not to acknowledge so directly. Because of the often heavy emphasis on deficits and negative changes after head injury, it is important when interpreting evaluation findings with children and adolescents and their parents to include both capacities and deficits. Interpretation of evaluation findings can become a natural time for continuing the ongoing process of education about head injury, keeping in perspective the components of injury as well as normal development. However, evaluation findings may be utilized and presented quite differently when the audience shifts to teachers and therapists who are concerned about alterations in management techniques and possible program changes, or attorneys and insurance representatives who are concerned about financial and legal settlements, or for judges who are concerned about competency determination.

Summary

The cognitive aspects of traumatic brain injury in children and adolescents and their processes of recovery and improvement are not likely to be understood as a unitary phenomenon. Instead, cognitive functioning after head injury is affected by multiple processes, as well as multiple variables such as age, developmental level, preinjury functioning, specific injury characteristics, and complications. This complexity has not been appreciated in research (Boll & Barth, 1981) and is only beginning to be utilized in recent research efforts (Filley, Cranberg, Alexander, & Hart, 1987). Children and adolescents after head injury are a heterogeneous group in terms of cognitive effects. However, it may be possible to derive subgroups that reflect specific patterns of deficits and strengths that could be useful in better understanding and aiding their learning. The approach being developed with children with learning disabilities could provide a useful model (Rourke, 1984; Rourke, Bakker, Fisk, & Strang, 1983).

In general, children and adolescents after traumatic brain injury have not received the best care if the cognitive and learning correlates of their disorder have not been carefully and explicitly addressed in a manner integral to their overall management (Boll, 1983). However, this often does not occur because of an underemphasis on the possible cognitive sequelae from head injury, as well as from a dearth of trained professionals with expertise in this area.

INTERVENTION

Cognitive Rehabilitation

From work with adults after head injury, the potential for greater levels of recovery with intensive therapy started the burgeoning of interest in cognitive rehabilitation approaches and program development. Several books have been recently published on cognitive rehabilitation with adults (Adamovich, Henderson, & Auerbach, 1985; Meier, Benton, & Diller, 1987; Prigatano, 1986; Trexler, 1982; Uzzell & Gross, 1986; Williams & Long, 1987). However, only one book has focused on the rehabilitation of children and adolescents after traumatic brain injury (Ylvisaker, 1985).

Experience with cognitive rehabilitation has raised hopes that individuals after traumatic brain injury can improve their functioning even many years after injury if they are taught in specific ways. This hope should be tempered with the realization that the degree of improvement possible still has limitations dependent on the degree of neurological impairment and the characteristics of the individual. We need to keep clearly in focus that what we are attempting to do through cognitive rehabilitation is to train and retrain a system with deficits. While improvements and more adequate functioning may be possible, return to preinjury levels of functioning or preinjury potential may not be realistic. Cognitive rehabilitation strategies basically involve the essential components of learning: persistent study with rapid and appropriate feedback while maintaining the individual's motivation to attend to the tasks and to work toward improving performance (Long, 1987).

There has been very little direct work with children and adolescents in cognitive rehabilitation; very few therapy programs are designed specifically with a developmental focus. Teaching and therapy approaches, though, have been developed to aid children in cognitive aspects of learning (Feuer-stein, 1980; Meichenbaum, 1976; Santostefano, 1985). However, the effectiveness of both cognitive approaches designed for children with other learning disorders and those developed for adults after head injury, needs to be demonstrated for head-injured children and adolescents. These approaches, though, do provide a starting place for designing cognitive rehabilitation intervention for children and adolescents after head injury.

To develop an effective cognitive rehabilitation program for any child or adolescent after head injury, several factors must be considered. There must be a clear understanding of current level of functioning, both in testing and in real-life learning settings. In addition to the components of cognitive functioning discussed earlier in this chapter, other factors such as the child's or adolescent's awareness of deficits and motivation for improvement must be considered. Development of therapy goals should focus on concerns such as what is interfering the most with the child's cognitive functioning, what can be most easily improved, and what is most important for the child and adolescent, the teacher, and parents. After consideration of goals, the specific forms of intervention and procedures can be designed.

Three basic forms of intervention have been utilized in improving cognitive functioning after traumatic brain injury: (1) component training, (2) compensatory training, and (3) functional and integrative training. Although these approaches can be utilized separately, it is more common for them to be combined depending on the specific area of functioning being addressed, the characteristics of the child's strengths and deficits, and the nature of the setting within which the child is expected to function.

Component training involves direct remediation of deficits, usually in basic cognitive processes such as attention, memory, perceptual motor skills, linguistic skills, reasoning, and speed of processing. Intensive, carefully designed retraining programs utilizing this approach have improved the performance of adults after head injury (Ben-Yishay, Rattok, Ross, Lakin, Ezrachi, Silver, & Diller, 1982). Direct training in the areas of deficit or weakness is especially appropriate for utilization with young children (Haarbauer-Krupa, Henry, Szekeres, & Ylvisaker, 1985). They have a special need for intensive, systematic practice of component skills that they are in the process of developing. Young children also may not yet have the ability to engage in learning of compensatory strategies. Component training has also been recommended for immediate intervention with children as soon after injury as feasible (Rourke et al., 1983; Rourke, Fisk, & Strang, 1986). According to this rationale, the longer treatment is delayed, the greater the chance that deficits become entrenched and become more resistant to intervention. The specific circumstances that would argue for utilization of component training include remediation of well-circumscribed deficits that clearly interfere with functioning, remediation of mild deficits in the presence of well-developed strengths, and as a last resort, an attempt to improve functioning when there are too few strengths available to compensate effectively.

Criticism of the component training approach has centered on its single-minded focus, especially when it is used exclusively and functional skills have been ignored. Because of the direct focus on deficit areas, component training can be a slower and more frustrating approach than utilization of strengths. Children and adolescents must be willing and able to cooperate and tolerate working directly in the area of their deficits, without jeopardizing self-confidence or causing emotional distress. The advantage to this approach is that if the area of deficit can be improved significantly, the child or adolescent may be able to function and learn at a more normal level.

Compensatory strategy training can take two forms depending on who is doing the compensating: (1) alterations in the environment, including changes in expectations from others, use of environmental cues and support from others, and physical alterations of space, and (2) utilization of compensatory strategies by the head-injured individual through use of external aids (lists, appointment books, typewriters, tape recorders) or internal strategies (self-instruction, rehearsal, mental organization, verbalization techniques). After injury, even young children are likely to begin to develop their own compensations for deficits. However, the goal of cognitive rehabilitation in this area is the deliberate mastery of as functional and efficient compensation strategies as possible. Focusing intervention on utilizing strengths for compensation is usually more effective with older children and adolescents than deficit training (Rourke et al., 1983; Rourke et al., 1986). They are likely to respond more positively, be less emotionally resistive, and experience less frustration and a greater sense of control. Compensation strategies, though, must belong to the child or adolescent and be supported by teachers and parents for functional use on a daily basis. Specific approaches and techniques for compensation training are beyond the scope of this chapter and can be found in other sources (Haarbauer-Krupa et al., 1985; Ylvisaker, Szekeres, Henry, Sullivan, & Wheeler, 1987).

Functional and integrative training involves the generalization and application of cognitive skills in real-life settings. The approach to functional integration can involve directly teaching skills in the setting in which they will be used, as well as focusing on the transfer of skills learned in the therapy setting to real-life settings. Depending on the nature of the deficits, the characteristics of the individual and the setting, either of these approaches can be appropriate. The approach can also involve the mastery of general strategies for application in several settings, as well as specific training for tasks in a particular setting. Since head-injured children and adolescents do not automatically or easily integrate skills, generalize learning to new settings, or maintain improvements over time, an emphasis on functional and integrative training is always a component of effective cognitive rehabilitation. For children and adolescents, learning within the classroom setting is often a focus of the functional and integrative emphasis of therapy. Specific strategies and techniques for use in the school setting can be found in several sources (Burns, Cook, & Ylvisaker, 1988; Cohen, Joyce, Rhoades, & Welks, 1985; DePompei & Blosser, 1987).

There has been little research on the effectiveness of cognitive intervention with children or adolescents. Only one published research study has utilized a comparison group of children who did not receive services with one that did. The Neurocognitive Education Project was designed as a research intervention program for head-injured children who were at least 1 year postinjury (Light, Neumann, Lewis, Morecki-Oberg, Asarnow, & Satz, 1987). It involved training tutors to work with the children on a one-to-one basis in both home and school settings. The purpose of the program was to teach the children to recognize their own strengths and weaknesses to learn to use their brain better by mastering cognitive strategies. The approaches involved an integration of neuropsychological and educational knowledge and methods. Intervention programs were tailored for each child based on pretutoring evaluations, with goals designed for using strengths in remediating deficits. The specific techniques included identifying strengths, cuing and fading of cues, social and cognitive modeling, verbal mediation, summarizing, generalization, creative implementing of cognitive strategies, and cooperative teacher-learner interaction. After approximately 5 months of tutoring, improvements were measured in adaptive behavior areas but less so in cognitive functioning.

Intervention techniques and programs for the remediation and enhancement of learning in head-injured children and adolescents are clearly in the very beginning stages. Work with head-injured adults and experience with other learning-impaired children has provided some direction. However, we are far from the goal of being able to design effective interventions that are geared to the child's developmental level and stage of recovery and improvement, directed at specific deficits, utilizing current strengths, and with applicability to educational and noneducational settings.

Use of Computers in Cognitive Rehabilitation

The adaptation and development of computer applications for use with adults after head injury and in educational settings with children have generated considerable interest and fascination over the past several years. With the increasing availability of computers for use at home, at school, and in cognitive therapy, there has also been increasing concern about the appropriate utilization of this technique in the rehabilitation of head-injured individuals. At present, there is little research to support the effectiveness of computer programs in cognitive rehabilitation (Lynch, 1986). However, because of the recent development in this area, the paucity of research is hardly surprising. An important distinction should be made. When considering whether the use of computers is appropriate and helpful in cognitive rehabilitation, the computer is actually less important than the software or the computer programs and the way in which these programs are used with children and adolescents. The computer and computer programs have the potential for being powerful tools in cognitive rehabilitation, but they are only tools and cannot supplant teachers, therapists, and parents to guide their use with children and adolescents after head injuries.

Computers have the advantage of being patient, consistent, and nonjudgmental tutors that can give immediate and continual feedback about performance. Learning tasks can be flexibly designed to meet individual needs for speed, for cuing, and for level of task complexity. Working on the computer can be enjoyable and motivating for some children and adolescents. The computer format can be utilized to present basic level learning in a way that is not demeaning or perceived as babyish, which is particularly important for children and adolescents after head injury. It is sometimes easier to be confronted with a deficient performance from the impersonal machine. Computers can also be utilized in the accurate monitoring of individualized learning at a reasonable cost, including collection of data for therapy and research purposes (Long, 1987).

However, all of these advantages hinge on the adequacy of the computer programs being utilized. If programs are not carefully selected, they can be expensive forms of tasks that are better learned through other means such as pencil-and-paper formats. Poorly designed programs can be very frustrating to normal learning children, much less to children after head injury, and can in actuality be much less flexible than a skilled therapist using traditional materials (Ylvisaker et al., 1987). Probably the most important possible disadvantage of computer use in cognitive retraining is the inappropriate use of programs that do not meet the needs of the individual. Existing software usually does not address issues related to improving the functional abilities of head-injured individuals in real-life settings.

Computers can be put to several quite different uses in working with children and adolescents after head injury. Computer activities can be an adjunct to cognitive-based therapy, either in the presence of the therapist or through independent use of programs that have been specifically chosen by the therapist. Other than use in direct or indirect therapy activities, though, computers can fulfill learning, recreational, and compensatory needs of children and adolescents after head injury. Many of the commercially available games (Lynch, 1982) and educational programs are useful in helping head-injured children and adolescents more profitably occupy their free time when it can be particularly difficult for them to engage in less-structured activities. For those children and adolescents who have fine-motor limitations, even of a relatively mild nature affecting writing speed and hand fatigue, word-processing programs can offer a useful alternative to writing papers and assignments. This can be especially important for children and adolescents in the upper grades and in high school by helping them to complete longer papers at a reasonable level with the minimum of frustration. The use of a spell-check program and an outlining program can provide direct compensation for acquired deficits in accuracy and organization.

Educational skills programs can be particularly useful in helping recently injured children or adolescents to regain previous academic mastery levels while promoting self-confidence. Complex learning and computer programming can be addressed through the individual or group use of detective or adventure role-playing games, as well as through learning a computer language such as LOGO (Papert, 1980). Considerable experience in enhancing the learning of handicapped and nonhandicapped children in language and mathematical areas utilizing the LOGO system could be applicable to use with children and adolescents after head injuries (Weir & Watt, 1981).

Computer-assisted instruction appears most effective when paired with traditional teaching, though it may be as effective as traditional teaching by itself (Lieber & Semmel, 1985). However, information learned through the computer may not be retained or generalized as successfully as when it is learned in traditional or applied learning settings. In educational settings, computer-assisted instruction has been found most effective with older children (older than 8 years of age) and adolescents who already have some familiarity with the material and are good achievers and when used for the purposes of drill and practice (Long, 1987). The effectiveness of computer-assisted instruction has been attributed more to using this means to implement sound educational practice rather than to the special features of computer technology (Ragosta, 1982).

One concern about the use of computers in childhood is that of increasing social isolation through interacting with a machine rather than other people. This is an important issue for children and adolescents after head injury, for whom social isolation is often a key issue (see Chapter 6). Two approaches have been utilized in meeting this criticism: one is the use of computers in conjunction with face-to-face instruction and therapy; the other is use of group sessions of computer instruction, during which children work cooperatively on problem-solving tasks.

In studies with children with learning disabilities, computers have been most useful in providing a special kind of practice of skills that are first introduced by the teacher. Mastery of basic academic skills in reading, math, and spelling is important since deficits in these areas impede learning of more complex processes such as comprehension (Torgesen, 1986). However, the inappropriate use and reliance on computer tasks may actually interfere with learning in those children who benefit the most from teacher-aided and group instruction. Since not all children with learning difficulties learn in the same way, the use of even a variety of computer approaches may not be appropriate in meeting their needs.

Within the past several years, a number of software packages have been developed and marketed for the purpose of cognitive retraining of individuals after head injuries. No matter how well-designed the software may be, a critical factor in its successful utilization is ensuring that it fits the needs of the individual using it. Because of the wide variation in levels of functioning, strengths, and deficits of individuals after head injury, no standard cognitive retraining package can by itself provide remediation or retraining for any head-injured person. In summary, computers can be a useful and effective adjunctive strategy for cognitive rehabilitation but do not supplant therapy or teaching and are certainly not magic or simple solutions to the complex cognitive difficulties of head-injured children and adolescents. The overriding issue remains whether the skills learned through the use of the computer generalize and enhance the functional abilities of head-injured children and adolescents.

Model Programs

In the past five years, there has been a virtual explosion of postacute therapy programs designed for the rehabilitation and remediation of the cognitive, social and emotional, and vocational deficits experienced by many adults after head injuries. These programs are usually based in the community and focus on amelioration of functional impairments that interfere with the ability of head-injured adults to live independently and to be gainfully employed. Although children and adolescents may need the comprehensive and integrated services offered by a therapeutic program designed for head-injured individuals, these services are not commonly available to them through either therapeutic or educational programs. The school system is often relied on to provide for both the educational and the therapeutic needs of children and adolescents after head injury, even though traditional educational systems may not have the expertise or the staff to do so. Community-based programs designed for head-injured adults are being requested to serve younger and younger children. However, these programs may lack expertise with the developmental and educational needs of children and adolescents.

Several models are proposed for the design of therapeutic programs that have the potential to meet the specific needs of head-injured children and adolescents:

- Therapeutic programs designed for head-injured children and adolescents. For those children and adolescents who are not able to learn successfully in a school-based academic setting, at least temporary involvement in a therapy program specifically designed for the remediation of head-injury sequelae would be appropriate. The kinds of deficits that could necessitate such a therapy program include severe memory, attention and concentration, and language impairments. Those children and adolescents who are not able to learn effectively in a classroom setting because of behavioral control deficits, significantly slowed processing of information, and fatigue may also benefit from involvement in a structured therapy program. Such programs could be designed as full-day programs in which children and adolescents could be involved for relatively short transition periods (several weeks to several months) or for more extensive therapy involvement as with adults (6 months to 2 years). If a child or adolescent is involved primarily in a therapy program for any length of time, an essential part of the program should focus on academic skills and eventual return to an education setting. Other drawbacks of separate therapy programs for children and adolescents after head injury consist of increased social isolation from friends and the difficulty in forming reasonable groupings according to developmental as well as functional levels. Very few community-based therapy programs are in operation for children and adolescents. Those that do exist or are in the planning stages are primarily connected with programs for head-injured adults.
- Combination of therapy and school programs. This model has the potential to meet both the specific needs related to head injury and the educational and social needs of many children and adolescents. However, the combination of two programs and two sets of personnel must be carefully coordinated to utilize best the two programs in an integrated manner for the individual child. In many geographical areas, transportation time and cost could prohibit the use of this alternative. Involvement in the therapy program could be on a tutorial basis,

possibly after school hours (Light et al., 1987). However, the energy level of the child, as well as recreational and play needs, must be taken into account when planning for after-school programs.

- Programs for head-injured children and adolescents based in special education schools or programs. This is probably becoming the most available option for children and adolescents who have deficits that impair their functioning to such an extent that they are not able to benefit from regular or special educational programming designed for children with other learning difficulties. Most of these programs are based in special private or public schools that have extensive experience in working with children and adolescents who have a wide range of severe learning and physical handicaps. Some of the school programs are affiliated with hospitals and can provide a continuum of service for head-injured children and adolescents from acute care through rehabilitation and postacute programming in their school setting.

- Adaptations of regular education programs. These are discussed more fully in Chapter 7. Some children and adolescents after head injury are able to return to their regular class programs but may need adaptations such as a reduced course load, an extra study period, resource room or tutorial support, and a coordinator to help organize their program on a daily basis, as well as to plan on a longer-term basis. For this model to be fully successful, consultation with professionals who are experienced in the management of head-injured children and adolescents is often necessary. Very few regular school programs have the expertise to plan independently and carry out an adapted program without such consultation. For children and adolescents who have been involved in rehabilitation programs, the rehabilitation staff can often provide consultation as part of their routine follow-up care.

In summary, therapeutic intervention of head-injured children and adolescents presents specific difficulties and challenges. Although many of the approaches and techniques that have been developed for use with head-injured adults and for use with children with other learning difficulties may be useful, they must be carefully evaluated and applied in intervention with head-injured children and adolescents. Attempts at easy answers such as computer packages for head-injury remediation are not likely to be successful.

REFERENCES

Adamovich, B.B., Henderson, J.A., & Auerbach, S. (1985). *Cognitive rehabilitation of closed head injured patients: A dynamic approach.* San Diego: College-Hill Press.

Baddeley, A., Harris, J., Sunderland, A., Watts, K.P., & Wilson, B.A. (1987). Closed head injury and memory. In H.S. Levin, J. Grafman, & H.M. Eisenberg (Eds.), *Neurobehavioral recovery from head injury*. New York: Oxford University Press.

Bawden, H.N., Knights, R.M., & Winogron, H.W. (1985). Speeded performance following head injury in children. *Journal of Clinical and Experimental Neuropsychology*, 7, 39–54.

Bayley, N. (1969). *Bayley Scales of Infant Development: Birth to two years*. New York: Psychological Corp.

Ben-Yishay, Y., Rattok, J., Ross, B., Lakin, R., Ezrachi, O., Silver, S., & Diller, L. (1982). Rehabilitation of cognitive and perceptual deficits in people with traumatic brain damage: A five year clinical research study. In Y. Ben-Yishay (Ed.), *Working approaches to remediation of cognitive deficits in brain damaged persons* (Rehabilitation Monograph No. 64). New York University Medical Center: Institute of Rehabilitation Medicine.

Benton, A.L. (1974). *The Revised Visual Retention Test* (4th ed.). New York: Psychological Corp.

Black, P., Blumer, D., Wellner, A.M., & Walker, A.E. (1971). The head-injured child: Time-course of recovery, with implications for rehabilitation. *Proceedings of the International Symposium on Head Injuries* (pp. 131–137). Edinburgh: Churchill Livingstone.

Boll, T.J. (1983). Neuropsychological assessment of the child: Myths, current status and future prospects. In C.E. Walker & M.C. Roberts (Eds.), *Handbook of clinical child psychology*. New York: John Wiley & Sons.

Boll, T.J., & Barth, J.T. (1981). Neuropsychology of brain damage in children. In S.B. Filskov & T.J. Boll (Eds.), *Handbook of clinical neuropsychology*. New York: John Wiley & Sons.

Brink, J.D., Garrett, A.L., Hale, W.R., Woo-Sam, J., & Nickel, V.L. (1970). Recovery of motor and intellectual function in children sustaining severe head injuries. *Developmental Medicine and Child Neurology*, 12, 565–571.

Brooks, D.N. (1976). Wechsler Memory Scale performance and its relationship to brain damage after severe closed head injury. *Journal of Neurology, Neurosurgery, and Psychiatry*, 39, 593–601.

Brooks, D.N. (1987). Measuring neuropsychological and functional recovery. In H.S. Levin, J. Grafman, & H.M. Eisenberg (Eds.), *Neurobehavioral recovery from head injury*. New York: Oxford University Press.

Brown, T.L., & Morgan, S.B. (1987). Cognitive training with brain-injured children: General issues and approaches. In J.M. Williams & C.J. Long (Eds.), *The rehabilitation of cognitive disabilities*. New York: Plenum Press.

Burgemeister, B.B., Blum, L.H., & Lorge, I. (1962). *Columbia Mental Maturity Scale* (3rd ed.). New York: Harcourt Brace Jovanovich.

Burns, P.G., Cook, J., & Ylvisaker, M. (1988). Cognitive assessment and intervention. In R.C. Savage & G.F. Wolcott (Eds.), *An educator's manual*. Southborough, MA: National Head Injury Foundation.

Buschke, H. (1974). Components of verbal learning in children: Analysis by selective reminding. *Journal of Experimental Child Psychology*, 18, 488–496.

Campanelli, P.A. (1970). Sustained attention in brain damaged children. *Exceptional Children*, 36, 317–323.

Carey, S. (1984). Cognitive development: The descriptive problem. In M. Gazzaniga (Ed.), *Handbook of cognitive neuroscience*. New York: Plenum Press.

Carper, J.M., Cohen, R.F., & Mapou, R.L. (1987). A scale for rating disorders of arousal and attention. Paper presented at the 95th Annual American Psychological Association Convention, New York.

Chadwick, O., Rutter, M., Brown, G., Shaffer, D., & Traub, M. (1981). A prospective study of children with head injuries: II. Cognitive sequelae. *Psychological Medicine, 11*, 49–61.

Chadwick, O., Rutter, M., Shaffer, D., & Shrout, P.E. (1981). A prospective study of children with head injuries: IV. Specific cognitive deficits. *Journal of Clinical Neuropsychology, 3*, 101–120.

Cicerone, K.D., & Tupper, D.E. (1986). Cognitive assessment in the neuropsychological rehabilitation of head-injured adults. In B.P. Uzzell & Y. Gross (Eds.), *Clinical neuropsychology of intervention*. Boston: Martinus Nijhoff Publishing.

Cohen, S.B., Joyce, C.M., Rhoades, K.W., & Welks, D.M. (1985). Educational programming for head injured students. In M. Ylvisaker (Ed.), *Head injury rehabilitation: Children and adolescents*. San Diego: College-Hill Press.

Cull, C., & Wyke, M.A. (1984). Memory function of children with spina bifida and shunted hydrocephalus. *Developmental Medicine and Child Neurology, 26*, 177–183.

Denman, S.B. (1984). *Denman Neuropsychology Memory Scale*. Charleston, SC: Sidney B. Denman.

DePompei, R., & Blosser, J. (1987). *School re-entry: Problems and suggested solutions*. Unpublished manuscript. University of Akron, Department of Communicative Disorders, Akron, OH.

Douglas, V., & Peters, K. (1979). Toward a clearer definition of the attentional deficit of hyperactive children. In G. Hale & M. Lewis (Eds.), *Attention and cognitive development*. New York: Plenum Press.

Ewing-Cobbs, L., Fletcher, J.M., Landry, S.H., & Levin, H.S. (1985). Language disorders after pediatric head injury. In J.K. Darby (Ed.), *Speech and language evaluation in neurology: Childhood disorders*. San Diego: Grune & Stratton.

Feuerstein, R. (1980). *Instrumental enrichment: An intervention program for cognitive modifiability*. Baltimore: University Park Press.

Filley, C.M., Cranberg, M.D., Alexander, M.P., & Hart E.J. (1987). Neurobehavioral outcome after closed head injury in childhood and adolescence. *Archives of Neurology, 44*, 194–198.

Flavell, J.H. (1971). First discussant's comments: What is memory development the development of? *Human Development, 14*, 272–278.

Fletcher, J.M., Ewing-Cobbs, L., McLaughlin, E.J., & Levin, H.S. (1985). Cognitive and psychosocial sequelae of head injury in children: Implications for assessment and management. In B.F. Brooks (Ed.), *The injured child*. Austin: University of Texas Press.

Fletcher, J.M., & Taylor, H.G. (1984). Neuropsychological approaches to children: Towards a developmental neuropsychology. *Journal of Clinical Neuropsychology, 6*, 39–56.

French, J.L. (1964). *Manual: Pictorial test of intelligence*. Boston: Houghton Mifflin.

Fromm-Auch, D., & Yeudall, L.T. (1984). Normative data for the Halstead-Reitan Neuropsychological Tests. *Journal of Clinical Neuropsychology, 5*, 221–238.

Gaddes, W.H. (1985). *Learning disabilities and brain function: A neuropsychological approach* (2nd ed.). New York: Springer-Verlag.

Gaidolfi, E., & Vignolo, L.A. (1980). Closed head injuries of school-age children: Neuropsychological sequelae in early adulthood. *Italian Journal of Neurological Science, 2*, 65–73.

Goethe, K.E., & Levin, H.S. (1984). Neuropsychological consequences of head injury in children. In R. Tarter & G. Goldstein (Eds.), *Advances in clinical neuropsychology*. New York: Plenum Press.

Grabe, M. (1986). Attentional processes in education. In G.D. Phye & T. Andre (Eds.), *Cognitive classroom learning: Understanding, thinking, and problem solving*. Orlando, FL: Academic Press.

Haarbauer-Krupa, J., Henry, K., Szekeres, S.F., & Ylvisaker, M. (1985). Cognitive rehabilitation therapy: Late stages of recovery. In M. Ylvisaker (Ed.), *Head injury rehabilitation: Children and adolescents*. San Diego: College-Hill Press.

Hagen, J., & Hale, G. (1973). The development of attention in children. In A. Pick (Ed.), *Minnesota Symposium on Child Psychology, Vol. 7* (pp. 117–140). Minneapolis: University of Minnesota Press.

Hartlage, L.C., & Telzrow, C.F. (1986). *Neuropsychological assessment and intervention with children and adolescents*. Sarasota, FL: Professional Resource Exchange.

Hecaen, H. (1976). Acquired aphasia in children and the ontogenesis of hemispheric functional specialization. *Brain and Language, 3*, 114–134.

Herbert, M. (1964). The concept and testing of brain-damage in children: A review. *Journal of Child Psychology and Psychiatry, 5*, 197–216.

Hiskey, M. (1966). *Hiskey-Nebraska Test of Learning Aptitude*. Lincoln, NE: Union College Press.

Hulicka, I.M. (1966). Age differences in Wechsler Memory Scales scores. *Journal of Genetic Psychology, 109*, 135–145.

Hynd, G.W., & Obrzut, J.E. (1986). Clinical child neuropsychology: Issues and perspectives. In J.E. Obrzut & G.W. Hynd (Eds.), *Child neuropsychology, Vol. 2*. San Diego: Academic Press.

Jastak, S., & Wilkinson, G.S. (1984). *Wide Range Achievement Test* (rev. 1984 ed.). Wilmington, DE: Jastak Associates.

Kail, R. (1979). *The development of memory in children*. San Francisco: W.H. Freeman & Co.

Kaufman, A.S., & Kaufman, N.L. (1983). *Kaufman Assessment Battery for Children*. Circle Pines, MN: American Guidance Service.

Kimura, D., & McGlone, J. (1979). Children's stories for testing LTM. In D. Kimura & J. McGlone (Eds.), *Neuropsychological test manual*. London, Ontario: D.K. Consultants.

Kirk, U., & Kelly, M.S. (1986). *Scoring scale for the Rey-Osterrieth Complex Figure*. Unpublished manuscript.

Kleges, R.C., & Sanchez, V.C. (1981). Cross-validation of an index of premorbid intellectual functioning in children. *Journal of Consulting and Clinical Psychology, 49*, 141.

Klonoff, H., Crockett, D.D., & Clark, C. (1984). Head injuries in children: A model for predicting course of recovery and prognosis. In R.E. Tarter & G. Goldstein (Eds.), *Advances in clinical neuropsychology, Vol. 2*. New York: Plenum Press.

Klonoff, H., & Low, M.D. (1974). Disordered brain function in young children and early adolescents: Neuropsychological and electroencephalographic correlates. In R.M. Reitan & L.A. Davison (Eds.), *Clinical neuropsychology: Current status and applications*. New York: John Wiley & Sons.

Klonoff, H., Low, M.D., & Clark, C. (1977). Head injuries in children: A prospective five year follow-up. *Journal of Neurology, Neurosurgery, and Psychiatry, 40*, 1211–1219.

Klonoff, H., & Paris, R. (1974). Immediate, short-term and residual effects of acute head injuries in children: Neuropsychological and neurological correlates. In R. Reitan & L. Davison (Eds.), *Clinical neuropsychology: Current status and applications*. New York: John Wiley & Sons.

Knights, R.M. (1970). *Smoothed normative data on tests for evaluating brain damage in children*. Ottawa, Ontario: Author.

Krupski, A. (1986). Attention problems in youngsters with learning handicaps. In J.D. Torgesen & B.Y.L. Wong (Eds.), *Psychological and educational perspectives on learning disabilities*. Orlando, FL: Academic Press.

Leiter, R.G. (1948). *Leiter International Performance Scale*. Chicago: Stoelting Co.

Levin, H.S. (1981). Aphasia in closed head injury. In M.T. Sarno (Ed.), *Acquired aphasia*. New York: Academic Press.

Levin, H.S., Benton, A.L., & Grossman, R.G. (1982). *Neurobehavioral consequences of closed head injury*. New York: Oxford University Press.

Levin, H.S., & Eisenberg, H.M. (1979). Neuropsychological impairment after closed head injury in children and adolescents. *Journal of Pediatric Psychology*, *4*, 389–402.

Levin, H.S., Eisenberg, H.M., Wigg, N.R., & Kobayashi, K. (1982). Memory and intellectual abilities after head injury in children and adolescents. *Neurosurgery*, *11*, 668–673.

Lieber, J., & Semmel, M.I. (1985). Effectiveness of computer application to instruction with mildly handicapped learners. *Remedial and Special Education*, *6*, 5–12.

Light, R., Neumann, E., Lewis, R., Morecki-Oberg, C., Asarnow, R., & Satz, P. (1987). An evaluation of a neuropsychologically based reeducation project for the head-injured child. *Journal of Head Trauma Rehabilitation*, *2*, 11–25.

Long, C.J. (1987). The current status of computer-assisted cognitive rehabilitation. In J.M. Williams & C.J. Long (Eds.), *The rehabilitation of cognitive disabilities*. New York: Plenum Press.

Lynch, W. (1986). Microcomputers and cognitive retraining. *Journal of Head Trauma Rehabilitation*, *1*, 79–82.

Lynch, W.J. (1982). The use of electronic games in cognitive rehabilitation. In L.E. Trexler (Ed.), *Cognitive rehabilitation: Conceptualization and intervention*. New York: Plenum Press.

McCarthy, D.A. (1972). *Manual for the McCarthy Scales of Children's Abilities*. New York: Psychological Corp.

Meichenbaum, D. (1976). Cognitive factors as determinants of learning disabilities: A cognitive-functional approach. In R. Knights & D. Bakker (Eds.), *The neuropsychology of learning disorders: Theoretical approaches*. Baltimore: University Park Press.

Meier, M., Benton, A., & Diller, L. (Eds.) (1987). *Neuropsychological rehabilitation*. New York: Guilford Press.

Miller, P., & Weiss, M. (1981). Children's attentional allocation, understanding of attention, and performance on the incidental learning task. *Child Development*, *52*, 1183–1190.

Neumann, E.M., Morecki-Oberg, C., & Light, R. (1987). *The Neuro-Cognitive Education Project: Teacher's manual*. Pomona, CA: Children's Service Center, Casa Colina Hospital.

Papert, S. (1980). *Mindstorms: Children, computers, and powerful ideas*. New York: Basic Books.

Picton, T.W., Stuss, D.T., & Marshall, K.C. (1986). Attention and the brain. In S.L. Friedman, K.A. Klivington, & R.W. Peterson (Eds.), *The brain, cognition, and education*. Orlando, FL: Academic Press.

Plaisted, J.R., Gustavson, J.L., Wilkening, G.N., & Golden, C.J. (1983). The Luria-Nebraska Neuropsychological Battery—Children's revision: Theory and current research findings. *Journal of Clinical Child Psychology, 12*, 13–21.

Prigatano, G.P. (1986). *Neuropsychological rehabilitation after brain injury.* Baltimore: Johns Hopkins University Press.

Ragosta, M. (1982). *Computer-assisted instruction and compensatory education: The ETS/LAUSD study-overview of the final report.* Washington, DC: U.S. National Institute of Education.

Reitan, R.M., & Davison, L.A. (Eds.) (1974). *Clinical neuropsychology: Current status and applications.* New York: John Wiley & Sons.

Richardson, F. (1963). Some effects of severe head injury: A follow-up study of children and adolescents after protracted coma. *Developmental Medicine and Child Neurology, 5*, 471–482.

Rosenthal, R., & Allen, T. (1980). Intratask distractibility in hyperkinetic and nonhyperkinetic children. *Journal of Abnormal Child Psychology, 8*, 175–187.

Rourke, B.P. (1981). Neuropsychological assessment of children with learning disabilities. In S.B. Filskov & T.J. Boll (Eds.), *Handbook of clinical neuropsychology.* New York: Interscience.

Rourke, B.P. (1984). Quantitative approaches to the neuropsychological assessment of children. In R.E. Tarter & G. Goldstein (Eds.), *Advances in clinical neuropsychology, Vol. 2.* New York: Plenum Press.

Rourke, B.P., & Adams, K.M. (1984). Quantitative approaches to the neuropsychological assessment of children. In R.M. Tarter & G. Goldstein (Eds.), *Advances in clinical neuropsychology, Vol. 2.* New York: Plenum Press.

Rourke, B.P., Bakker, D.J., Fisk, J.L., & Strang, J.D. (1983). *Child neuropsychology: An introduction to theory, research, and clinical practice.* New York: Guilford Press.

Rourke, B.P., Fisk, J.L., & Strang, J.D. (1986). *Neuropsychological assessment of children: A treatment-oriented approach.* New York: Guilford Press.

Rutter, M., Chadwick, O., & Shaffer, D. (1983). Head injury. In M. Rutter (Ed.), *Developmental neuropsychiatry.* New York: Guilford Press.

Rutter, M., Chadwick, O., Shaffer, D., & Brown, G. (1980). A prospective study of children with head injuries: I. Design and methods. *Psychological Medicine, 10*, 633–645.

Samuels, S., & Edwall, G. (1981). The role of attention in reading with implications for the learning disabled student. *Journal of Learning Disabilities, 14*, 353–361, 368.

Santostefano, S. (1985). *Cognitive control therapy with children and adolescents.* New York: Pergamon Press.

Santostefano, S., Rutledge, L., & Randall, D. (1965). Cognitive styles and reading disability. *Psychology in the Schools, 2*, 57–62.

Satz, P., & Bullard-Bates, C. (1981). Acquired aphasia in children. In M.T. Sarno (Ed.), *Acquired aphasia.* New York: Academic Press.

Seidenberg, M., Giordani, B., Berent, S., & Boll, T.J. (1983). IQ level and performance on the Halstead-Reitan Neuropsychological Test Battery for Older Children. *Journal of Consulting and Clinical Psychology, 51*, 406–413.

Selz, M., & Reitan, R.M. (1979). Rules for neuropsychological diagnosis: Classification of brain function in older children. *Journal of Consulting and Clinical Psychology, 47*, 258–264.

Spreen, O., & Gaddes, W.H. (1969). Developmental norms for 15 neuropsychological tests age 6 to 15. *Cortex, 5*, 171–191.

Squires, L.R. (1986). Memory and the brain. In S.L. Friedman, K.A. Klivington, & R.W. Peterson (Eds.), *The Brain, cognition, and education*. Orlando, FL: Academic Press.

Stankov, L. (1983). Attention and intelligence. *Journal of Educational Psychology, 75*, 471–490.

Teeter, P.A. (1986). Standard neuropsychological batteries for children. In J.E. Obrzut & G.W. Hynd (Eds.), *Child neuropsychology, Vol. 2*. San Diego: Academic Press.

Terman, L.M., & Merrill, M.A. (1960). *Stanford-Binet Intelligence Scale*. Boston: Houghton Mifflin.

Thorndike, R.L., Hagen, E.P., & Sattler, J.M. (1986). *Stanford-Binet Intelligence Scale* (4th ed.). Chicago: Riverside Publishing Co.

Tindal, G., & Marston, D. (1986). Approaches to assessment. In J.K. Torgesen & B.Y.L. Wong (Eds.), *Psychological and educational perspectives on learning disabilities*. Orlando, FL: Academic Press.

Torgesen, J.K. (1986). Computer-assisted instruction with learning-disabled children. In J.K. Torgesen & B.Y.L. Wong (Eds.), *Psychological and educational perspectives in learning disabilities*. Orlando, FL: Academic Press.

Tramontana, M.F., Klee, S.N., & Boyd, T.A. (1984). WISC-R interrelationships with the Halstead-Reitan and Childrens' Luria Neuropsychological batteries. *Clinical Neuropsychology, 6*, 1–8.

Trexler, L.E. (1982). *Cognitive rehabilitation: Conceptualization and intervention*. New York: Plenum Press.

Uzzell, B.P., & Gross, Y. (Eds.) (1986). *Clinical neuropsychology of intervention*. Boston: Martinus Nijhoff Publishing.

van Dongen, H.R., & Loonen, M.C.B. (1977). Factors related to prognosis of acquired aphasia in children. *Cortex, 13*, 131–136.

van Zomeren, A.H., Brouwer, W.H., & Deelman, B.G. (1984). Attentional deficits: The riddles of selectivity, speed and alertness. In N. Brooks (Ed.), *Closed head injury: Psychological, social and family consequences*. Oxford: Oxford University Press.

Wechsler, D. (1967). *Manual for the Wechsler Preschool and Primary Scale of Intelligence*. New York: Psychological Corp.

Wechsler, D. (1974). *Manual for the Wechsler Intelligence Scale for Children* (rev. ed.). New York: Psychological Corp.

Wechsler, D. (1987). *Manual for the Wechsler Memory Scale* (rev. ed.). San Antonio: Psychological Corp.

Weir, S., & Watt, D. (1981). Logo: A computer environment for learning disabled students. *Computer Teacher, 8*, 11–17.

Williams, J.M., & Long, C.J. (Eds.). (1987). *The rehabilitation of cognitive disabilities*. New York: Plenum Press.

Ylvisaker, M. (Ed.) (1985). *Head injury rehabilitation: Children and adolescents*. San Diego: College-Hill Press.

Ylvisaker, M., Szekeres, S.F., Henry, K., Sullivan, D.M., & Wheeler, P. (1987). Topics in cognitive rehabilitation therapy. In M. Ylvisaker & E.M.R. Gobble (Eds.), *Community re-entry for head injured adults*. Boston: Little, Brown & Co.

Chapter 5

Behavioral Components

Ellen Lehr and Joseph A. Lantz

INTRODUCTION

The behavioral effects of traumatic brain injury in children and adolescents are discussed in this chapter. The focus is upon those behaviors that tend to be long-term and persistent. This is in contrast with the immediate behavioral presentation of traumatic brain injury and coma as observed in the acute and rehabilitation hospital settings discussed in Chapter 2. The behaviors discussed here are those confronting parents, family members, school personnel, friends, and the child or adolescent after returning home and to the community. Approaches to understanding these behaviors and appropriately responding to them are also discussed. The purpose of this chapter is to provide parents and professionals with a knowledgeable, flexible approach in understanding and responding to the behavior of head-injured children and adolescents. The goal of this approach is to improve behavioral control and limit the adverse impact of behavioral difficulties. This includes a description of the more common types of behaviors observed in children and adolescents after traumatic brain injury.

NORMAL LEARNING AND BEHAVIOR

Children are excellent observers of their parents' behavior. What parent has not been amazed and perhaps embarrassed to see children repeat an activity, phrase, or statement that was never intentionally communicated to them or knowingly said or done in their presence? Both with and without realizing it, parents daily employ behavioral techniques in raising their children. The loving smile and caress, extended individual attention, verbal praise, withdrawal of attention, and slap of a hand all have an effect on behavior through communicating either a positive or negative response.

Through these processes of behavioral management and learning, children learn what is acceptable and unacceptable behavior, what draws favorable responses or punishment from parents, teachers, and other significant people in their lives. This is also how children learn that through their behavior they have an impact upon their environment. They come to see that they can influence the world and thus exert a direct effect in meeting their needs.

Through the process of successfully interacting with their world, children develop a sense of competency and control. They do not only mirror the behavior and values of their parents. They also incorporate the lessons learned directly and indirectly through contact with relatives, siblings, teachers, other important adults, and countless other sources of social and educational contact. As children grow and mature, these lessons ideally become incorporated into their moral and ethical sense of the world and how they wish to conduct their lives. Reinforcements, both positive and negative, often become more internalized but might also include environmental reinforcers such as financial and social success or ostracism and failure.

For parents of children and adolescents who have had traumatic brain injuries, the parenting strategies and techniques that they had utilized effectively before injury may no longer be successful in teaching and maintaining appropriate behavior. However, this realization usually occurs when parents have less access to professional resources than in the period immediately after injury (Jacobs, 1989). Parents may find themselves at a loss as to how to deal with their child. They may have little information about the possible long-term behavioral components of traumatic brain injury, be confused as to what behavior is related to injury and what is not, and have little direction in attempting to manage behavioral changes more adaptively for their child and the family as a whole. Some of the strategies they try may even be counterproductive and make existing problems more difficult to change (Deaton, 1987; Kozloff, 1974, 1979).

BEHAVIORAL EFFECTS OF TRAUMATIC BRAIN INJURY

Little is known about the specific behavior patterns that may be associated with specific types of traumatic brain injuries in children and adolescents except that there is likely to be an increase in behavioral variability and no one unvarying picture of behavioral deficit (Boll, 1983). Descriptively children tend to demonstrate one of several general patterns of behavioral sequelae: little readily apparent behavioral change after injury, exacerbations of preinjury behavior to unacceptable levels, marked changes in behavior, and behavioral reactions to other head-injury deficits. In general, severe traumatic brain injuries are likely to be associated with an increase in behavioral difficulties (Divak, Herrie, & Scott, 1985; Goethe & Levin, 1984). However, the behavioral impact of a particular injury is not always directly correlated with the severity of injury. Neither is the behavioral impairment always directly correlated with the severity of cognitive deficits. A mild traumatic brain injury might have significant behavioral effects while a more severe injury might produce little obvious behavioral change. Much depends upon premorbid personality styles, behavior patterns, and family dynamics.

Behavior can be distinguished from cognitive and social-emotional aspects of functioning, even though all three are interrelated and interact with each other. In the most basic sense, behavior is overt expression and action that usually occurs in a social environment. In other words, the expression of anger or irritability in yelling, hitting, or speaking sarcastically is behavior, even though the anger itself may be an emotional reaction to injury-related impairments and irritability may be a reflection of cognitive and neurological changes subsequent to injury. Specific behavioral effects have rarely been the focus of research on the effects of head injury in children and adolescents. The behavioral impact of traumatic brain injury can perhaps be understood best as a loss in the degree of control the child or adolescent is able to exert over functioning, relative to the range of developmentally acceptable behavior for the age. This can result in a less stable and predictable pattern of behavior for any individual child or adolescent.

Frequently observed behavioral effects include irritability, impulsiveness, disinhibition, decreased frustration tolerance, fatigue, reduced anger control, hypoactivity, reduced motivation and initiative, aggressiveness, and hyperactivity (Black, Blumer, Wellner, & Walker, 1971; Brink, Garrett, Hale, Woo-Sam, & Nickel, 1970; Klonoff & Paris, 1974; Richardson, 1963). In extreme circumstances behavioral effects can also include antisocial behaviors. These behaviors are often the expression of the effect of reduced cognitive and emotional control. In one study of the effects of severe head trauma in children and adolescents, half of those with residual behavioral disturbances were characterized by problems with overarousal or excessive behavior and half with problems with underarousal or diminished behavior (Filley, Cranberg, Alexander, & Hart, 1987). Although intervention directed at improving cognitive and psychosocial functioning may also have an effect on improving behavior, intervention focused directly on behavioral aspects can often be more quickly effective in ameliorating the immediate personal and environmental impact.

There are several misconceptions about the behavior of children and adolescents after traumatic brain injury (Deaton, 1987). Behavioral problems after injury are often assumed to be unchangeable because they are neurological in nature. Although neurological deficits may in fact make intervention more difficult and place limits on potential control, most children and adolescents after even severe injury are capable of relearning some, if not all, old skills and mastering at least some new behaviors. Injury-related behavioral problems are perceived of as consisting solely of reductions of maladaptive behaviors, such as hyperactivity or increased expression of anger. Instead a major goal of behavioral intervention often is focused on relearning or increasing the occurrence of self-care and individually responsible behaviors and socially adaptive behaviors. The third misconception is that the overt result of inappropriate behaviors is intended by the head-injured child or adolescent. For an intervention to be successful, the underlying intention, not only the result, of the problem behavior must first be identified. For example, a child after injury may be ostracized by other children for telling loud, inappropriate jokes and talking all the time in a group. The head-injured child may be attempting to make friends through these overtures and increase these inappropriate social behaviors as other children withdraw.

Excessive Behavior

Socially disruptive behaviors that occur at a high rate of frequency or with increased intensity often prompt immediate concern and an evident need for intervention. After head injury in children and adolescents, behaviors related to hyperactivity, impulsiveness, irritability, anger outbursts, and social disinhibition fall into this classification as excessive behaviors. The actual expression of these general classes of behavior varies widely. It can include actions such as breaking toys, talking loudly, loss of physical control during play, turning rough-housing into fighting, running across streets without looking, mouthing off, swearing, and being constantly on the go. Both parents and teachers complain that the children are less compliant than before injury and that the strategies that previously were successful in controlling their behavior are less so after injury. Because these behaviors can be so disruptive in home, neighborhood, and classroom settings, assistance is frequently sought to reduce their occurrence and intensity.

Hyperactivity

Since hyperactivity has traditionally been associated with neurological impairment in children, it is discussed separately. Hyperactivity, or increased physical activity, can occur after head injury in children, but it is not necessarily part of the sequelae of traumatic brain injury in children and adolescents (Rutter, 1982). There have been inconsistent research findings that younger children, especially those younger than 10 years of age at the time of injury, may have a higher incidence of hyperactivity after injury than older children (Brink et al., 1970). However, hyperactivity has not been well defined in studies of head injury effects in children and adolescents; therefore reports of increased activity level may also be referring to the combination of impulsiveness, irritability, disinhibition, and shortened attention span. Also few studies have controlled for the incidence of hyperactivity in children before injury compared with the increases subsequent to injury. In older children and adolescents, an increase in motor behavior may be expressed in fidgeting rather than overt physical activity levels. In order to assess hyperactivity more accurately in children after traumatic brain injury, measures such as the Connor's Parent Symptom Questionnaire and the Connor's Teacher Rating Scale (Connors, 1970; Trites, Laprade, & Blouin, 1982) should be used in clinical studies.

From clinical experience, it is likely that some children and adolescents do experience heightened levels of activity that can interfere with learning and safety. Whether these disorders involve new behavior or exacerbation of previous increased activity levels probably varies from child to child. The so-called hyperactive impulse disorder as a sequelae from acquired neurological insult first gained prominence in children surviving encephalitis. In these children, it was related to dysfunction of the lower brain centers and the brain stem area rather than higher brain or cortical areas (Benton, 1963). A combination of medication and behavior management techniques is likely to succeed in helping to control hyperactivity in head-injured children and adolescents, similar to the approaches utilized with other hyperactive children (Barkley, 1981; Pelham, Schnedler, Bender, Nilsson, Miller, Budrow, Ronnei, Paluchowski, & Marks, 1988).

Diminished Behavior

There has been little research on the effects of hypoactivity, reduced motivation, apathy, reduced initiative, and fatigue on children's and adolescent's functioning after head injury. From clinical observation, these reductions in expected levels of behavior can be very frustrating for parents and staff (Wood, 1987) but not necessarily for the children and adolescents themselves. When cognitive functioning is relatively unimpaired, reductions in activity and initiative can be perceived as laziness, or described by the children and adolescents as boredom. They may also devise explanations for why they find it difficult to engage in activity, such as "It's easier for you to do it," which helps to disguise the reductions in behavior that they are experiencing. However, these impairments likely have significant impact on learning and development in all areas of functioning after injury by reducing the self-driven exploration often taken for granted during the developmental years and limiting the experience of competence.

Although diminished behavior may have significant and even severe implications for head-injured children's and adolescents' developmental potential, it can be difficult to evaluate accurately its occurrence and effects. Complaints of reductions of behavior are more likely to be vague and less immediately pressing than those prompted by excessive behaviors. It is especially important when assessing these behaviors to observe the child or adolescent and directly measure what they *do* rather than relying on what they and the adults around them *say*. Factors such as speed, duration, and quantity become essential, especially as they impact on daily life and learning.

Extreme Behavior Disorders

For a very low percentage of children and adolescents after traumatic brain injury, behavior disorders may become severely incapacitating or even dangerous to themselves and other people. Uncontrolled physical aggression and self-injurious behavior may require comprehensive management in settings such as day and residential treatment programs.

Although most children and adolescents who sustain traumatic brain injury do not become violent, the combination of head injury and experience of family violence or abuse may be factors in increasing violent behavior in adulthood. Recent research with convicted murders on death row found that all of the 15 individuals studied had histories of severe head injury (Lewis, Pincus, Feldman, Jackson, & Bard, 1986). In all but one case, the initial injury had occurred in childhood. In addition, most of this group of murderers had multiple head injuries over the developmental period and continuing into adulthood. The causes of injury included accidents and child abuse.

BEHAVIORAL INTERVENTION

Introduction

Rarely do head-injured children and adolescents request help with their behavior, either to increase adaptive behaviors or to decrease the behaviors that get them into difficulties. Instead the effect of their behavior on other people prompts concern. The responsibility for intervention usually is initiated and implemented by the adults in the child's or adolescent's life, especially their parents and teachers. Despite this, it is important to elicit the cooperation of the child or adolescent to whatever extent is possible in any behavioral intervention attempt.

As discussed in Chapter 4, traumatic brain injury can lead to significant cognitive and learning deficits. These deficits can present limitations for the utilization of behavior techniques but rarely to the point of making them useless (Divak et al., 1985). Neurologically based learning and memory deficits impede rapid mastery of new learning and generalization of responses in behavioral areas. Behavioral interventions may therefore need to be implemented over an extended period, may have less degree of success than with noninjured individuals, and rely more heavily on environmental approaches than on self-mastery.

To increase the effectiveness of behavioral management interventions with children and adolescents after traumatic brain injury, the following general guidelines are recommended.

- Directly involve the child or adolescent as much as possible in the behavioral program to increase motivation and awareness of the program's rationale (Newcombe, 1981). The intention to help should be expressed in a caring and empathetic manner.
- Take baseline data to identify the existing form and frequency of behavior, as well as the variables that may be contributing to the occurrence or lack of the behavior. Then operationally define the behavior and the goal to achieve as a function of intervention (Gelfand & Hartmann, 1984).
- Provide explicit behavioral directives and tangible, extrinsic rewards (Muir, Haffey, Ott, Karaica, Muir, & Sutko, 1983). This is important because of the decreased awareness of subtle social cues and the reduced awareness of the effect of one's own behavior after head injury.
- Make interventions simple, with complex behaviors broken into small, well-defined steps, and applied persistently and consistently (Newcombe, 1981; Kazdin, 1984). These procedures aid in reducing confusion and in compensating for injury-related learning and memory deficits.
- Allow increased time for the program to be successful. Traumatically brain-injured children and adolescents need to experience consequences many times before incorporating new learning and behaviors (Barin, Hanchett, Jacob, & Scott, 1985).

- Intervene in the setting when and where the behavior occurs (Kazdin, 1984). Talking about how to behave in a particular setting is likely to be less successful with head-injured children and adolescents than actually intervening in the setting itself.
- Teach generalization specifically (Deaton, 1987). Because of injury-related cognitive deficits, generalization of behavioral changes to other situations may be difficult for the child or adolescent to accomplish without direct intervention in this area.

Levels of Intervention

Specific behavioral interventions vary according to the needs and capacities of children and adolescents after traumatic brain injury. Depending on the degree of cognitive, emotional, and physical abilities of the child or adolescent, intervention may be designed to rely on environmental control, behavioral change strategies, or self-control techniques. If the implementation of a behavioral program relies on other people, such as parents and teachers, then their capacities and limitations must also be carefully considered. Not all of the possible behavioral techniques and strategies that can be used with children and adolescents after head injury can be discussed here. Instead a range of techniques has been chosen to illustrate the potential of some of these procedures. For an introduction to behavioral procedures in general a recommended resource is *Child Behavior Analysis and Therapy* (Gelfand & Hartmann, 1984).

Environmental Control Strategies

The effect of the environment on the behavior of children and adolescents in the period immediately after traumatic brain injury is well known to those who work in acute-care and rehabilitation hospital settings. Providing a carefully structured environment with control over stimuli such as visual distractors, sound level, number of people, as well as the length and timing of demands placed on the child or adolescent is likely to be the intervention approach most useful for maintaining appropriate behavior and reducing behavioral difficulties in the early stages of recovery or for those who have been severely injured (Grimm & Bleiberg, 1986; Howard & Bleiberg, 1983). However, understanding the effect of the environment on the traumatically brain-injured child or adolescent is often very important in the latter stages of recovery and for those less severely injured. Environmental control strategies directly involve the modification of the antecedents of behavior, and therefore their manipulation can avoid the expression of the behavior itself. If the environmental aspects that trigger problem behaviors can be controlled (and sometimes they cannot), rapid change can often be effected.

EXAMPLE

Jose

Jose, a 14-year-old bilingual boy, had severe cognitive and language deficits since being injured in a bicycle accident. After he returned home from the hospital, he had daily episodes of angry outbursts that culminated in spitting or hitting out at his brothers and sisters. His family was overwhelmed by his behavior and felt that he no longer loved them. When they were asked to keep a record of what occurred before his outbursts, a specific environmental antecedent began to emerge. After his injury, Jose had severe difficulty understanding language and had not recovered his abilities in both languages. He was most functional in English, with little or no comprehension of Spanish. His outbursts occurred when his family were speaking rapidly in Spanish, especially if they were joking or arguing. The severity of his outbursts increased when he was out of the room and overheard family interactions. He would rush into the room, lash out, and accuse his family of talking about him. When his family began to speak in English at home and made specific attempts to make certain he understood what they were talking about, Jose's unprovoked outbursts decreased markedly.

The primary rationale for the use of environmental control techniques is that the loss of behavioral control is a reaction to an impaired brain attempting unsuccessfully to understand a complex environment. It is an attempt to simplify or alter the environment to the level that the head-injured child or adolescent is able to manage appropriately and minimize behavioral expressions of confusion, frustration, or failure. Rarely can these procedures be identified or implemented by the head-injured child or adolescent directly. Instead these techniques depend on other people to evaluate what specifically is overwhelming the head-injured child, monitoring the environment for the head-injured child, and implementing procedures to reduce the environmental complexity.

Techniques that are frequently utilized include establishment of routines, development of schedules, written lists, redirection, and planning for breaks in activities. Routines and schedules can aid in many areas to help the head-injured child or adolescent know what to expect and how to perform. They can also be utilized to complete daily activities such as self-care routines more efficiently. Redirection has become a classic technique in the management of traumatic brain-injured individuals. It utilizes the shortened attention span and distractability that usually are a component of head injury to change the focus of a child's or adolescent's behavior to a more acceptable direction. After getting the child's attention, the topic of conversation is changed, or the child is asked to engage in a different activity. In this way, control is maintained over the head-injured individual's behavior. Because of fatigue and difficulty dealing with complex situations, the length of activities and demands placed on the head-injured child or adolescent should be carefully monitored. Planning for breaks in activities and rest periods before the child becomes overly fatigued or overwhelmed is often successful in avoiding behavioral outbursts related to these aspects of head-injury functioning.

Stimulus Control

Sometimes the behavior that head-injured children or adolescents demonstrate is appropriate for one setting but not for another. However, they may not be able to distinguish under which circumstances a specific behavior is appropriate and when it is not. Through techniques such as cuing, instructions, prompting, and modeling, adults can help head-injured children and adolescents to focus on the relevant aspects of a situation that can guide them in behaving appropriately.

EXAMPLE

Andy

Andy was an exuberant 8-year-old boy who had a severe traumatic brain injury 2 years previously. One of the first social behaviors that had emerged as he recovered was that of telling jokes. This was encouraged by his family and other children as it presented a normal way of interacting with him while much of his social behavior was otherwise quite impaired. However, as he improved, Andy continued to rely on telling jokes as a social gambit whenever he was not sure of how to behave. This became an immediate concern for his family when Andy engaged in joke telling at the funeral of a relative. After discussing with him when it was appropriate to tell jokes and when it was not, his parents arranged a cuing procedure with him. They agreed to talk about what was appropriate behavior for new or anxiety-provoking situations before Andy entered them to prepare him for what to expect and how they wanted him to behave. In the situation itself, they arranged for a secret signal so that they could cue him to stop telling jokes if it were not appropriate.

Direct Consequation

Head-injured children and adolescents may also be expected to make significant changes in their behavior. When they demonstrate the capacity to make cause-and-effect connections and can retain them over an extended period, behavioral techniques that rely on learning principles can be utilized. However, the procedures at this level continue to be initiated and implemented primarily by the adults in children's or adolescents' environment.

Reinforcement

In basic terms, reinforcement is anything that increases a desired behavior by its presence (positive reinforcer) or by its removal (negative reinforcer) in response to an individual's behavior. Reinforcers can take a variety of forms including primary reinforcers such as food, physical contact, toys and activities; social reinforcers such as attention and praise; or secondary reinforcers such as point systems and token economy systems. Any or all of these can be used to increase appropriate behaviors and have been found to lead to lasting behavioral changes in traumatically brain-injured individuals (Eames & Wood, 1985; Wood, 1984; Wood & Eames, 1981).

EXAMPLE

Kurt

Kurt, a 15-year-old adolescent boy, had multiple severe physical deficits after traumatic brain injury. Despite his deficits, though, it appeared that he had the capacity to push his wheelchair independently using one of his feet and one of his hands. This was a major goal for him to accomplish before he could return home and to school after discharge from a rehabilitation hospital. However, he refused to do so, saying, "It's faster if you do it." The benefits of pushing his wheelchair by himself had been pointed out to him repeatedly, but he persisted in engaging people in verbal reasons why he could not until, to save time, they relented and pushed him.

It was determined through physical therapy sessions that Kurt did have the skills to push his wheelchair independently but preferred not to do so. A reinforcement program was designed in which he would be able to play computer games (one of his favorite therapy activities) with the therapist if he pushed his chair from the elevator to the therapy room. The therapist met him at the elevator and timed how long it took for him to push himself to the room. It was explained to Kurt that the longer it took him, the less time there would be to play computer games. She also would not engage in talking with him if he did not push his wheelchair. His times were then charted on a graph in the therapy room. During the first week, he took an average of 20 to 25 minutes to get to the therapy room. However, this rapidly decreased, and by the third week he was pushing his chair at the same speed as the therapist was walking, taking about 3 to 4 minutes to get to the room. He was quite proud of his speed and engaged in races with the therapist to see if he could beat his time and go faster than she could walk. It was then pointed out to him that if he pushed himself, he could go to the game room on his own during his free time and down to the cafeteria to pick out his food. Within another week, he was independently moving around the hospital and in his neighborhood on weekend visits without specific reinforcement needed.

Punishment

In behavior management, the term *punishment* has a specific definition. It is anything that decreases the likelihood of a response that it follows. Therefore if a child is told to stop hitting or there will be a spanking, and the hitting increases after the spanking, it is no longer functioning as a punishment for that child. With head-injured children and adolescents, punishment procedures such as physical restraint may be useful to reduce dangerous behaviors such as self-abuse. However, these procedures are rarely effective by themselves. They should be combined with reinforcement for positive appropriate behaviors in order to produce lasting changes.

EXAMPLE

Michelle

Michelle was an 11-year-old girl who had recovered quite well from severe traumatic brain injury. However, she demonstrated significant behavioral disinhibition in social settings. The specific behavior that caused concern for her parents was her persistent swearing at home whenever she became annoyed or frustrated.

Since her teenage brothers also demonstrated more of this behavior at home than their parents wished, they designed a family
program to reduce swearing among all the children. Every time
the children swore, they had to put a quarter from their allowance
into a kitty; the one who swore the least got the money to spend
at the end of the week. By the end of a month, the kitty was
empty but continued to be present as a reminder. To avoid the
punishment procedure, Michelle and her parents developed alternative ways for her to express her feelings, including acceptable
expressive words that she could use instead of swear words.

Time-Out

Time-out is a form of negative control that has been particularly effective
in managing disruptive or dangerous behavior in individuals after head
injury (Muir et al., 1983; Sand, Trieschman, Fordyce, & Fowler, 1970). It
is a procedure that entails removing the person from situations where
positive reinforcement may be obtained. One method is to designate a
specific place as a time-out room, corner, or chair to which a child is sent
immediately after the prohibited behavior. The time-out area should be
nonstimulating and nonrewarding, with no toys or activities available. The
child should remain in the time-out setting until he or she has calmed down
and remains calm for a minute or 2. Then the child needs to return to the
previous environment to have the opportunity to be reinforced for more
appropriate behaviors. It is especially important for head-injured children
and adolescents to understand which behavior is being focused on, what
the time-out procedure is, as well as what the expected behavior is and
that it will be reinforced. Time-out is not the same as breaks or rest periods
for head-injured children to avoid behavioral expressions of fatigue and
overstimulation. Breaks and rest periods should be gauged so that the child
does not demonstrate the inappropriate behavior; time-out is used as a
consequence of a specific prohibited behavior. However, part of the effectiveness of time-out with head-injured children and adolescents may
indeed consist of the fact that it removes them from the situation and
allows for a break from demands.

EXAMPLE

Ben

Ben was a 10-year-old boy, who at 2 years after severe head
injury continued to have difficulty controlling his temper when
he could not have what he wanted when he wanted it. His temper

tantrums consisted of yelling and screaming, escalating into hitting, kicking, and throwing any objects within his reach. His parents explained to him that they would no longer tolerate this behavior but would give him two warnings to control himself; if he did not, he would have to sit in the time-out chair until he remained quiet for 1 minute. If after that time he was quiet, he would be able to leave the chair. A timer was used so that Ben would know how much time he had left in time-out. After he was calm, his parents agreed to discuss and find alternatives with him for better handling what he wanted and postponing gratification. Initially Ben was resistant to time-out and he had to be reminded about the procedure. Gradually he began to comply more easily and compared his time-out procedure with warnings and penalties in ice hockey, his favorite game. He began to call the time-out chair his penalty box and actively worked with his parents on strategies to keep him in the game.

Self-Control Techniques

The use of self-monitoring and control is the highest level of intervention. The focus here is upon enabling the child or adolescent to monitor and control one's own behavior. This level of intervention may be appropriate for children and adolescents who have sustained relatively mild traumatic brain injuries. More severely injured survivors may also reach this level, usually after treatment through environmental interventions and the use of specific behavioral techniques designed and implemented by other people. Self-control procedures have been utilized with children and adolescents to decrease impulsivity (Meichenbaum & Goodman, 1977), decrease disruptive behavior (Bolstad & Johnson, 1972; Drabman, Spitalnik, & O'Leary, 1973), decrease overactivity (Bornstein & Quevillon, 1976), and increase academic achievement (Felixbrod & O'Leary, 1973).

To use self-control procedures, the individual must have developed some awareness of deficits and behavioral difficulties, the circumstances under which these are most likely to occur, and the impact of their behavior on themselves and other people. Effective methods of altering one's behavior or removing oneself from a difficult situation must be learned and practiced. Although children and adolescents may have help in setting up a self-control program, they themselves provide the impetus for selecting behaviors they want to change, collect data on their own behavior, chose the techniques with which they feel most comfortable, and even provide their own reinforcement.

EXAMPLE

Kathryn

Before her traumatic brain injury, Kathryn was an attractive 17-year-old girl with many friends. However, her severe injury interrupted her high school education, and she was not able to graduate with her class. Most of her friends went on to college or lost touch with her because of her long hospitalization. Two years after injury, Kathryn was ready to resume her social life, but she expressed feelings of shyness and lack of confidence in making new friends. She was able to define this as a primary issue for herself and was motivated to find ways to alter it. A social skills group for older adolescents and young adults was forming, and Kathryn expressed interest in participating. The group focused on relaxation and imagery exercises to decrease anxiety in social situations, practice in conversational skills relating to making friends and dating, and individual homework assignments to increase social interaction outside the group. Kathryn was successful in using the self-control techniques to decrease her anxiety when interacting with other people. She enrolled in a community college course to help complete credits toward her high school graduation and was able to utilize her social skills in making friends in this setting. By the end of the group sessions, she had begun to date again, though not seriously, and had developed a close friendship with one of the other group members.

PROCESS OF BEHAVIORAL CONSULTATION

Having discussed the general nature of behavioral management and some of the specific techniques that can be utilized with children and adolescents after traumatic brain injury, the rest of the chapter presents the process through which these behaviors are identified, assessed, and altered. The stages in this process include identification and definition of the target behavior, collection of baseline data of the existing behavior, identification of salient variables, formulation of a treatment plan, implementation of the treatment plan, and programming for generalization and maintenance of the behavior.

Identification and Definition of Target Behavior

This discussion of behavioral consultation is primarily intended for the period when the child has returned home from the acute hospital setting or rehabilitation hospital. In those settings the focus is generally upon the initial adjustment of the child and family. This is often a period of shock, disbelief, and great uncertainty. Unrealistic fantasies or erroneous perceptions may exist regarding the extent, impact, and potential recovery of the child. It is often a time of significant disruption in the family life. Once the injured child has returned to home and school, parents and the children gradually begin to see and appreciate the impact of the injury and how it affects their lives. It is a period of observing, learning, and struggling to accept the many difficult, painful changes brought on by the injury. At this point parents begin to develop a more accurate sense of their child's behavioral challenges and how they might begin to address them. They come to realize that they must resume responsibility for their child's future and that of their family. Relationships with treating professionals become that of colleagues collaborating with parents in managing their child's care.

Descriptions of a child's or adolescent's behavior alterations after traumatic brain injury may be vague and initially difficult to define. To intervene, specific behaviors need to be defined precisely and in a measurable way. For example, a child may be described as unable to play as before injury. Analysis could show that the level of play may be appropriate but the length of time the child engages in play may be very brief. The target for intervention then may focus on increasing the period the child can engage in play activites.

Collection of Baseline Data of the Existing Behavior

After the behavior is defined in an operational way satisfactory to all of the participants, it should be assessed to determine its characteristics in the environment. The baseline or initial measurement of behavior includes the function of the behavior, its underlying cause, immediate precipitants, consequences, and important dimensions such as duration, frequency, and intensity. Through the collection of this information in an organized, clearly defined way, the specifics about the behavior can be uncovered in terms of where it occurs and does not occur, with whom, under what conditions, and with what results. Because head-injured children's or adolescents' behavior may be quite variable, it is especially important to collect as accurate information as possible over time to clarify the consistencies of their behavior as well. Once the relationship of the environment and the behavior are clearly understood, the development of intervention approaches often becomes obvious.

Identification of Salient Variables and Resources

Some of the controlling variables of a specific behavior cannot be completely altered. This is especially so for individuals who have sustained neurological impairment. Behavioral outbursts may be related to seizure activity that may only partially be controlled by medication. However, other variables such as the amount of environmental stimulation, the level of demands, the fatigue level of the child, and the reinforcement for maintaining behavioral control may be effective in helping to manage the situation. Other relevant variables include cognitive capacities, memory intactness, and personality characteristics. However, not only the head-injured child's or adolescent's capacities and characteristics must be taken into account. It is also important to consider the strengths and limitations of the family members, home situation, teachers, classmates, classroom environment, therapists, etc. All of these may be involved in terms of how they impact on the child's behavior and how they can be utilized as resources for change.

Formulation of a Treatment Plan

It is important to make sure that complete information about the behavior and the resources available to aid in altering it have been thoroughly evaluated before designing the treatment plan. This includes the cooperation and collaboration of all those involved in the plan to ensure its success. Relying on resources that are not available or over which there is little control, either on the child's or adolescent's part or on that of other people in the environment, is likely to lead to unsuccessful intervention. If this is done several times, it not only can be very frustrating to the head-injured child, family, or teachers but also lead to the perception that behavioral approaches are not useful. Although the treatment plan is carried out by people who may have little formal training in behavioral approaches, the plan itself should be designed by an expert in this area. Each treatment plan is unique to the individual and the circumstances, incorporating one or more of the possible behavioral techniques available. A general guideline is to use as few resources as possible but as many as necessary to achieve the goal of the treatment plan (Jacobs, 1988).

Implementation of the Treatment Plan

While the plan is in process, it is essential that information about the controlling variables and behaviors continue to be collected. Without on-going data, it is difficult, if not impossible, to evaluate the effectiveness of the intervention. Although a treatment plan may initially appear successful, it is necessary to determine if change is being maintained. If circumstances have altered or the program is not effective, alterations can be made on the basis of the data that have continued to be collected. When a treatment program is not successful, several factors could be operating: it is not being implemented consistently, additional resources may required, the strategy may not be appropriate or may not be powerful enough, the target behavior may not be well-defined, the behavior may be very entrenched and requires lengthy intervention before change occurs, or the head-injured child or adolescent may not be able to perform the expected behavior due to organically based limitations (Deaton, 1987).

Programming for Generalization and Maintenance

For continued success, treatment programs should incorporate procedures for maintenance and generalization. This is especially important for individuals who have sustained neurological impairment. Hard-won changes can be jeopardized if the old pretreatment contingencies return. However, the maintenance of a program rarely involves as much effort as the initial implementation, especially if naturalistic contingencies can be established. Utilization of new behaviors in other than the targeted situation is usually desirable. For the head-injured child or adolescent, though, generalization of newly mastered behaviors in other situations may be difficult or even impossible to achieve. Generalization may need to be approached gradually or specifically taught. Some head-injured children and adolescents may not be able to generalize their behavior, and functional skills must then be taught in each expected setting.

SUMMARY

Traumatic brain injury in children and adolescents presents a variety of behavioral changes and challenges. Some of these are directly related to neurological sequelae, others are in reaction to attempts to cope with injury, and still others are exacerbations of preinjury characteristics and difficulties. Often behavioral components of injury significantly determine outcome, from the child's and other people's viewpoint. However, intervention approaches can be designed to meet the specific needs of these children to increase behavioral control and foster adaptive, independent behavior.

REFERENCES

Barin, J.J., Hanchett, M.M., Jacob, W.L., & Scott, M.B. (1985). Counseling the head injured patient. In M. Ylvisaker (Ed.), *Head injury rehabilitation: Children and adolescents.* San Diego: College-Hill Press.

Barkley, R.A. (1981). *Hyperactive children: A handbook for diagnosis and treatment.* New York: Guilford Press.

Benton, A.L. (1963). Behavioral indices of brain injury in school children. *Child Development, 33,* 201–208.

Black, P., Blumer, D., Wellner, A.M., & Walker, A.E. (1971). The head injured child: Time-course of recovery, with implications for rehabilitation. *Proceedings of the International Symposium on Head Injuries* (pp. 131–137). Edinburgh: Churchill Livingstone.

Boll, T.J. (1983). Neuropsychological assessment of the child: Myths, current status and future prospects. In C.E. Walker & M.C. Roberts (Eds.), *Handbook of clinical child psychology.* New York: John Wiley & Sons.

Bolstad, O.D., & Johnson, S.M. (1972). Self-regulation in the modification of disruptive classroom behavior. *Journal of Applied Behavior Analysis, 5,* 443–454.

Bornstein, P., & Quevillon, R. (1976). The effects of a self-instruction package on overactive preschool boys. *Journal of Applied Behavior Analysis, 9,* 179–188.

Brink, J.D., Garrett, A.L., Hale, W.R., Woo-Sam, J., & Nickel, V.L. (1970). Recovery of motor and intellectual function in children sustaining severe head injuries. *Developmental Medicine and Child Neurology, 12,* 565–571.

Connors, C.K. (1970). Symptom patterns in hyperkinetic, neurotic and normal children. *Child Development, 41,* 667–682.

Deaton, A.V. (1987). Behavioral change strategies for children and adolescents with severe brain injury. *Journal of Learning Disabilities, 20*(10), 581–589.

Divak, J.A., Herrie, J., & Scott, M.B. (1985). Behavior management. In M. Ylvisaker (Ed.), *Head injury rehabilitation: Children and adolescents.* San Diego: College-Hill Press.

Drabman, R.S., Spitalnik, R., & O'Leary, K.D. (1973). Teaching self-control to disruptive children. *Journal of Abnormal Psychology, 82,* 10–16.

Eames, P., & Wood, R. (1985). Rehabilitation after severe brain injury: A special unit approach. *International Rehabilitation Medicine, 7*(3), 130–133.

Felixbrod, J.J., & O'Leary, K.D. (1973). Effects of reinforcement on children's academic behavior as a function of self-determined and externally-imposed contingencies. *Journal of Applied Behavior Analysis, 6,* 241–250.

Filley, C.M., Cranberg, M.D., Alexander, M.P., & Hart, E.J. (1987). Neurobehavioral outcome after closed head injury in childhood and adolescence. *Archives of Neurology, 44,* 194–198.

Gelfand, D.M., & Hartmann, D.P. (1984). *Child behavior analysis and therapy.* New York: Pergamon Press.

Goethe, K.E., & Levin, H.S. (1984). Behavioral manifestations during the early and long-term stages of recovery after closed head injury. *Psychiatric Annals, 14*(7), 540–546.

152 PSYCHOLOGICAL MANAGEMENT OF TBI IN CHILDREN AND ADOLESCENTS

Grimm, B.H., & Bleiberg, J. (1986). Psychological rehabilitation in traumatic brain injury. In S. Filskov & T. Boll (Eds.), *Handbook of clinical neuropsychology*. New York: John Wiley & Sons.

Howard, M., & Bleiberg, J. (1983). *A manual of behavior management stategies for traumatically brain-injured adults*. Chicago: Education and Training Center, Rehabilitation Institute of Chicago.

Jacobs, H.E. (1988). Yes, behavior analysis can help, but do you know how to harness it? *Brain Injury, 2*(4), 339–346.

Jacobs, H.E. (1989). Family reaction and treatment. In A. Christensen & D. Ellis (Eds.), *Neuropsychological treatment of head injury*. Boston: Martinus Nijhoff Publishing.

Kazdin, A.E. (1984). *Behavior modification in applied settings*. Homewood, IL: Dorsey.

Klonoff, H., & Paris, R. (1974). Immediate, short-term and residual effects of acute head injuries in children: Neuropsychological and neurological correlates. In R. Reitan & L. Davison (Eds.), *Clinical neuropsychology: Current status and applications*. New York: John Wiley & Sons.

Kozloff, M.A. (1974). *Educating children with learning and behavior problems*. New York: John Wiley & Sons.

Kozloff, M.A. (1979). *A program for families of children with learning and behavior problems*. New York: John Wiley & Sons.

Lewis, D.O., Pincus, M.D., Feldman, M.A., Jackson, M.A. & Bard, B. (1986). Psychiatric, neurological, and psychoeducational characteristics of 15 death row inmates in the United States. *American Journal of Psychiatry, 143*, 838–845.

Meichenbaum, D.H., & Goodman, J. (1977). Training impulsive children to talk to themselves: A means of developing self-control. In A. Ellis & R. Grieger (Eds.), *Handbook of rational emotive therapy*. New York: Springer Publishing.

Muir, C.A., Haffey, W.J., Ott, K.J., Karaica, D., Muir, J.H., & Sutko, M. (1983). Treatment of behavioral deficits. In M. Rosenthal, E.R. Griffith, M. Bond, & J.D. Miller (Eds.), *Rehabilitation of the head injured adult*. Philadelphia: F.A. Davis.

Newcombe, F. (1981). The psychological consequences of closed head injury: Assessment and rehabilitation. *Injury, 14*, 111–136.

Pelham, W.E., Schnedler, R.W., Bender, M.E., Nilsson, D.E., Miller, J., Budrow, M.S., Ronnei, M., Paluchowski, C., & Marks, D.A. (1988). The combination of behavior therapy and methylphenidate in the treatment of attention deficit disorders: A therapy outcome study. In L.M. Bloomingdale (Ed.), *Attention deficit disorder, Vol. 3: New research in attention, treatment, and psychopharmacology*. Oxford, Eng.: Pergamon Press.

Richardson, F. (1963). Some effects of severe head injury: A follow-up study of children and adolescents after protracted coma. *Developmental Medicine and Child Neurology, 5*, 471–482.

Rutter, M. (1982). Developmental neuropsychiatry: Concepts, issues, and prospects. *Journal of Clinical Neuropsychology, 4*, 91–115.

Sand, P.L., Trieschman, R.B., Fordyce, W.E., & Fowler, R.S. (1970). Behavior modification in the medical rehabilitation setting: Rationale and some applications. *Rehabilitation Research Practice Review, 1*, 11.

Trites, R.L., Laprade, K., & Blouin, A.G. (1982). Factor analysis of the Conner's Teacher Rating Scale based on a large normative sample. *Journal of Consulting and Clinical Psychology, 50*, 615–623.

Wood, R.L. (1984). Behavior disorders following severe brain injury: Their presentation and psychological management. In N. Brooks (Ed.), *Closed head injury: Psychological, social, and family consequences.* Oxford, Eng.: Oxford University Press.

Wood, R.L. (1987). *Brain injury rehabilitation: A neurobehavioral approach.* Rockville, MD: Aspen Publishers.

Wood, R.L., & Eames, P. (1981). Application of behavior modification in the rehabilitation of traumatically brain injured patients. In G. Davey (Ed.), *Applications of conditioning theory.* London: Methuen.

Chapter 6

Psychosocial Issues

Ellen Lehr

INTRODUCTION

This chapter attempts to examine the experience and perception of the psychosocial effects of traumatic brain injury from the children's and adolescents' point of view, from their family's point of view, and from their friends' point of view. Although it is well recognized that the psychosocial aspects of head injury are often most critical in terms of determining the levels of perceived stress and functional disability, both for the injured individual and the family, this area has received much less attention than physical or cognitive effects of head injuries (Bond, 1975; Brooks, 1984; Lezak, 1987; Oddy, 1984). The available literature that focuses on psychosocial aspects of traumatic brain injury for children, adolescents, their families, and friends is even more sparse than that concerning head-injured adults.

Several factors that can lead to higher risk of psychosocial sequelae after traumatic brain injury have been identified. However, prediction of psychological and social effects after injury is much more complex and less consistent with injury characteristics than prediction of cognitive effects. Psychosocial effects are likely related to a combination of factors occurring together rather than to single variables (Rutter, Chadwick, & Shaffer, 1983). The factors that interact to increase the likelihood of psychosocial sequelae in children and adolescents after head injuries include the following.

The first factor involves the severity of injury. Those children and adolescents who sustain severe injuries are more likely to experience difficulties in psychosocial areas as they recover. However, this is clearly a complex relationship since those children with the most severe injuries whose functioning is markedly compromised to the point of not being aware of what has happened to them or those survivors at the extreme end of the spectrum who remain in persistent vegetative state, have fewer or literally no psychosocial concerns.

Preinjury behavior and personality have been identified as a critical factor in the occurrence of psychosocial disorders after head injury. Those children who have been functioning well in psychosocial areas before injury are less likely to develop new disorders in this area after injury than those children who were experiencing difficulty in psychosocial areas before injury. However, even those children who were functioning well psychosocially before injury are still at increased risk for developing new disorders in this area after head injury. In one of the few follow-up studies that included measurement of psychosocial functioning (Rutter et al., 1983), one-fourth of children with a history of normal preaccident adjustment developed a new psychiatric disorder by 1 year after head injury, but one-half children with difficulties before injury did so.

A third factor has been called *psychosocial adversity*. This is actually a composite measure reflecting the characteristics of the child's family and living setting and is composed of such variables as large family size, overcrowding, parental psychiatric disorder or criminal behavior, low social status, the child's involvement in foster care because of family difficulties, and discordant family relationships (Rutter et al., 1983). Psychosocial disorders were most frequent in children after head injuries when a severe injury was combined with increased psychosocial adversity. Brain injury may increase the child's vulnerability to adverse environmental circumstances (Shaffer, Chadwick & Rutter, 1975), and the development of disturbance in the child after injury may have a further negative effect on family cohesiveness and happiness, especially in families already experiencing a high level of stress or disorganization.

There also appears to be a higher risk for psychosocial disorders after traumatic brain injury in those children and adolescents who experience posttraumatic epilepsy (seizures). From the Isle of Wight study (Rutter, Graham, & Yule, 1970), 35% of children with seizures or structural damage to the central nervous system or both had a handicapping psychiatric disturbance compared with 7% in the nonepileptic and undamaged population. In a follow-up study of children after head injury, the most unfavorable psychosocial prognosis was found in those children with posttraumatic epilepsy, despite optimal antiepileptic treatment (Kleinpeter, 1976). In adults, there is a close relationship between temporal lobe epilepsy, the most common type of seizure disorder after blunt head injury, and psychosocial disturbance, especially if seizures develop within the first year after injury (Lishman, 1973). Children with epilepsy have been found to have a tendency to social isolation (Bolter, 1986), but this was especially so for those with temporal lobe epilepsy (Stores, 1978).

The occurrence of psychosocial disorders after traumatic brain injuries in children and adolescents is not necessarily directly related to visible physical impairment. In fact, those children with obvious physical sequelae after injury may be less likely to have psychiatric impairment than those children with milder or no physical impairment. This may be related to awareness of what they cannot do, as well as to other people's level of expectation (Seidel, Chadwick, & Rutter, 1975).

NEUROLOGICAL ASPECTS OF PSYCHOSOCIAL SEQUELAE

The neurology of emotion is not well understood, either for adults or especially for children and adolescents. However, it is likely that certain areas or functional systems of the brain are more involved than others in terms of emotional control and response (Lishman, 1968, 1973). Understanding and expression of emotions may also involve a separate neural processing system that is integrated with cognitive processing (LeDoux, 1984). The two hemispheres of the brain appear to contribute differently to psychosocial sequelae after traumatic brain injury (Bryden & Ley, 1983). The right hemisphere is specialized both to perceive and to express emotion so that emotional stimuli are comprehended more accurately when they are able to gain access to this hemisphere of the brain (Gianotti, 1983). Adult patients after right-hemisphere brain injury therefore have difficulty understanding the emotional tone of what people are saying, the emotional expressions of their faces and body postures, as well as difficulty integrating the complexity of social interaction. They may also have difficulty in the communication of emotion through their speech and facial expression. In general, they appear apathetic, indifferent to emotions, or even euphoric.

In contrast, adults after left-hemisphere brain injury appear depressed and anxious, sometimes catastrophically so (Goldstein, 1952). However, their reaction, even though dramatic and accentuated, is nevertheless a psychologically appropriate emotional response. They are often able to express their emotional experience of being injured even when their language is significantly impaired. The left hemisphere therefore may normally have an inhibitory effect on emotional expression, and together with the ability to use verbalization to cope with the effects of injury, it may aid in maintaining emotional control (Gianotti, 1983).

Interestingly adults after diffuse traumatic brain injury often appear similar to those with focal right-hemisphere injuries, even though both hemispheres of their brain have been involved. The theory for how this might occur has been developed recently from research findings that the right hemisphere has more white matter or nerve fibers than the left hemisphere (Goldberg & Costa, 1981). Right-hemisphere processing of information has been known to be more integrative and holistic than left-hemisphere processing and more reliant on nerve connections within the hemisphere itself, not only for adequate development but also for maintenance of adequate functioning. Since one of the primary mechanisms of head injury is stretching and shearing damage of the axons (which are white matter parts of the nerves)—even though this damage may be present in both hemispheres of the brain—it may therefore more seriously disrupt right-hemisphere functioning.

Rourke (1987) has extended this theory to children. It has been recognized that a group of children with nonverbal learning disabilities not only have difficulty learning in specific cognitive and academic areas but also have significant deficits in social perception, social judgment, and social interaction skills with a marked tendency toward social withdrawal and even social isolation as they get older. They are also at greater risk for developing social and emotional types of psychopathology. Rourke has hypothesized that the primary mechanism for this constellation of characteristics is disruption of white matter functioning whether it occurs prenatally as in learning disabilities or through disease or trauma in the developmental period. The severity of the syndrome is postulated to be related to the amount of white matter that is disordered or destroyed. With increasing amount of white matter dysfunction, the ability to deal with learning, especially in novel situations, becomes more impaired. The effects of the syndrome are less apparent at 7 or 8 years of age than they are at 10 to 14, and even more so as adulthood approaches. Developmentally the effects of this syndrome become more apparent and debilitating with age, not because of increasing damage but because of increasing expectations of being able to cope more independently in a more complex social environment. The social inappropriateness of individuals with this syndrome is related to attempts to apply previously acquired skills in a rigid, stereotypic, perseverative fashion to situations in which such a limited skill repertoire is not necessarily adaptive.

Other parts of the brain have also been implicated in psychosocial functioning, especially the frontal parts of both hemispheres and the limbic system, which lies between the frontal lobes and the brain stem. Interruption of the connections among these parts of the brain, the hemispheres and the brain stem, as well as focal injury to any one or more of them, is likely implicated in psychosocial aspects of traumatic brain injury. As presented in Chapter 3, the frontal parts of the brain are undergoing development throughout childhood and into adolescence. The executive functions of the frontal lobe, which are expected to be partially operative at least by adolescence, clearly affect psychosocial capacities (Lezak, 1982). Lack of foresight, tact and concern, the inability to plan ahead or judge the consequences of actions, and disinhibition all interfere with the ability of an individual to function adequately in a social world. Adults with damage to the frontal parts of both hemispheres of their brain have been known to demonstrate the most severe examples of irresponsible and antisocial conduct (Lishman, 1973).

Although we are beginning to understand more about brain function and dysfunction as it affects social and emotional capacities, we know less about the effect of traumatic brain injury in these areas with children than we do with adults. Few studies with children and adolescents have attempted to relate the nature and location of injury with psychosocial sequelae. In one of the few studies in this area (Filley, Cranberg, Alexander, & Hart, 1987), discrete frontal injury or clinical evidence of diffuse axonal injury was implicated in severe and persistent emotional sequelae in children and adolescents after severe head injury. They found two patterns of deficits. One was characterized by overarousal including inattentiveness, irritability, hyperactivity, impulsiveness, inappropriate behavior, and aggressiveness. The other pattern involved underarousal demonstrated through apathy, poor motivation, and social withdrawal.

PSYCHOSOCIAL EFFECTS OF TRAUMATIC BRAIN INJURY ON CHILDREN AND ADOLESCENTS

The research on psychosocial effects is usually derived from parent's reports or from professional's observation but rarely from the child's or adolescent's perspective. Because of this, clinical observations and drawings are utilized in this chapter in order to include the child's or adolescent's personal experience as much as possible.

Three possible aspects to psychosocial components of functioning after head injury consist of (1) emotional reaction to injury and deficits, (2) neurological aspects of injury that directly affect emotional perception and control, and (3) preinjury personality or characteristics that may have been maladaptive or may become so after being intensified by injury (Prigatano, 1986). These components interact and can affect both the prognosis for adaptive functioning and the type of intervention that might be effective.

In adults who have had head injuries, changes in emotional areas are usually referred to as *personality changes* (Prigatano, 1986), changes from the type of person we knew before (Lishman, 1973). These changes may be gross and obvious or detectable only by those who knew the person well before injury. At times they are significantly more apparent to others than they are to the injured individuals themselves. In children, personality is undergoing development, but some basic components of personality are evident even in young infants. These individual characteristics in infants and children are often referred to as *temperament* rather than personality and are characterized both by continuity and change over the developmental period (Chess & Thomas, 1984; Thomas & Chess, 1980). For the purposes of this discussion, the terms *psychological* and *emotional changes* are utilized rather than *personality changes* as with adults. However, no matter what it is called, what is well recognized by the families, friends, teachers, and therapists of head-injured children and adolescents is the importance of these factors in teaching, befriending, and in general living with children and adolescents after injury. For the children and adolescents themselves, changes in psychosocial functioning cause significant emotional distress and confusion that can be difficult for them to understand and deal with.

The characteristics of psychosocial sequelae of head injury in children and adolescents consist of a constellation of social disinhibition or acting in socially inappropriate ways, irritability, increased emotionality, reduced judgment and motivation, perseveration, lowered tolerance for frustration, and egocentricity seen through insensitivity to others, unawareness of their impact on others, and an increase in demanding behavior. It is difficult to make clear distinctions between aspects of cognitive and psychosocial components since they interact and affect each other. For example, perseveration can affect the flexibility of how a child or adolescent learns and integrates new ideas and concepts. However, it can also contribute to psychosocial difficulties when it interferes with understanding and ability to comply with parental demands or expectations without persistent arguments that do not take into account the parents' perspective or changes in circumstances.

From the children's or adolescents' point of view, they often feel a vague or more immediate sense of not being like themselves, of being out of control or crazy. Traumatic brain injury can threaten not only their sense of physical integrity but also their sense of emotional and social integrity. The sense of self and of self-confidence that they have been developing over time and that is usually taken for granted is often significantly jeopardized by alterations in emotional and self-perception and control. Children and adolescents often directly express these feelings in interviews, through their drawings and play. Figure 6-1 was drawn by a 12-year-old girl shortly before she was discharged from a rehabilitation hospital. Before her severe head injury, she was described as dramatic and stubborn, but afterward she was markedly disinhibited with exaggerated affect and emotional control difficulties. Her drawing is of a boy "with the wind blowing and his hair's all over his face." She added mittens and a hat that "just

Figure 6-1 Drawing of a Boy by a 12-year-old Girl 2 1/2 Months after Injury

blew off." Drawings by other adolescents are effective in communicating their sense of anger (Figure 6-2), their struggle with alterations in physical prowess (Figure 6-3), and concern about sexuality after injury (Figure 6-4).

In the Rutter group's findings (Rutter et al., 1983), the main increase in psychiatric disturbance took place during the months immediately fol-

Figure 6-2 Drawing of a Face by a 16-year-old Boy 1 Year after Injury

Figure 6-3 Drawing of a Boy by a 13-year-old Boy 5 Months after Injury

lowing injury, when social disinhibition was at its peak. Afterward, though, there was no substantial falling off in psychiatric problems over the 2 1/4-year follow-up period. There was a tendency for the characteristic pattern of socially embarrassing behavior to diminish so that the disorders of the severe group were less clearly distinctive as time progressed.

Probably two processes that are intertwined cause the initial rise in psychosocial disturbances and the prolonged nature of the increase in disorders in this area. The first is likely to be a direct expression of loosened behavioral and emotional controls in conjunction with altered cognitive abilities that interfere with the accurate perception of complex social interaction, of one's own effect on others, and of one's own behavior and emotion. In conjunction with the often rapid recovery and improvement in cognitive functioning, the head-injured child or adolescent is then able to realize more fully the impact of injury and react emotionally to these felt changes. This second process is therefore related to increased awareness of the effect of injury in terms of the child's or adolescent's emotional response and attempts to cope with alterations after injury. This is con-

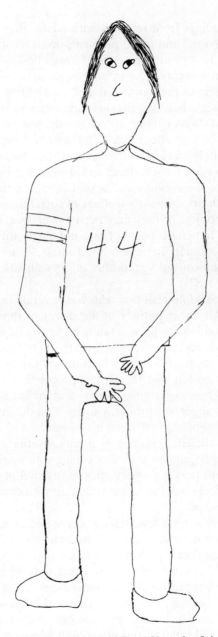

Figure 6-4 Drawing of a Boy by a 15-year-old Boy 1 Year after Injury

sistent with the findings from research with adults after head injuries for whom severe behavioral and social problems occur most frequently in the second half of the first posttrauma year (Lezak, 1987).

As children or adolescents become more aware of the effects of traumatic brain injury in terms of their own reduced capabilities, they are able to grieve for their losses, become anxious sometimes to the point of panic about their reduced ability to cope with demands, and directly express their anger at having to live an altered life. They can become depressed to the point of being acutely suicidal and wish that they had not survived. At times, especially in adolescence, drugs and alcohol may be utilized to blunt the felt intensity of these emotions. Sexual acting out may be used as a way of dealing with or combating feelings of social isolation. These reactions may be temporary, or they may persist over several years. Feelings of anger are likely to persist, but they may not necessarily interfere markedly with daily functioning. In head-injured adults, 70% continued to have difficulties with anger control 5 years after injury with little or no abatement over time (Lezak, 1987).

For example, one adolescent boy who was severely injured at 13 years of age expressed his anger initially at the driver of the car who was responsible for his accident by perseverating on saying he was going to "kill the old lady." Gradually over the next 2 years and as financial settlements were pursued, the focus of his anger became in "taking her for all she is worth." However, he felt that the only appropriate punishment was for the "old lady" and him to exchange places, and for her to have to live the way he had to. His anger was primarily focused on the unfairness of being punished by being handicapped when it was her "fault" and she was not being punished at all. His preoccupation with wanting to be the way he had been before injury and his difficulty coping with significant, pervasive deficits continued to persist 4 years after injury and at times reached a level of psychological disorganization requiring medication and inpatient psychiatric management.

Interestingly there is little research on severe and persistent psychiatric disorders after traumatic brain injury in children and adolescents. Even in adults the relationship between head injury and psychiatric disorders is not clear (Bond, 1984). Bender (1956) found that only 86 of 5,000 children who had been hospitalized for psychiatric reasons at Bellevue had a precipitant incident of head injury. She concluded that there was a very low incidence of posttraumatic chronic psychosis in children and adolescents. For those head-injured children and adolescents who were treated at Bellevue, Bender postulated that the accidents may have been related to delusional ideas and that the head injury was a sequelae of preexisting psychosis. She found a high incidence of psychopathology and alcoholism in the parents of these children. Outcome for these children depended on their families' capabilities before injury and their response to injury.

From clinical experience, if a child or adolescent has a history of significant psychiatric disorder before injury, these preexisting difficulties are likely to reemerge with recovery, even from very severe injuries. Often both the family and the treatment team are hopeful that this will not occur and may become quite resistant to the possibility. Head injury and coma recovery can be seen as a second chance both for themselves and their child or adolescent, which will "knock some sense" into the patient's head. For the severely injured child or adolescent, these hopes are sustained through early and middle stages of recovery when they are somewhat docile and tractable but are often dashed in the later stages with reemergence of preinjury personality and behavior, which is possibly even exacerbated. When this happens, the family can become very angry and feel betrayed by their head-injured child or adolescent for becoming worse rather than better.

Robert, who was severely injured in an unexplained fall from a window when he was 16, was an example of how preexisting psychiatric difficulties can reemerge after head injury. He had a history of drug and alcohol use since the age of 12 and had been in several residential treatment programs with little success. Attempts to return home to live were also unsuccessful and usually ended in his being kicked out and going to live with friends. At the time of injury, his source of income appeared to come from his friends and possibly from sexual encounters. He apparently was not involved in drug dealing or overt criminal activities. His parents were contacted through identification found on Robert in the emergency room. They visited him frequently throughout his acute-care and rehabilitation hospitalizations and planned to take him home to try again.

Toward the end of his rehabilitation stay, though, Robert became acutely paranoid, delusional, and felt that his roommate was trying to kill him. This occurred after posttraumatic amnesia and confusion had resolved. He appeared to be increasingly out of contact with reality, which was expressed throughout his drawings and statements. Figures 6-5 and 6-6 were drawn in art therapy sessions and his preoccupation with Moy the boy persisted for several weeks. Figure 6-7 was a drawing of a person requested during formal psychological and neuropsychological testing before discharge. He stated that the drawing was of the examiner and then went on talking about how it was so "dirty" and "sexy" and how could the examiner "stand to look at it." Since Robert was threatening to run away and had also expressed suicidal intentions, he was admitted to an adolescent psychiatric program for management and treatment. Over the next several years, he improved in cognitive areas but continued to function marginally in psy-

Figure 6-5 Drawing of a Boy by a 16-year-old Boy 3 Months after Injury

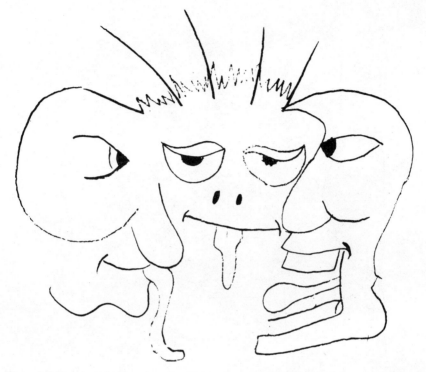

Figure 6-6 Drawing of a Face by a 16-year-old Boy 3 Months after Injury

chosocial areas. He denied use of drugs but was not able to work, attend school, or establish any interpersonal relationships for longer than a few weeks at a time. Even ongoing contact with psychiatric services of the most basic nature could not be sustained.

For a thorough evaluation of the psychosocial and emotional aspects of traumatic brain injury in children and adolescents, information from a variety of sources is necessary. As much as possible, an accurate description of the children's or adolescents' preinjury functioning in these areas should be obtained. Parents, teachers, friends, and the children or adolescents themselves all have their own perspectives, which must be integrated to have a more complete picture of long-standing traits and personality style as they were evident across different situations and in different interactions. Having parents complete report measures such as the Personality Inventory for Children (Wirt, Lachar, Klinedinst, & Seat, 1977) shortly after their children's injury may be helpful in gaining a somewhat more objective measure than that derived only through unstructured interviewing.

Accurate evaluation of psychosocial changes after injury also must incorporate information about how others perceive the children's or adoles-

Figure 6-7 Drawing of a Woman by a 16-year-old Boy 4 Months after Injury

cents' psychosocial functioning, as well as their own perceptions about themselves. Because individuals after head injury are likely to be more unaware of their psychosocial functioning than is usually the case, this information often cannot be directly elicited from them. However, similarities or discrepancies in reports can be very useful in determining the degree of unawareness present and can give information about who is feeling what kind of emotional stress (Fordyce & Roueche, 1986). Even when both the children and their parents report psychosocial sequelae after head injury, they may perceive problems in different areas and propose quite different solutions.

Techniques for eliciting the children's and adolescents' perception and experience of psychosocial difficulties can include their own report on personality measures such as the Early School Personality Questionnaire (Cattell & Coan, 1966), the Children's Personality Questionnaire (Porter & Cattell, 1959), the High School Personality Questionnaire (Cattell, Cattell, & Johns, 1958), and the Millon Adolescent Personality Inventory (Millon, Green, & Meagher, 1977); self-esteem scales such as the Piers-Harris Children's Self Concept Scale (Piers & Harris, 1969), the McDaniel-Piers Young Children's Self-Concept Scale (McDaniel & Piers, 1973), the Self-Esteem Inventory (Coopersmith, 1967), and the Tennessee Self-Concept Scale (Fitts, 1965); human figure drawings (Koppitz, 1968); as well as their responses to projective measures such as those utilizing story telling like the Thematic Apperception Test (Bellack, 1975), the Children's Apperception Test (Bellack, 1975), the Tasks of Emotional Development (Cohen & Weil, 1975), the Michigan Picture Test-Revised (Hutt, 1980), the Roberts Apperception Test for Children (McArthur & Roberts, 1982), and the Rorschach (Exner & Weiner, 1982; Rorschach, 1966). Specialized techniques have also been developed to assess children's and adolescent's perception of emotional cues and social situations, but most of these have been used in research rather than clinical settings (O'Sullivan & Guilford, 1975; Platt & Spivak, 1975; Selman, 1976).

FAMILY EXPERIENCE AND PERSPECTIVE

Except in unusual circumstances, families are essential in the recovery and eventual functioning level of their head-injured child or adolescent. It is within the family context that the head-injured child or adolescent continues to live and develop long after injury. Family functioning as a whole, therefore, is likely to be critical to the adequacy of the development of the head-injured child as well as other family members (Foster, Berger, & McLean, 1981). However, when working with the families of children and adolescents after head injury, it is important to remember that *family* is not synonymous with *parents*. Rather the entire family must be considered, including siblings, grandparents, aunts, uncles, cousins, and other relatives who are important to any one particular family's functioning. It cannot be assumed that there is necessarily a united family perspective about how the head-injured child or adolescent affects family interaction and contributes to family stress. Rather each family member has an individual reaction and way of coping with the child's injury that impinges and alters family functioning, just as changes in the child's functioning also affect family interactions.

Few data are available on how families react to their children's head injuries and how these reactions might influence the children's psychosocial functioning after injury. From work with head-injured adults, family cohesion appears to be resistant to physical disability, but much less so to mental handicaps, especially memory and personality impairments (Brooks, 1984; Oddy, Humphrey, & Uttley, 1978; Lezak, 1978). Whether this is similar for the families of injured children is open to question and likely to be related to the age of the child at the time of injury.

From a prospective study (Rutter et al., 1983), the initial impact on the parents of their child's severe injury was considerable. Parents had doubts about whether their children would survive severe injury and expressed worries about their unusual behavior as they regained consciousness. Almost half of the parents were described as experiencing persisting emotional disturbances of their own in reaction to their children's injury. Marital tensions were reportedly increased initially after injury, but it was unusual for this to continue over more than a few months. (However, other reports have not been so positive and have found a higher incidence of divorce in parents of severely injured children with persisting deficits [Lezak, 1988].) Parents of children who had mild head injuries or orthopedic injuries did not report the same intensity of concern about their children's well-being nor the same degree of emotional reaction to their children's injury.

Rutter and his group (Rutter, 1983) also observed a tendency for parents to become more overprotective of their children after injury, which was demonstrated by their doing more for their children, allowing them less autonomy and independence, and being less strict in disciplining the injured child. Parents reported being especially afraid of using physical punishment if their children were taking anticonvulsant medication. Even though their sample size was small, in that they studied only 28 mildly and 28 severely injured children and their families, there appeared to be a tendency for heightened parental changes to be related to increased risk of psychosocial difficulties for the children after injury. However, the nature of this relationship is not clear as to whether the parental changes are in fact in response to greater changes in their children. In other words, the parents whose behavior changed the most and whose emotional reaction was the most severe may in fact be responding to more severe changes in their children. It seems likely that both of these factors are involved but not equally so in each case.

Some parents may experience such severe emotional distress of their own in reaction to their children's injuries that they are less available and have less energy to deal with the children themselves. This emotional stress on the parents' part may increase the likelihood of psychosocial difficulties for the children. However, the alternative might occur. The actual changes in children's behavior and personality after injury may increase parental stress and directly alter parental behavior. That parental reaction is important in protecting or in making children more vulnerable to psychosocial stress after injury is reasonable. Determining what is driving the stress is especially important in developing effective intervention, that is, whether intervention efforts need to be directed to reducing parental distress so that parents are more available for taking care of children or whether intervention should be directed at helping the parents to contain or better manage the children's altered behavior.

In Chapter 2, the process of head injury recovery and improvement was discussed from the point of view of the child, the family, and the professionals working with them. The family's understanding of head injury as it affects their child and themselves is an ongoing process that can take a considerable amount of time before they feel comfortable and at least somewhat in control of what has happened to all of them. Initially family members usually have little or no experience or understanding of head-injury issues, either in general or specifically as these issues relate to themselves and their child. In addition, family members are expected to learn about head injury at a time of extreme crisis and emotional stress.

Some reactions of family members, though, can be very difficult for professionals to deal with constructively. Family members may insist, despite severe head injury and obvious deficits, that their child or adolescent is no different than before injury. They may focus on the similarities to preinjury behavior and personality with little emphasis on changes after injury. Hospital, rehabilitation, and school personnel may become frustrated in trying to plan for the child in the face of the parents' denial of deficits and may feel that the child's parents cannot be trusted to manage the child safely at home. Sometimes spending time with family members in gathering a comprehensive picture of the child or adolescent before injury can be helpful in clarifying the real differences related to injury. This can also help in bridging the gulf that occurs when family and professionals each emphasize what they know the best, for example, the family's knowledge about their child's preinjury functioning and the professional staff members' knowledge about head injury effects. Also allowing the family time to become more fully aware of the extent and characteristics of psychosocial changes after injury can relieve some of the tension between family and professionals. However, this usually does not occur until after discharge from the acute-care or rehabilitation hospital. As the family becomes more cognizant of the child's deficits, it is important for professionals not to react to this awareness in an I-told-you-so manner and thus further distancing the family when they may be most in need of support and services.

Some families or some individual family members may be so devastated by a child's injury that they may not be able to mobilize the energy and emotion to care for the child during recovery. At times, this severe reaction is related to guilt concerning the injury and a questioning of the parents or siblings about their own capacity to relate or care for the child since it was their "fault" that the child was injured. However, it can also be in reaction to the individual family member's own injuries or the injury or death of other family members. For some families, whose psychological and financial resources are already being stretched, a child's head injury may be the last straw in overwhelming an already overloaded system. In these circumstances, crisis support should be available for family members and for the family as a whole to help them literally live from day to day. If the family cannot mobilize sufficiently to care for the child adequately, alternatives such as in-home help, involvement of the extended family, or residential placement should be considered.

Although it may be less common with parents of children than with spouses or parents of adults, parents sometimes have the reaction that the head-injured child is not "their child" after injury. From clinical observation, parents often seem to relate their child's behavior or psychosocial functioning after injury to how they behaved at an earlier stage of development, rather than as a personality change in the child. However, when this reaction occurs in negative ways, it can be quite devastating for both the parents and the child. In extreme instances, the child's emotional and behavioral control deficits may be attributed to such circumstances as getting blood transfusions from a bad person or to the devil getting into the victim. However, psychosocial and emotional changes are not always perceived as negative. For children and adolescents who have had a history of preinjury control difficulties and who experience a constriction of affect and behavior after injury, these changes may be easily seen as positive by their families with an expressed wish that they continue, rather than hoping for a complete recovery. Children and adolescents who were considerably shy or withdrawn before injury may literally enjoy the experience of disinhibition. Their families may also prefer to have their previously quiet children and adolescents act in a more outgoing way both with themselves and with other people.

Several periods or transitions are likely to be particularly stressful for families of children and adolescents who have had traumatic brain injuries. The period immediately after injury is often a time of family crisis and disorganization. Although this is especially true after severe injuries, when it is not clear if the child or adolescent will survive, it probably is so in an abbreviated manner even after mild injuries. However, this is also a time when families may receive very little if any professional support or information about head-injury effects in terms of what to expect over either the short- or the long-term.

Because it is so important for children and adolescents to be at home with their families, as well as because of their often rapid physical and medical progress, they are likely to be discharged from acute-care hospitals quicker than adults. If children and adolescents after moderate or severe head injury are not involved in rehabilitation, they might return home before they are fully oriented and in a period of confusion. Families may have little preparation for what their children and adolescents are going through and therefore feel quite overwhelmed by attempting to care for them. Families may also receive little preparation for possible delayed effects of head injury in those children and adolescents who initially appear to be doing quite well after injury. For those who are involved in rehabilitation programs, return to home, school, and community can be quite difficult even when well-planned. The reality of the children's and adolescents' deficits, especially their effect on family functioning, can be experienced only after they return home. At that time, the wish that everything would be as it was before injury is severely challenged in the face of day-to-day experience. Anniversaries of the date of injury can also be stressful, especially if important hoped-for goals have not been reached, for example, being able to walk normally and returning to regular class programming.

Another stress-provoking period involves the negotiations and settlements of legal and financial claims. Often this involves a recapitulation of the events surrounding the accident and injury, sometimes with further knowledge and understanding of what happened. Feelings that family members and the injured child or adolescent thought were in the past and could be at least partially forgotten reemerge and can threaten the present stability and coping ability of family members. In one family, when the siblings realized that their brother and parents were going to receive payment for pain and suffering, the brothers and sisters became adamant that they also should be compensated. This was handled sensitively by setting up a college fund with a part of the settlement money for all of the siblings to share. However, it was quite surprising for the parents and the head-injured brother to find out that perceptions and feelings of the other brothers and sisters were expressed in a different and perhaps more clearly stated way when settlement issues arose.

For children and adolescents with persisting impairment after head injury, special occasions celebrating transitions for the children or parents can be poignant and painful. These families are continually faced with the reality of one of their members being dependent on them, possibly for the rest of their lives. It can be difficult to foster the normal developmental progression of leaving the family for the other children, when parents need to care for a perpetually dependent child (Lezak, 1988). Indeed it arrests the development of parents who may have been looking forward to a time of freedom from raising children and now find themselves restricted by the needs of their head-injured adult child.

Relationships among siblings have received little to no attention in research on head-injury effects in children and adolescents. Yet from clinical work, these relationships are often very important both for the head-injured sibling and for those siblings who have not been injured. Head injury in families is usually very much a family affair. Siblings may have felt responsible for the injury to their brother or sister, especially if they were taking care of them or were with them at the time of the accident. Even younger siblings may feel guilty about the circumstances of injury if they were aware of what their older brother or sister was doing (for example, drinking or driving dangerously) and their parents were not. After a head injury, the relationships among siblings can shift significantly. A younger, noninjured brother or sister may be expected to or may be eager to take on the responsibilities and privileges of an older sibling. However, with recovery or improvement the injured sibling is not likely to tolerate this usurping of rights. Changes in psychosocial functioning after injury are likely to be very apparent and often quite confusing to the head-injured child's or adolescent's brother or sister. Siblings may react with significant anger and a heart-felt wish that their family return to the way it was before injury, blaming their head-injured sibling for the changes (Figure 6-8). Expression of these feelings toward an impaired sibling, though understandable, can be difficult to tolerate, especially within the family itself.

Professionals with expertise in pediatric head injury must become allies with the injured child's or adolescent's family, especially their parents and siblings. This process, though, can be complicated by the fact that the information professionals often must present to family members can be so devastating. To be able to maintain the delicate balance of giving accurate information to the family, which can often be quite depressing for them, and supporting the family in coping with the changes that head injury has brought about, an accurate assessment of family functioning and needs must be developed.

It is especially important for professionals to respect the primacy of the family and to work within its system, only attempting to alter it if it is clearly maladaptive. This involves understanding the family's conception of its social world, its basic attitudes, and its definitions and perceptions of problems, especially in the light of traumatic injury to one of the family's members (Westin & Reiss, 1979). It is important to understand current family roles in terms of who makes what kind of decisions, how family

Figure 6-8 Drawing by a 13-year-old Brother of Boy Who Had Been Injured 8 Months Previously

members communicate with each other, how conflict is expressed and managed, how feelings are shared, how previous losses have been dealt with, how each family member has responded to the traumatic injury, what they have been told about it, and what their expectations are for the injured child or adolescent within the family context (Ball, Lehr, & Lebow, submitted for publication). When assessing family members' perception of the head-injured child's or adolescent's deficits and functioning, it is essential that professionals clearly differentiate the family's perceptions (Horobin & Voysey-Paun, 1981) from how the professionals might feel it it were their child.

EXPERIENCE OF FRIENDS

Even though having friends is such an important part of a child's or adolescent's life, the ways in which friendships are altered after head injury are basically unknown. Although social withdrawal and social isolation are recognized sequelae in adults after head injury (Oddy, 1984), the process of how this occurs, how it could be avoided, and how it can be altered has not been studied. From clinical work with head-injured children and adolescents, there appear to be two aspects to altered friendships after injury. One concerns the changes in the individual child or adolescent that interfere with the ability to maintain and initiate friendships. The other involves the perceptions and experience of the other children and adolescents, that is, what it is like for them to have a friend who has had traumatic brain injury.

Children as young as preschool age can experience alterations in their ability to perceive and function in social situations that interfere with interactions with other children in an age-appropriate manner. However, deficits in social cognition and social control are likely to be more evident, interfere more directly with development, and cause more distress in school-age children and adolescents. By the time children are 10 to 12 years of age, they are expected to begin to understand other people's complex behavior, especially as it is related to less visible, internal feelings and motives (Leahy & Shirk, 1984). They can also begin to make comparisons between themselves and others in terms of psychological characteristics, heightening their own self-awareness, as well as their awareness of others. By the time of school attendance, children are expected to function as a member of a group, to understand and even create group rules. In terms of social competence, children and adolescents are developing the ability to perceive, understand, and act in social settings. They also are developing the ability to alter their own behavior depending on the specific nature of the social situation. From the earlier section of this chapter on the psychosocial aspects of head injury in children and adolescents, it is easy to see how deficits in insight, empathy, and emotional control interfere with their ability to understand and interact in social settings, either with one or with many children.

Unlike siblings, who must continue to interact with their brother or sister after head injury, friends have the option of maintaining or ending their relationship with their head-injured peer. Other children and adolescents may be quite confused about the overt and subtle psychosocial changes that they perceive in their friend after head injury. Alterations in social cognition and social behavior on the part of their head-injured friend may be perceived as rejecting and lead them to believe that the friend does not want them to be around. They may be perplexed at their friend no longer being able to understand joking or teasing, not being able to keep up with group banter, embarrassing them with socially disinhibited behavior, and not having shared their experiences while being hospitalized. Other children and adolescents may feel that they cannot do anything to alter their head-injurea friend's behavior, especially if the person is not as reactive to peer pressure as before injury. Even with the best intentions, they may gradually distance themselves from the head-injured child or adolescent.

The impact of loss of friends for children and adolescents after head injury is often most apparent in their play or leisure activities. Instead of riding bicycles, playing ball, going to Scouts, or going to the movies with other children and adolescents, the head-injured child or adolescent may be left to pursuits such as watching television, reading, or playing computer games alone. Rarely do children and adolescents after head injury or their parents prefer this situation, but seldom are they able to alter the cycle once it has begun.

INTERVENTION

Intervention focused on psychosocial aspects of childrens' and adolescents' functioning usually involves a combination of approaches to be successful. This is generally true for interventions with children and adolescents, whether they have sustained traumatic head injury or not, and reflects the importance of having the child or adolescent, parents, other family members, and teachers involved in intervention efforts in order to have an impact on the various aspects of the child's or adolescent's psychosocial functioning. After traumatic head injury, multiple psychosocial intervention approaches are often essential since psychosocial components of functioning and recovery are necessary for adaptive behavior and further development. Although intervention approaches are presented according to the target person and system, namely the head-injured child or adolescent, their families, and their friends, these approaches in reality should occur in an integrated rather than an isolated manner.

Intervention with Head-Injured Children and Adolescents

Only recently have psychotherapists taken seriously the psychotherapy needs of individuals after traumatic brain injury (Ball, 1988; Morris & Bleiberg, 1986; Prigatano, 1986). The focus of individual psychotherapy is to help people after traumatic brain injury understand and cope with what has happened to them. Because of possible cognitive and awareness limitations, this must be done in a way that makes sense to the person, is relatively easy to remember, fits what is known about traumatic brain injury in general and in specific, and must explain what the individual experiences. It necessarily involves the therapist assuming an active teaching role in the beginning. Gradually, issues of what the injury means to the individual, including grappling with issues of "why me," emerge. The work of therapy involves being able to achieve a sense of self-acceptance and forgiveness for those responsible for the injury, making realistic commitments to learning and to other people, improving behavior in social situations and in deficit areas, as well as fostering a sense of realistic hope (Prigatano, 1986).

This process, which has been developed for therapeutic work with adults after traumatic head injuries, is very appropriate for older children and adolescents as long as developmental and overall functioning levels are taken into consideration. For young children, adaptations of this model can be made into a play therapy approach that is more developmentally appropriate. However, no matter what the age of the child, it is important for the child to agree to therapy and to be involved in the process. It is also important for the child and adolescent and the parents to be aware that psychotherapy after traumatic head injury can often be a painful process, involving grief over lost capacities and potential, awareness of altered functioning, defensiveness, and adjustment that allows for continued growth and development.

Group Approaches

Group therapy has the potential for being very effective with children and adolescents after head injury but has rarely been utilized in any systematic manner. Depending on the goals of intervention, groups could be composed of only children and adolescents who have experienced traumatic head injury or a combination of head-injured and non-head–injured children and adolescents. In groups for head-injured children and adolescents, the focus could be on utilizing each other for support and on directly altering or practicing social behavior in a therapeutic setting. Direct teaching and experience with social skills is often more successful in a group than in an individual therapy setting. Techniques that have been useful with other children and adolescents with social skills deficits are likely to be successful with head-injured children and adolescents, including verbalizations of nonverbal social behavior, imagery, self-instruction, and step-by-step social problem solving (Cartledge & Milburn, 1980; Shure, 1981). From long-term follow-up with children and adolescents who have nonverbal learning disabilities, it has become clear that early and intensive therapy is essential in attempting to remediate and minimize the profound social deficits that can become apparent in later adolescence and adulthood (Rourke, 1987).

Groups that involve head-injured and noninjured children and adolescents can consist of naturally occurring group activities, with extra support and teaching available to both the adult leaders and the noninjured children as necessary. Classmates and friends of children and adolescents after head injury often benefit from information about traumatic head injuries to enable them to allay some of their fears and maintain their relationships. Close friends and siblings may be involved in more intense group intervention focused on their own support and education and help for the head-injured child or adolescent to cope more adaptively with injury effects.

Intervention with Families

In contrast with individual psychotherapy, the focus for family approaches is not necessarily on the head-injured family member, even though this may be the ostensible reason for therapy involvement. Rather the goal of family teaching and intervention is to maintain and reconstitute the family as an entity that can foster the development of all of its members despite the stress and changes imposed by traumatic brain injury. Family intervention can take a variety of forms (Rosenthal, 1984) including education of family members about head-injury effects in their child or adolescent, family support groups, parenting techniques both in dealing with the head-injured child and with the other siblings, home-based intervention for intractable behaviors, and family therapy. Materials are being developed to aid family members in understanding head injury in children and adolescents (Deaton, 1987). Otherwise much of the education of family members depends upon the clinical experience of the professional team working with them. Family support groups are available in most parts of the country, usually through state and local organzations affiliated with the National Head Injury Foundation. However, these groups may not have members with head-injured children; especially parents or family members of young head-injured children may not feel much in common with groups focused on adolescents and adults after head injury. Parents may also benefit from specialized guidance in caring for and raising their child or adolescent after head injury. At least for the short-term and possibly longer, they cannot necessarily rely on their usual strategies, nor as easily understand or interpret their child's behavior (Horobin & Voysey-Paun, 1981). Resources for guidance in parenting a special child may be available through other groups specialized in the care of handicapped children, even though they may not specifically be geared to head-injured children. Involvement in family therapy can be useful to manage crises and to enable the family to manage developmental challenges in an adaptive way for all family members (Wiley, 1983).

Coordination and Timing of Intervention

Even though multiple intervention approaches may be necessary and appropriate in ameliorating the psychosocial effects of head injury in children and adolescents, this does not mean that all of these efforts take place simultaneously or continuously. Instead the purpose of and participants in intervention vary according to the individual and system needs at any time. However, it is helpful if not essential for one person or a psychosocial team experienced in the long-term psychosocial management of pediatric head injury to be very familiar with each child or adolescent, his or her family, friends, and teachers. Intervention can then take on an anticipatory focus rather than merely a crisis-oriented one. This is especially important in work with children and adolescents since psychosocial aspects of injury are likely to manifest themselves in a variety of ways over an extended period.

A model that has been useful in clinical work with children and adolescents after head injury involves the therapist working directly with the child or adolescent and family in the rehabilitation setting, evaluating both the neuropsychological and psychosocial aspects of injury, as well as family functioning under crisis. The therapist is closely involved in planning for discharge and return to school, including meetings with friends, classmates, and teachers. (If the child or adolescent is not involved in an inpatient rehabilitation program, initial contact is usually through referral for evaluation and treatment on an outpatient basis.) Routine contact is maintained either through clinic visits or telephone calls, initiated both by the therapist and the family. If the period immediately after injury is particularly stressful, individual and family intervention may be initiated at this time. Neuropsychological evaluations at 6 month and yearly intervals provide an opportunity to assess psychosocial functioning over a longer period.

The therapist may not be the provider of all intervention services but rather serves the function of coordinator and monitor, recommending which psychosocial interventions are appropriate at different times (Ball, 1988). Specific interventions may be time-limited and problem-focused. When they are completed, the therapist again retires to the background until needed for further consultation or direct involvement. Through planned psychosocial interventions utilizing models such as the one presented here, it is possible that the psychosocial sequelae of head injury in children and adolescents can be minimized if not avoided, both for themselves and for those who care for them.

REFERENCES

Ball, J.D. (1988). Psychotherapy with head-injured patients. *Medical Psychotherapy, 1*, 15–22.

Ball, N.A., Lehr, E., & Lebow, J. *Family assessment in the rehabilitation setting.* Manuscript submitted for publication.

Bellack, L. (1975). *The Thematic Apperception Test, the Children's Apperception Test, and the Senior Apperception Test in clinical use* (3rd ed.) New York: Grune & Stratton.

Bender, L. (1956). Personality problems of the child with a head injury. *Psychopathology of children with organic brain disorders.* Springfield, IL: C.C. Thomas, pp. 66–96.

Bolter, J.F. (1986). Epilepsy in children: Neuropsychological effects. In J.E. Obrzut & G.W. Hynd (Eds.), *Child Neuropsychology, Vol. 2: Clinical practice.* San Diego: Academic Press.

Bond, M.R. (1975). Assessment of the psychosocial outcome after severe head injury. In *Ciba Foundation Symposium, No. 34, Symposium on the Outcome of Severe Damage to the Central Nervous System.* Amsterdam: Elsevier.

Bond, M. (1984). The psychiatry of closed head injury. In N. Brooks (Ed.), *Closed head injury: Psychological, social, and family consequences.* Oxford, Eng.: Oxford University Press.

Brooks, N. (1984). Head injury and the family. In N. Brooks (Ed.), *Closed head injury: Psychological, social, and family consequences.* Oxford, Eng.: Oxford University Press.

Brown, G., Chadwick, O., Shaffer, D., Rutter, M., & Traub, M. (1981). A prospective study of children with head injuries: III. Psychiatric sequelae. *Psychological Medicine, 11*, 63–78.

Bryden, M.P., & Ley, R.G. (1983). Right-hemispheric involvement in the perception and expression of emotion in normal humans. In K.M. Heilman and P. Satz (Eds.), *Neuropsychology of human emotion.* New York: Guilford Press.

Cartledge, G., & Milburn, J.F. (1980). *Teaching social skills to children.* New York: Pergamon Press.

Cattell, R.B., Cattell, M.D., & Johns, E. (1958). *High School Personality Questionnaire.* Champaign, IL: Institute of Personality and Ability Testing.

Cattell, R.B., & Coan, R.W. (1966). *Early School Personality Questionnaire.* Champaign, IL: Institute of Personality and Ability Testing.

Chess, S., & Thomas, A. (1984). *Origins and evolution of behavior disorders: From infancy to early adult life.* New York: Brunner/Mazel.

Cohen, H., & Weil, G.R. (1975). *Tasks of emotional development: A projective test for children and adolescents.* Brookline, MA: T.E.D. Associates.

Coopersmith, S. (1967). *The antecedents of self-esteem.* San Francisco: Freeman.

Deaton, A. (1987). *Pediatric head trauma: A guide for families.* New Kent, VA: Cumberland, A Hospital for Children and Adolescents.

Exner, J.D., & Weiner, I.B. (1982). *The Rorschach: A comprehensive system. Assessment of children and adolescents, Vol. 3.* New York: John Wiley & Sons.

Filley, C.M., Cranberg, M.D., Alexander, M.P., & Hart, E.J. (1987). Neurobehavioral outcome after closed head injury in childhood and adolescence. *Archives of Neurology*, *44*, 194–198.

Fitts, W.H. (1965). *Tennessee Self-Concept Inventory*. Nashville: Counselor Recordings and Tests.

Fordyce, D.J., & Roueche, J.R. (1986). Changes in perspective of disability among patients, staff, and relatives during rehabilitation of brain injury. *Rehabilitation Psychology*, *31*, 217–229.

Foster, M., Berger, M., & McLean, M. (1981). Rethinking a good idea: A reassessment of parent involvement. *Topics in Early Childhood Special Education*, *1*, 55–65.

Gianotti, G. (1983). Laterality of affect: The emotional behavior of right- and left-brain–damaged patients. In *Hemisyndromes: Psychobiology, neurology, psychiatry*. San Diego: Academic Press.

Goldberg, E., & Costa, L.D. (1981). Hemisphere differences in the acquisition and use of descriptive systems. *Brain and Language*, *14*, 144–173.

Goldstein, D. (1948). *Language and language disturbances*. New York: Grune & Stratton.

Goldstein, K. (1952). The effect of brain damage on the personality. *Psychiatry*, *15*, 245–260.

Heilman, K.M., Watson, R.T., & Bowers, D. (1983). Affective disorders associated with hemispheric disease. In K.M. Heilman & P. Satz (Eds.), *Neuropsychology of human emotion*. New York: Guilford Press.

Horobin, G., & Voysey-Paun, M. (1981). Sociological perspectives. In P. Black (Ed.), *Brain dysfunction in children: Etiology, diagnosis, and management*. New York: Raven Press.

Hutt, M.L. (1980). *Michigan Picture Test* (rev. ed.). New York: Grune & Stratton.

Kleinpeter, U. (1976). Social integration after brain trauma during childhood. *Acta Paedopsychiatrica*, *42*, 68–75.

Koppitz, E. (1968). *Psychological evaluation of children's human figure drawings*. New York: Grune & Stratton.

Leahy, R.L., & Shirk, S.R. (1984). The development of social cognition: Conceptions of personality. *Annals of Child Development*, *1*, 175–200.

LeDoux, J.E. (1984). Cognition and emotion: Processing functions and brain systems. In M. Gazzaniga (Ed.), *Handbook of cognitive neuroscience*. New York: Plenum Press.

Lezak, M.D. (1978). Living with the characterologically altered brain injured patient. *Journal of Clinical Psychiatry*, *39*, 592–598.

Lezak, M.D. (1982). The problem of assessing executive functions. *International Journal of Psychology*, *17*, 281–297.

Lezak, M.D. (1987). Relationships between personality disorders, social disturbances, and physical disability following traumatic brain injury. *Journal of Head Trauma Rehabilitation*, *2*, 57–69.

Lezak, M.D. (1988). Brain damage is a family affair. *Journal of Clinical and Experimental Neuropsychology*, *10*, 111–123.

Lishman, W.A. (1968). Brain damage in relation to psychiatric disability after head injury. *British Journal of Psychiatry*, *114*, 373–410.

Lishman, W.A. (1973). The psychiatric sequelae of head injury: A review. *Psychological Medicine*, *3*, 304–318.

McArthur, D.S., & Roberts, G.E. (1982). *Roberts Apperception Test for Children.* Los Angeles: Western Psychological Services.

McDaniel, E., & Piers, E. (1973). *Longitudinal study of elementary school effects: Design, instruments and specifications for a field test.* West Lafayette, IN: Purdue University, Purdue Educational Research Center.

Millon, T., Green, C.J., & Meagher, R.B. (1977). *Millon Adolescent Personality Inventory manual.* Minneapolis: Interpretive Scoring Systems.

Morris, J., & Bleiberg, J. (1986). Neuropsychological rehabilitation and traditional psychotherapy. *International Journal of Clinical Neuropsychology, 8,* 133–135.

Oddy, M. (1984). Head injury and social adjustment. In N. Brooks (Ed.), *Closed head injury.* Oxford, Eng.: Oxford University Press.

Oddy, M., Humphrey, M., & Uttley, D. (1978). Subjective impairment and social recovery after closed head injury. *Journal of Neurology, Neurosurgery, and Psychiatry, 41,* 611–616.

O'Sullivan, M., & Guilford, J.P. (1975). Six factors of behavioral cognition: Understanding other people. *Journal of Educational Measurement, 12,* 255–271.

Piers, E., & Harris, D. (1969). *The Piers-Harris Children's Self-Concept Scale.* Nashville: Counselor Recordings and Tests.

Platt, J.J., & Spivak, G. (1975). Unidimensionality of the Means-Ends Problem-Solving Procedure (MEPS). *Journal of Clinical Psychology, 28,* 3–5.

Porter, R.B., & Cattell, R.B. (1959). *Children's Personality Questionnaire.* Champaign, IL: Institute for Personality and Ability Testing.

Prigatano, G. (1986). *Neuropsychological rehabilitation after brain injury.* Baltimore: Johns Hopkins University Press.

Rosenthal, M. (1984). Strategies for intervention with families of brain-injured patients. In B.A. Edelstein & E.T. Couture (Eds.), *Behavioral assessment and rehabilitation of the traumatically brain damaged.* New York: Plenum Press.

Rorschach, H. (1966). *Rorschach Ink Blot Test.* New York: Grune & Stratton.

Rourke, B.P. (1987). Syndrome of nonverbal learning disabilities: The final common pathway of white-matter disease/dysfunction? *Clinical Neuropsychologist, 1,* 209–234.

Rutter, M., Chadwick, O., & Shaffer, D. (1983). Head injury. In M. Rutter (Ed.), *Developmental neuropsychiatry.* New York: Guilford Press.

Rutter, M., Graham, P., & Yule, W. (1970). A neuropsychiatric study in childhood. *Clinical Developmental Medicine, 35/36.*

Seidel, U.P., Chadwick, O.F.D., & Rutter, M. (1975). Psychological disorders in crippled children. A comparative study of children with and without brain damage. *Developmental Medicine and Child Neurology, 17,* 563–573.

Selman, R.L. (1976). Toward a structural analysis of developing interpersonal relations concepts: Research with normal and disturbed adolescent boys. In A. Pick (Ed.), *Annual Minnesota symposium of child psychology.* Minneapolis: University of Minnesota Press.

Shaffer, D., Chadwick, O., & Rutter, M. (1975). Psychiatric outcome of localized head injury in children. In R. Porter & D. FitzSimons (Eds.), *Outcome of severe damage to the central nervous system* (Ciba Foundation Symposium No. 34, new series). Amsterdam: Elsevier-Excerpta-Medica-North Holland.

Shure, M. (1981). Social competence as a problem-solving skill. In J.D. Wine & M.D. Smye (Eds.), *Social competence.* New York: Guilford Press.

Stores, G. (1978). School-children with epilepsy at risk for learning and behavior problems. *Developmental Medicine and Child Neurology, 20*, 502–508.

Thomas, A., & Chess, S. (1980). *The dynamics of psychological development.* New York: Brunner/Mazel.

Westin, M.T., & Reiss, D. (1979). The family's role in rehabilitation. *Journal of Rehabilitation, 45*, 26–29.

Wiley, S.D. (1983). Structural treatment approach for families in crisis: A challenge to rehabilitation. *American Journal of Physical Medicine, 62*, 271–286.

Wirt, R.D., Lachar, D., Klinedinst, J.D., & Seat, P.D. (1977). *Multidimensional description of child personality: A manual for the Personality Inventory for Children.* Los Angeles: Western Psychological Services.

Chapter 7

School Management

Ellen Lehr

CASE STUDY

Jason

Jason was 13 years old when the snow mobile he and his friend were riding on was hit by a car while crossing a country road. He sustained a severe closed head injury and was comatose for 6 days. After a 3-week stay in a small community hospital, Jason came home. Although he was able to talk, walk, and take basic care of himself, he was also quite confused. On his return home, he threatened his father with his BB gun for causing his accident. At this time, he did not understand what had happened nor could he remember the explanations his parents had repeatedly told him.

Shortly after his return home, Jason returned to his junior high school. However, not until at least a month after discharge from the hospital did his parents report his memory for daily events was accurate. Jason himself was surprised when his parents told him about threatening his father and did not remember his return to school. At the end of his first semester after injury, Jason was failing in all his courses. He was extremely tired at the end of each school day and usually fell asleep when he got home in the afternoon. After waking from his nap, he would eat dinner and attempt to do his homework.

Even though he spent several hours on his assignments, Jason often could not complete them all. He was very slow, had difficulty remembering what he was supposed to do and in understanding material the teacher had explained in class that day. Despite studying by himself and with the help of his parents, Jason was often not able to finish his daily homework and usually failed quizzes and tests. Not only was he not able to catch up on the work he had missed because of his time in the hospital, he was daily falling further and further behind. When he was seen for a neuropsychological evaluation 5 months after his accident, Jason was extremely frustrated, considering dropping out of school, and complained of spending all of his time on school work with nothing to show but grief for it.

INTRODUCTION

Although it is a compilation of the case histories of several actual children, the above scenario illustrates the kind of problems children can experience on return to school after a relatively severe head injury with few physically visible sequelae. The specific difficulties are heightened for Jason since he received no evaluation of the effects of his head injury on his learning, memory, or energy level. Instead because he looked so good, it was assumed that he would be able to learn as well as he did before his injury. No planning was done before he returned to school to assess whether and what kind of difficulty he might face and how his school program might be altered even on a temporary basis.

Probably because of the generally good physical recovery of many children and adolescents after traumatic head injury and the prevailing myth that they do not experience the severity of cognitive and psychosocial sequelae of adults, schools have rarely been made aware of the educational issues these children present. In contrast with the relatively well-recognized difficulty adults may have in returning to their preinjury employment, little attention has been paid to the difficulty children may have in returning to school. Only in the past five years has this issue received attention both from medical and school personnel. Especially if head-injured children or adolescents have received treatment only in an acute-care hospital setting, it has been easy to assume that because they no longer require medical management at discharge, they are able to resume their previous educational programming. Only recently have possible school difficulties been anticipated for children and adolescents before failure. It continues to be quite common for head-injured children to be evaluated only when parents request assessment after prolonged experience of educational frustration and failure (Shaffer, Bijur, Chadwick, & Rutter, 1980).

Much of the information in this chapter is from clinical experience with reference to the few research studies conducted in this area. Although a number of the studies on the cognitive and psychosocial effects of head injury on children have mentioned that subsequent educational achievement has been adversely affected, there have been no comprehensive research efforts to determine the specific effects of pediatric head injury on learning in an educational setting. Nor have there been any systematic efforts to evaluate which educational programs or techniques might be most successful with particular groups of head-injured children and adolescents. Considering how crucial future learning is to children and adolescents in general and especially after traumatic brain injury, this lack is difficult to explain and should be a focus of future work. Specific therapeutic and educational techniques useful in interventions focusing on cognitive, behavioral, and psychosocial sequelae after head injury are not presented in this chapter since they have been included in Chapters 4, 5, and 6.

In terms of planning a return to school, traumatically brain injured children and adolescents are likely to have the following characteristics in common. They are likely to have experienced a loss of school time. The length of absence from school is variable, but most children with moderate to severe injuries are likely to be behind in their schoolwork simply because of missed school days, regardless of specific head injury effects. They are likely to have experienced an alteration in the processes that underly learning, such as attention, memory, concentration, speed of processing, and response. They are also likely to tire more easily, both physically and mentally. This is possible even after mild head injury, though the effects may be less pronounced and more transient than in moderate to severe injuries. They are likely to have a period of initial unawareness of the impact of the head injury on subtle cognitive and psychosocial aspects of functioning, with the result that the child or adolescent is able to experience frustration but does not realize where the difficulties are coming from. The child or adolescent may deny difficulties, making it harder for others to adapt activities and expectations appropriately, including those that are school-related.

In considering whether, when, and how a child should return to school after a head injury, many aspects should be kept in mind. Planning must be done on an individual basis since the effects of head injuries vary so widely. The needs of any one child depend on age, severity of the injury, kind of school program before injury, child's preinjury functioning level, physical and cognitive functioning level postinjury, and the time since injury (acuteness).

Age Effects

Since the passage of Public Law 94–142 in 1975, all children with handicaps are entitled to appropriate educational services between the ages of 3 and 21 years. With the recent revisions in the law, services now are mandated from birth on. For the youngest of these children, their first infant or preschool experience may occur after injury, and they may qualify for educational services on the basis of their injury from the beginning of their contact with the educational system. Age effects have been discussed more fully in Chapter 3. Here only the application to school settings is briefly presented.

For children who are injured before or during the primary grade period, learning and mastery of basic academic skills in reading, spelling, math, and writing is the major focus of their educational program. Depending on each child's specific postinjury difficulties, this may require specialized teaching approaches. While some children appear to have little difficulty in mastering these skills, others have deficits that interfere in one or all academic areas. Of equal importance during these early school years is the mastery of the behavioral aspects of learning, such as being able to attend for longer periods, maintain task focus, learn in a group setting, take turns, and help others. Children at school also learn to be more responsible and independent in caring for themselves by having to put on and take off outdoor clothing, going to the toilet in the school bathroom, choosing their own food, and eating with other children in the school cafeteria. As discussed in Chapter 3, it is just in these behavioral areas that the effects of traumatic brain injury may be most evident in this age period. In fact, in young children who are or have recovered relatively well from their injuries, behavior difficulties are likely to be the most important limiting factor in school.

Placement in small classes of 8 to 10 children is often appropriate for behavior management of attention, distractability, slow processing of information, and attainment of social skills. However, these classes may not be available for young children unless they are classified as behavior-disordered, mentally retarded or learning-disabled, which may or may not be appropriate classifications for children after head injuries. Preschool, kindergarten, and first-grade classes that are called *noncategorical*, *generic*, or *transitional* may be quite appropriate for some children after head injuries in that they are often smaller and provide for more individual attention. What is essential for children injured in the early school years is that they have a good start in learning basic academic and social skills, without having to fail several grades before intervention is provided.

During the middle school years, roughly grades 4 through 8, children are expected to have mastered many basic academic skills. Their primary task is to apply these basic skills to completing longer and more complicated assignments in a variety of areas such as social studies and science. The emphasis is on increasing independence in learning, abstraction, and comprehension rather than on rote acquiring of information. The effects of head injuries, both in terms of immediate and delayed effects, often interfere directly in exactly these areas of higher cognitive functioning. Because during this period children are just beginning to be able to learn in this more integrated way, the transition for children injured at this time is even more difficult.

High school years are probably the most difficult time for head injuries to occur in terms of school needs and management. Because of the limited time span, either of 3 or 4 years, any extended loss of school time or impairment in learning ability often has an immediate impact on class placement and can even affect graduation date. It is also usually very important for high school students to be a member of their class, including all of the social activities associated with this such as junior and senior proms, class rings, and trips. In addition, high school classes are often taught in sequences with up to 4 years of courses building on each other. These sequences can be very difficult to interrupt and still complete at a later date without repeating a semester or a year of school. For adolescents who sustain head injuries during the high school years, the psychosocial needs centering on being a member of their school class may be more important than their academic mastery and skill level. However, after they graduate from high school, they are no longer eligible for either the special education or the vocational services available through the school system.

An important focus of a head-injured high school student's program is incorporating long-range planning for vocational and college programs after graduation (Savage & Carter, 1984; Telzrow, 1985). This transition needs to be planned explicitly and carefully as much in advance as possible, with possible postponement of awarding the high school diploma to enable the student to utilize school services such as work-study programs and college preparatory courses until the adolescent is clearly capable of handling the transition to the higher education or work setting.

Severity of Injury

The degree of injury severity is of critical importance in planning and implementing school programming for children and adolescents after traumatic brain injuries. Possible transitory learning, attention and concentration, memory, and fatigue effects after mild injury may go unrecognized by teachers, parents, medical personnel, and even the child or adolescent (Boll, 1983; Gulbrandsen, 1984). The child or adolescent may be accused of being lazy, not trying, and having developed behavioral or emotional problems. This is especially important for those children who are injured in the middle of the school year, when the academic pace is at its quickest.

There is usually little reason for these children and adolescents not to return to their preinjury school programs, but they may require slightly reduced course loads, rest periods, tutoring, and other support services. What they do not need is the pressure to perform and the experience of failure, while not understanding what has happened to them. Unfortunately there is very little research documentation on the effects of mild head injuries in children and adolescents. (See Chapter 8 for more information on mild head injuries.)

For children who are returning to school shortly after having sustained moderate head injuries or who are experiencing good recoveries from severe injuries, school planning requires considerable thought and flexibility. Because of their extremely good physical recovery, cognitive and behavioral effects of their traumatic brain injuries are often minimized. In addition, these children and adolescents do not fit neatly into any of the recognized special education classifications or the services designed to meet other special education students' needs (Cohen, 1986; Savage & Carter, 1984; Telzrow, 1985). Since they are usually in a period of rapid change and recovery on their return to school, programming needs to be timely, creative, organized, and flexible. Even though special education programs are mandated to be evaluated annually, these children may need their programs evaluated every marking period for the first 3 to 12 months after injury. Their functioning level in terms of cognitive and learning abilities and deficits also needs to be reevaluated on a frequent basis, at a minimum on a yearly basis. This rapid change in functioning levels is not something that schools have much experience with, and it places significant stress on both the children's teachers and on the administrative staff to implement and alter programs and services as rapidly as the children may require.

Although many children and adolescents recover quite well from even very severe injuries, others have visible physical, sensory, and cognitive impairments that are prolonged, if not permanent. The need for special classroom programming and special education services for a significant proportion of children after severe injuries has been recognized for many years (Brink, Garrett, Hale, Woo-Sam, & Nickel, 1970; Flach & Malmros, 1972; Fuld & Fisher, 1977; Heiskanen & Kaste, 1974; Richardson, 1963). These children and adolescents often require a wide spectrum of services including therapeutic and educational services, but access to them in an efficient manner may be difficult. For example, the physical therapy, occupational therapy, speech and language therapy and sensory-impaired services may not be available in the same building as self-contained learning-disability classes or behavior-disordered services. The entire spectrum of special education services, including those for the most profoundly and multiply handicapped, could be appropriate and necessary for any one of the wide range of traumatically brain-injured children and adolescents. In general, these children may require the most complex array of combined services that a school system has been expected to deliver, and they may require them throughout their school years.

Period since Injury

For some children and adolescents in the period immediately after acute-care or rehabilitation hospitalization, therapy services may be more appropriate than educational programming. They may require intervention directly related to their postinjury cognitive processing deficits and require a period for relearning of previously mastered academic skills. This is not a time to expect or demand new learning. During this period, head-injury recovery needs and effects are at their most predominant and possibly their most critical. Unfortunately very few programs, either based in outpatient therapy settings or school settings, are specifically designed for the acute-period learning needs of head-injured children and adolescents, even on a temporary basis.

As the immediate postinjury effects begin to ameliorate, the children's or adolescents' ability to begin to handle a school-based academic program increases. They also need to be immersed again in their own world of daily activities, including school and social contact with noninjured children. However, they continue to be in a period of rapid gains in cognitive and psychosocial areas. During this period, awareness of the impact of injury increases with its subsequent emotional reaction. School staff need to be apprised of this so they do not perceive it as development of behavior problems or a rejection of learning activities.

Children and adolescents may experience longer periods of improvement than adults do, and this may extend as long as 3 to 5 years even after relatively mild injuries. After a year postinjury, long-standing and possibly permanent impairments begin to either be suspected or readily apparent. The pace of improvement probably begins to slow after approximately a year. However, school programs continue to need to be altered, at least on a yearly basis for several years to incorporate increasing challenge, mainstreaming, and independence.

Preinjury Functioning Level

Preinjury functioning level in school-related areas is often best determined by previous classroom programming, academic performance, and testing scores. Results of standardized testing, utilizing measures such as the Iowa Basic Skills Tests and the Stanford Achievement Tests, can offer a reasonable estimate of a child's preinjury scholastic performance in a variety of areas, including an estimate of possible preinjury learning disabilities, their extent, and type (Goldstein & Levin, 1985). These objective achievement tests are routinely given to all school-age children, and comparison with national norms allows for comparisons across different tests and groups. They can therefore be utilized to follow school-age childrens' and adolescents' progress longitudinally after injury. Unfortunately, despite the importance of learning more about the effect that traumatic brain injury may have on school-related learning, little or no research has focused on comparing academic achievement before traumatic brain injury with the rate and degree of academic achievement after injury.

Some children and adolescents may have been experiencing learning difficulties and possibly receiving special education services before their injury. It is important that their preinjury difficulties be clearly considered in planning their return to school. At times, these children's functioning after injury is attributed to their preinjury difficulties without thoughtful evaluation of the possible changes related to injury. Their class placement and programming may also require alterations related to injury sequelae and should not be assumed to be appropriate.

PREVIOUS RESEARCH

Academic and Educational Sequelae of Head Injury

The effect of cognitive sequelae on academic performance is not clear, though there are indications that scholastic achievement is significantly affected by relatively mild (Klonoff, Low, & Clark, 1977) as well as moderate and severe injuries (Ewing-Cobbs, Fletcher, & Levin, 1985; Heiskanen & Kaste, 1974) and may improve less rapidly than cognitive abilities (Rutter, Chadwick, & Shaffer, 1983). Most of the research on academic effects of traumatic brain injury have looked only at the types of school placements and programming of children after injury, especially whether they could return to their preinjury educational setting, rather than effects on learning per se. Rarely have standardized, objective measures of academic attainment been used, much less on a longitudinal basis to assess progress or lack of progress over several years. The effect of traumatic brain injury on academic performance may be more significant for younger children, that is, those who have not mastered the basics of reading, spelling, and arithmetic before injury, as well as for those children who are more severely injured (Brink et al., 1970; Chadwick, Rutter, Thompson, & Shaffer, 1981; Shaffer et al., 1980). However, only with very recent research has the relationship of altered cognitive processes after traumatic brain injury to specific academic learning difficulties been examined, though this has been better known clinically. Levin and Benton (1986) have suggested that difficulty after TBI in controlled processes of learning involving attention, memory, and speed of information processing interferes more significantly in mathematical calculation than in reading decoding and can coexist with normal IQ.

It is relatively well known that scholastic achievement is often significantly affected by moderate and severe head injury (Ewing-Cobbs et al., 1985). However, the extent of this effect is not as clearly understood. In order to assess fully the effect of head injuries of children's future learning, it is critical to include an accurate history of preinjury academic functioning. For example, a child who was in gifted programming before injury and functions at grade level after injury is performing well below what would be expected and demonstrates a significant decrease in academic areas. However, this child would be unlikely to qualify for special education services and would usually not be considered as having academic difficulties according to many research criteria. Most research that looks at the academic sequelae of pediatric head injury has utilized rather gross indicators such as need for special education services postinjury, whether children could return to their preinjury educational program, or whether they were functioning below grade level after injury. However, just because these measures are relatively coarse, they are likely to identify those children with the most noticeable academic difficulties after injury. They are likely to miss those children with subtle difficulties. Therefore, the research is likely to underestimate rather than overestimate the academic and learning difficulties of children and adolescents after injury.

Effect on School Placement and School Performance

The effect of severe head injury in interfering with the subsequent school performance of children and adolescents appears to be relatively well substantiated. In their classic study, Brink and group (Brink et al., 1970) found that only 8 of their 34 pediatric severe head trauma patients (comatose for more than 1 week) were in regular education programs 1 to 7 years after injury. Even some of those in regular programs (including junior colleges and night school) were not felt to be performing to the standard expected from their scores on intelligence tests. Nineteen of the 34 were in special education programs including those for the physically handicapped, emotionally handicapped, and educably and trainably mentally retarded. Similar findings were established in other studies (Burkinshaw, 1960; Heiskanen & Kaste, 1974; Lehr, 1984; Richardson, 1963). There are indications that the longer a child is in coma, the worse subsequent performance in school is likely to be. Heiskanen and Kaste (1974) found that only 1 of the 9 children they studied who were in coma for more than 2 weeks was doing even moderately well in school. All of the children they followed who were in coma for longer than 1 month were educationally subnormal.

Even children with mild injuries may demonstrate subsequent learning difficulties, though there has been much less research in this area. Klonoff, et al. (1977) found that 25% of the younger children and 33% of the older children they studied had school learning difficulties after injury. Their criteria were relatively objective and restrictive, consisting of failure of an elementary school grade or placement in a remedial or slow learner class. Other children were considered as having normal educational progress.

In summary, the findings of school difficulties in children after head injury are not unexpected. However, the extent and nature of difficulties are not clear. Studies having different criteria for school difficulties (often quite subjective), were conducted when special education services varied considerably across states and countries, and rarely take into consideration children's preinjury school functioning. Despite the research, it is still difficult to assess either the frequency of school difficulties or their severity.

However, a study conducted by Savage (1985) presents a different perspective on school difficulties after traumatic brain injury. He surveyed the school records of more than 1,400 students in special education programs in Vermont. Overall 12% of the students in special education programs had a documented history of prior head injury that was not recognized as part of their present handicapping condition. Those special education classes with the highest percentage of children with previous head injuries included 20% of those in classes for the emotionally disturbed and 25% of 3- to 5-year-olds in early education programs.

Effect on Specific Academic Areas

Reading

Very little work has focused on learning of specific academic skills after head injury in children. One study (Shaffer et al., 1980) examined performance on tests measuring oral reading accuracy and comprehension in 88 children who had sustained open head injuries consisting of unilateral compound depressed skull fractures with confirmed brain involvement at least 2 years before the evaluation. All of the children had been age 12 or under at the time of injury and in regular school programs at the time of follow-up. When tested at 8 years of age or older, more than half of the children were reading 1 or more years behind their chronological ages, and one-third of them were 2 or more years behind. Reading difficulties after injury were similar in frequency for boys and girls.

The severity of injury appears to have an effect on reading mastery. Of those children who were not in coma after injury, 50% of them were reading at or above grade level. However, only 17% of those children who were in coma for 72 hours or longer were reading at or above grade level. For those children injured before they were 8 years old, the longer they were in coma, the more likely they were to show reading difficulties 2 years later. In other words, there was a direct relationship between injury severity and reading disorders. For children who were injured after 8 years of age, the relationship between the severity of injury and extent of reading difficulties was not significant. This is an expected finding if the assumption that head injury affects the ability to learn more extensively than it impairs an already mastered fund of knowledge holds true.

Two complications of injury, generalized brain swelling (edema) and late-onset seizures (after one week postinjury), also appeared to be related to a greater likelihood of reading difficulties. In attempting to determine the possible etiology of the reading difficulties in these head-injured children, the primary factor appeared to be the general effect of lowered intelligence subsequent to injury. Those children who had experienced a period of posttraumatic amnesia that lasted at least 3 weeks were more likely to have not only increased difficulty with reading but also increased difficulty in performing school work in general (Chadwick et al., 1981).

Mathematics

Only one study has examined the effect of head injury in children on math calculation (Levin & Benton, 1986). The findings from this study indicated that arithmetic calculation was more impaired than word recognition (as measured on the Wide Range Achievement Test) when tested at least 6 months after injury. Difficulties in calculation could exist even when IQ scores were not impaired, suggesting that subtle academic problems can persist even with normal IQs. Controlled processes requiring attention, memory, and speed of information processing appeared to be implicated in arithmetic difficulties after head injury.

Summary

Clearly these few studies have hardly begun to clarify the issues surrounding academic skill learning in children and adolescents after head injury. None of them utilized preinjury academic testing as baseline measures, though in some states this may be standardized for all students and relatively widely available. Nor had they examined or compared the wide range of possible academic skills, including word recognition, oral versus silent reading, reading comprehension, writing, mathematical concepts, mathematical reasoning, arithmetic computation, spelling recognition, spelling from dictation, and a fund of information in a variety of subject areas such as science and social studies.

TRANSITION FROM HOSPITAL TO SCHOOL

Appropriateness of Return to School

This is an important question for all children and adolescents after traumatic brain injuries. However, the answer is dependent not only on the child's functioning but also on the demands of the school program to be attended. For children with mild head injuries, this question is rarely even asked, and they are expected to function as they did before injury in the same academic setting. If they are in the group with significant sequelae and are expected to function soon after injury in a demanding academic setting, it is very likely that they experience frustration and probably failure in attempting to learn at the same level prior to injury. Here it is not so much a matter of return to school but of what adaptations should be made in their program.

For children with severe injuries, the probability of their being able to return immediately to their preinjury school programs is often unlikely. The basic criteria for even minimal functioning in an educational setting include resolution of posttraumatic amnesia and confusion, the ability to attend to a task for at least 15 to 20 minutes at a time, and the ability to function in a small group setting (Cohen, 1986). With the most severely involved children, though, they may not reach this level of functioning by the time of discharge home. However, they should not be excluded from school programs. Special education programs for children with severe, profound, or multiple handicaps may be appropriate.

Children and adolescents who are in a period of rapid improvement from moderate to severe injuries often present the most significant challenge in planning for return to school. If their return to school is not considered too precipitously, they usually meet the basic criteria, but they are usually unable to return with success to their preinjury school program. This can be difficult for the children or adolescents and their parents to accept, especially if there are few visible impairments after injury and if the children or adolescents are still unaware of deficits. It is especially difficult if the children or adolescents require a special education setting to learn, even on a temporary basis. At times, delay in return to academic learning in a school setting may be recommended for these children. Alternative approaches such as continuing in individual therapy through a hospital or community-based program for children after head injuries or learning in a tutorial setting may be considered. Isolation from other children is a major problem with this approach but can be handled by involvement in school social activities, including return for lunch if the school is close enough. For those children with marked hyperactivity, severe attention deficits, and significant concern about their safety in unstructured settings, immediate involvement in a structured school setting is essential. However, the usual process of evaluation and placement in special education programs is often too prolonged to meet their needs adequately and quickly.

Least Restrictive Setting

One of the cornerstones of special education is placement of the student in the least restrictive educational setting, that is, one that meets the child's special needs with the least possible separation from normal programming and normal children. For a child or adolescent on initial return to school after traumatic brain injury, the educational placement and services recommended by professionals experienced with head injury may appear more restrictive than necessary to school personnel, and even to the child and parents. However, a conservative approach to return to school with gradual resumption of more challenging activities and programming is often more successful and less likely to stress a child who is in recovery from injury.

School personnel may rely too much on the child's preinjury functioning level and not enough on postinjury difficulties. Immediate return to the previous school program, if it entails frustration and failure, is usually not in the best interest of the child. Rather a strategy of placing the child in the program allowing success at that point in recovery, with maximal flexiblity in terms of program adaptations and changes, often can aid rather than jeopardize return of functioning. Having the child experience the success of returning gradually to a more normalized setting through work and recovery is often more supportive of improvement and self-confidence than the experience of failure possible in an educational setting that is more demanding than can be handled initally after injury.

Special Education Procedures

Considering the issues that have already been presented, what then is the procedure in helping a child or adolescent return to school after a traumatic brain injury? The process is the same as for any other child whose teachers or parents have concerns about learning and wish to explore the appropriateness for special education services. Because special education services are mandated by federal law, the basic process is the same across all states, but there may be some differences in specific procedures.

When a child sustains an injury severe enough to require hospitalization, many people in the community, including school personnel, are often aware of it. However, with milder injuries, especially during vacation periods, parents may not inform school personnel that their child has been injured and that this might affect school performance. The initial step then is to notify the child's school of the injury and to ask for an evaluation of learning performance and possible consideration for school program adaptations or special education services. If the child or adolescent is hospitalized for a prolonged period, either in an acute or rehabilitation hospital, this initial contact with school personnel is often made by hospital staff with the parents' permission.

With more severe injuries, it is often clear that the child requires special education services after hospital discharge. Planning and evaluations may begin during the child's hospital stay to help make the transition back to school as easy and as appropriate as possible. Hospital and school staff can then coordinate their efforts and share information, both about preinjury and postinjury functioning in terms of initial school program recommendations. Because the long-term care of the severely injured child or adolescent is likely to be shared among a number of different people and facilities, it is important that each of them clarifies their role and services. For example, a child may be receiving therapy services at the hospital as well as at school because of the intensity of needs. However, hospital and school systems are not necessarily experienced in coordinating with each other, especially on a long-term basis. But for the child or adolescent returning to school after a traumatic brain injury, this is critical for successful reintegration.

When young children are injured, they may not have been attending school, and their parents need to register them before the procedure can begin. It is important for parents to be aware that their children are eligible for special education services at a much younger age than the mandated school attendance age. The initial federal law (P.L. 94–142) required educational services for all handicapped children from 3 to 21 years of age. However, recently services have been extended to children younger than 3. Children who have been attending private schools also may need to be registered with the public school system if public system special education services, either directly or through reimbursement, are being requested.

After the request for special education services has been made, the school system gathers information to plan and then conducts formal evaluations. Professionals who are familiar with the effects of head injuries in children and adolescents can be very helpful and are often essential during this phase. School personnel, such as school psychologists and special educators, are requested to evaluate the child but may have little to no experience with the learning and cognitive effects of traumatic brain injuries. They may overestimate the child's functioning level because of better preserved previous skills and underestimate the effects of processing difficulties, attention and concentration impairments, memory deficits, and fatigue. For children with multiple deficits after severe injuries, evaluation techniques may need to be very specialized or adapted to obtain a reasonable estimate of their functioning levels. These issues are not only pertinent for psychological and learning areas but also for physical and speech and language functioning. Few school-based personnel may have experience in the differences between traumatically acquired deficits and developmental or congenital disabilities.

The initial evaluation of a child after traumatic brain injury is only considered as a baseline measure of functioning at that particular time, not as a measure of ability that is necessarily predictive for the future. However, this is not the usual way that school-based evaluations are perceived. School systems have the option of either requesting outside evaluations or of accepting the evaluations completed by nonschool professionals with specific expertise. This is done quite frequently with children and adolescents after head injuries if they have been hospitalized and evaluated by hospital-based staff such as neuropsychologists, pediatric and child clinical psychologists, physical, occupational, and speech and language therapists.

After the evaluations are completed, a formal meeting of school personnel and the child's parents is held to develop an Individual Education Plan (IEP). At this meeting, the child is determined to have special education needs or not, with a delineation of the appropriate specific services. The IEP is not a binding legal document, but it is a statement of what the school system will provide, including the type of school program and classroom setting, the amount and kinds of therapy (usually in minutes per week), consultation services, special instructional services, and accessible facilities and transportation. It also includes the goals that school personnel will strive to meet while working with the child within a stated period, usually 3-, 6-, and 9-month periods. The IEP includes a plan for evaluation of the child's school program, which is mandated to occur at least annually, and for evaluation of the child's performance and abilities, which must occur at least every 3 years. For the child after head injury, evaluation of programming must occur much more frequently than is usually required, and transitions need to be identified and planned carefully. Evaluations of the child's functioning may occur as frequently as 3 to 6 months after injury in the initial postinjury period and at least annually afterward.

Special procedures and modifications in helping the student function in the school setting can be included in the IEP. These may include changes such as allowing the head-injured child or adolescent to take tests orally or without time limitations, to sit in the front of classrooms, and to use large-print books if double vision interferes with reading. If the head-injured student's behavior is difficult to manage in the school setting or physical limitations interfere significantly with independence, an aide may be recommended to carry out a behavior management program both in the classroom and in less-structured school activities. For other children and adolescents, a student buddy may help to maintain behavioral control and aid organization in school hallways during change of class times and provide help if necessary in bathrooms, in lunch rooms, or during recess periods. Most children and adolescents who are experiencing cognitive difficulties after head injury and are being mainstreamed benefit from checking in at the beginning of the school day and checking out at the end in order to help them organize daily schedules and homework assignments. This function can be performed by several school personnel, including the homeroom teacher, counselor, or learning-disability resource room teacher. All of these special modifications should be clearly specified in the IEP to avoid confusion about what adaptations are going to be made in the students' programs.

Sometimes the school program can be identified either at or even before the formal IEP meeting. When this happens, the date the child returns to school is usually known, and placement occurs quite quickly. Other times the appropriate program may be difficult to determine, or it may not be available in the child's school system and placement may be delayed. With children who have significant sequelae after head injuries, an ideal program that combines all of the recommended services is often not available, and compromises must be made.

Although it may not be formally included in the IEP, communication among the variety of people involved in the education of the child or adolescent after head injury should be emphasized as an issue, with a strategy designed to ensure a timely flow of information. This not only involves the school, child, and family but also all school personnel and nonschool professionals. Adequate communication not only facilitates change in the child's program with improvement but can also help to avoid major difficulties if a school program is not successful. As much as everyone involved attempts to plan for the best program possible, it may not work as planned, and considerable alterations may be needed. Formal monitoring may help to alleviate problems, but effective informal communication may ensure that changes are made more quickly, before problems become entrenched.

Types of Educational Services and Programs

Because of the extreme variability of head injuries and head injury sequelae, any of the programs and services available through the educational system for normal children and for children with special needs could be appropriate for any one child after injury. Even though special education services are mandated for all handicapped children, specific services are usually provided according to specific diagnostic classifications. These are often divided into programs for children with learning disabilities, mental retardation, behavior disorders, emotional disturbance, sensory handicaps (vision and hearing impairments), physical disabilities, multiple handicaps, and other health impairments. In addition to the guidelines in the federal legislation concerning the criteria for inclusion into any of these classifications, each state may have its own guidelines that supplement or operationalize the general categories of the federal law.

However, there is no classification specifically for children after traumatic brain injury, so that they often receive educational services under another diagnostic classification. It is important to emphasize that a child after head injury requires special education services of whatever classification due to acquired injury and that the educational label may be appropriate only for programming purposes. This is especially crucial for children who may require special education services on a short-term basis during the period of rapid recovery. However, it is also important for children who may require special education services over a long period. They may very well differ in important ways from children who have been traditionally diagnosed with learning disabilities, mental retardation, behavior disorders, etc. By emphasizing the etiology of their difficulties, it is less likely that these differences are overlooked and more likely that specific head injury concerns are incorporated into their programming.

The level of service in terms of intensity and departure from a regular class program varies considerably. While the child or adolescent is in the hospital, the student may receive educational services from a hospital teacher. Some childrens' hospitals have their own school programs, but others rely on itinerant teachers provided through the local public school system. Usually children must be hospitalized for a minimum of several weeks before hospital teaching can occur if it is provided through the school system. Some children and adolescents may also receive home teaching services if they are not medically able to return to school after discharge from the hospital. Once in a while, home teaching is recommended to provide educational services while a child is awaiting appropriate class placement.

The most restrictive educational setting, other than home or hospital teaching—which are usually considered as temporary—is a residential school program. Because of the prohibitive cost of these programs, they are usually recommended only for children or adolescents who are extremely difficult to manage. Very few head-injured children and adolescents are placed into residential programs, but for those with severe behavior and emotional disorders, this may be the only appropriate setting. However, only a few programs scattered across the country are able to manage, much less treat, this small but extremely difficult group of children and adolescents.

For children who can be managed at home and do not require 24-hour programming but have extensive needs, involvement in a public or private special education school may be appropriate. In rural or suburban districts, these may be collaborative programs across a larger geographical area to provide services for children with low-incidence handicaps. Those children and adolescents who have severe sequelae and multiple special education and therapy needs after head injury may require such programming especially since a wide range of services are likely to be available under one roof.

Since the late 1970s, though, most special education services have been provided through neighborhood schools. By placing special education classes and services in local schools, contact with normal children and mainstreaming into regular education classes can be provided more easily. For the child after a traumatic brain injury, this can mean that the student can receive special education services while continuing to attend the neighborhood school. However, it can also be difficult for a child to return to the school and not return to the former classroom. Involvement in a special education class can vary in terms of the amount of time the child spends in the self-contained classroom, which is smaller with more individualized instruction, and the amount of time the child is mainstreamed into regular educational programming.

For a child who can return to the preinjury class program but needs some special education services in order to succeed, a variety of services are available. The child may receive instruction part of the day in a resource room, which is a separate room staffed by a special education teacher in which students can spend up to approximately half of their school day. The time spent in the resource room is focused on a specific academic area, such as math, or on study skills in general. However, the student's primary class placement and most learning occurs in a regular school program. For head-injured children and adolescents, the resource room program can provide remedial help, as well as intervention directed toward specific deficits after injury. In junior high and high school programs, the resource room teacher may be the ideal person to help organize the head-injured adolescent's day and help to compensate for memory difficulties that interfere with remembering assignments and specific class-related material. For higher functioning adolescents after injury, the resource room may be a more productive place than the traditional study hall.

Some children and adolescents, especially those with milder injuries, may be able to return to their preinjury school programs but may need adaptations or tutoring. For example, they may require a shortened school day or a reduced course load. Rest periods may be incorporated into their school day through scheduled study hall periods or through arrangements to spend time in the school nurse's room. Those who were involved in advanced placement classes or gifted programs may especially need careful planning to ensure that they continue to be challenged but not overwhelmed on return to school. Consultation with classroom teachers on what they can expect of students returning to school after head injury is often extremely helpful in maintaining children and adolescents in mainstream programs when appropriate. Even though these children may not be deemed handicapped, it is important for everyone involved to recognize their needs and the adaptations being made for them.

Special services in addition to classroom programs are often available, including physical therapy, occupational therapy, speech and language therapy, counseling, social work, psychology, hearing impaired, visually handicapped, and vocational services. These are provided through the school system if they are deemed educationally relevant. Counseling services may be especially important for children and adolescents returning to school after head injuries, both in helping them to cope with possible frustration in attempting to resume their education and in helping their classmates understand and be prepared to accept their head-injured fellow student.

Although most of the services and programs presented have necessarily focused on the head-injured child or adolescent, there is also a need for training of teachers and other school personnel in traumatic brain injury issues as they affect learning and performance in academic settings. From a survey of special education teachers in Vermont, 75% had no training in the specific needs of students after traumatic brain injury (Savage, 1985). There is also critical need for training members of diagnostic teams and special education administrators who are responsible for decision making about whether and what special needs a child or adolescent has after head injury. However, head injury is rarely addressed in special education text-books or in teacher training programs.

CASE STUDY CONTINUED

Jason

Let us return to Jason, whose situation in school after injury was presented at the beginning of this chapter. At present, he is 19 years old and has recently graduated from high school. The intervening years have been difficult for him, especially in terms of academic achievement. Because his school had very limited services and very little understanding about his learning difficulties after injury, despite frequent conferences, he received many services outside the school system. He received therapy services through a local hospital focused on basic academic skills, cognitive problem solving and coping with the effects of injury.

He completed high school by the skin of his teeth, doing much of his academic work in lower-track courses and even correspondence courses. In his sophomore year of high school, his school started a resource room program, through which he received some study skill help. However, he was very interested and motivated to learn about mechanics, which he managed to incorporate not only into his school program but also into part-time and summer jobs. Although behaviorally he could be quite restless and fidgety at times, he was able to control this so that it did not interfere with conscientious work on the job. He took pride in his appearance and in completing his mechanical work thoroughly and neatly. Even though he had been offered a full-time job before graduation, he decided to ask to be able to work part-time until finishing a semester later than his classmates.

REFERENCES

Boll, T.J. (1983). Minor head injury in children: Out of sight but not out of mind. *Journal of Child Clinical Psychology, 12*, 74–80.

Brink, J.D., Garrett, A.L., Hale, W.R., Woo-Sam, J., & Nickel, V.L. (1970). Recovery of motor and intellectual function in children sustaining severe head injuries. *Developmental Medicine and Child Neurology, 12*, 565–571.

Burkinshaw, J. (1960). Head injuries in children: Observations on their incidence and causes with an enquiry into the value of routine skull x-rays. *Archives of Disease in Childhood, 35*, 205–214.

Chadwick, O., Rutter, M., Thompson, J., & Shaffer, D. (1981). Intellectual performance and reading skills after localized head injury in childhood. *Journal of Child Psychology and Psychiatry, 22*, 117–139.

Cohen, S.B. (1986). Educational reintegration and programming for children with head injuries. *Journal of Head Trauma Rehabilitation, 1*, 22–29.

Cohen, S.B., Joyce, C.M., Rhoades, K.W., & Welks, D.M. (1985). Educational programming for head injured students. In M. Ylvisaker (Ed.), *Head injury rehabilitation: Children and adolescents*. San Diego: College-Hill Press.

Ewing-Cobbs, L., Fletcher, J.M., & Levin, H.S. (1985). Neuropsychological sequelae following pediatric head injury. In M. Ylvisaker (Ed.), *Head injury rehabilitation: Children and adolescents*. San Diego: College-Hill Press.

Flach, J., & Malmros, R. (1972). A long-term follow-up study of children with severe head injury. *Scandinavian Journal of Rehabilitation Medicine, 4*, 9–15.

Fuld, P.A., & Fisher, P. (1977). Recovery of intellectual ability after closed head-injury. *Developmental Medicine and Child Neurology, 19*, 495–502.

Goldstein, F.C., & Levin, H.S. (1985) Intellectual and academic outcome following closed head injury in children and adolescents: Research strategies and empirical findings. *Developmental Neuropsychology, 1*, 195–214.

Gronwall, D., & Wrightson, P. (1974). Delayed recovery of intellectual function after minor head injury. *Lancet, 2*, 605–609.

Gulbrandsen, G.B. (1984). Neuropsychological sequelae of light head injuries in older children 6 months after trauma. *Journal of Clinical Neuropsychology, 3*, 257–268.

Heiskanen, O., & Kaste, M. (1974). Late prognosis of severe brain injury in children. *Developmental Medicine and Child Neurology, 16*, 11–14.

Klonoff, H., Low, M.D., & Clark, C. (1977). Head injuries in children: A prospective five year follow-up. *Journal of Neurology, Neurosurgery, and Psychiatry, 40*, 1211–1219.

Lehr, E. (1984). *Good recovery from severe head injury in children and adolescents*. Paper presented at the American Psychological Association Convention, Toronto.

Levin, H.S., & Benton, A.L. (1986). Developmental and acquired dyscalculia in children. In I. Fleming (Ed.), *Second European symposium on developmental neurology*. Stuttgart: Gustav Fisher Verlag.

Mahoney, W. J., D'Souza, B.J., Haller, J.A., Rogers, M.C., Epstein, M.H., & Freeman, J.M. (1983). Long-term outcome of children with severe head trauma and prolonged coma. *Pediatrics, 71*, 756–762.

Richardson, F. (1963). Some effects of severe head injury: A follow-up study of children and adolescents after protracted coma. *Developmental Medicine and Child Neurology*, *5*, 471–482.

Rutter, M., Chadwick, O., & Shaffer, D. (1983). Head injury. In M. Rutter (Ed.), *Developmental neuropsychiatry*. New York: Guilford Press.

Savage, R. (1985). *A survey of traumatically brain injured children within school-based special education programs*. Rutland, VT: Head Injury/Stroke Independence Project, pp. 1–6.

Savage, R.C., & Carter, R. (1984). Re-entry: The head injured student returns to school. *Cognitive Rehabilitation*, *2*, 28–33.

Shaffer, D., Bijur, P., Chadwick, O.F.D., & Rutter, M.L. (1980). Head injury and later reading disability. *Journal of the American Academy of Child Psychiatry*, *19*, 592–610.

Telzrow, C.F. (1985). The science and speculation of rehabilitation in developmental neuropsychological disorders. In L.C. Hartlage & C.F. Telzrow (Eds.), *The neuropsychology of individual differences: A developmental perspective*. New York: Plenum Press.

Chapter 8

Mild Head Injury

John F. Doronzo

CASE STUDY

Nathaniel

According to his parents, Nathaniel was a normal, delightful baby and toddler until he fell while they were on vacation when he was 2 1/2 years old. Although his parents were concerned about his fall, Nathaniel appeared to be more upset than hurt. He had no loss of consciousness or obvious injury. They calmed him and continued with their vacation activities. However, that evening Nathaniel had a grand mal seizure and was taken to the nearest emergency room. His mother reported a marked difference in his behavior and a decrease in this physical coordination after his injury. He was not as affectionate and cuddly, became more easily frustrated and irritable, and could not stay with his play activities for as long a period. During a medical evaluation at 3 years of age, he had a definite seizure disorder focusing primarily in the right side of his brain but sometimes extending to the left side. He was continued on medication for seizure management.

When he started preschool, his teacher described Nathaniel as having a short attention span and being frustrated because he did not seem to understand much of what was going on around him. He appeared to be slow both in following directions and in motor coordination, but he was not hyperactive. He was referred for services through an agency specializing in children with developmental delays and developmental disorders. However, when compared with the more severely involved children with whom this center primarily worked, Nathaniel seemed to be doing quite well. At home Nathaniel continued to have temper tantrums, cried easily, had difficulty staying with activities, and often appeared to be withdrawn.

On a psychological evaluation when he was 5 years old, Nathaniel was approximately a year behind in all cognitive and learning areas; it was recommended that he stay in preschool for another year rather than begin kindergarten in fall. At this time, he also began to have staring spells, which did not appear to be seizures but rather related to his learning and concentration difficulties. He continued to have an abnormal EEG and had two episodes of seizures while sleeping at night.

When he was 6 years old, Nathaniel fell off his bicycle as he went down an incline too quickly. He hit his head but again did not appear to be seriously injured apart from cuts and bruises on his legs and arms. However, he had a gran mal seizure the next morning. Since he had not had any seizures for a year, seizure medication had been discontinued 2 months previously but was begun again.

Nathaniel attended a regular private school for kindergarten and first grade; he continued to display difficulty in learning. At the end of first grade, there was again concern about whether he should be promoted to second grade or retained in first. Behaviorally Nathaniel was doing well in school. Psychological evaluation was completed again. Findings from the testing indicated that he was functioning cognitively in the borderline range, which was consistent with his below-grade-level academic learning. However, the observations of his difficulty expressing himself and his slow rate of learning basic academic skills concerned the evaluator, his parents, and his teacher and further evaluation was recommended to aid in special education programming.

Neuropsychological evaluation was completed before Nathaniel began in a new school that had special education services. Although he did not have behavior problems at school, his parents were very frustrated and concerned about his behavior at home. He had begun to tear things up and break his toys with a sense of enjoyment. They noted that he seemed to have a hard time keeping himself occupied unless it was something he was not supposed to be doing. Yelling at him and spanking seemed to have no effect. Nathaniel argued continually with his parents. Though they sensed that he wanted to be loved, he would push them away if they tried to hug him. However, what had made them extremely concerned was overhearing him say to one of his friends that he knew he was going to fail again in school, comments to his mother that "it wouldn't be a problem if I was dead," and his trying to set a fire in the shed. He also had become a daredevil on his bicycle, and they were very worried that he would have another accident. He sometimes appeared overly cocky, saying he knew how to do things that he had never tried before and being resistent to being shown how.

Nathaniel had been getting all Fs on his papers at the private school and had stopped bringing homework home. Even when he did, though, both he and his parents were very frustrated in trying to help him complete it. Even if he seemed to understand it at home, Nathaniel often could not do the same work at school the next day. However, he continued to love to do things with his hands and enjoyed putting models together.

The initial impression of Nathaniel during the evaluation was that of a very sad, quiet boy. He was cooperative and seemed to be trying to do his best, but he rarely smiled or talked spontaneously. His drawing of a 6-year-old boy who would be "happy" if he got "to go out to play" was very small with lines on the body, arms, and legs signifying "bones" (see Figure 8-1). Nathaniel brightened up considerably when the testing was over, and he talked about how much he was looking forward to getting a model airplane that could "really fly." He appeared very aware of his learning difficulties and seemed well on his way to giving up on being able to succeed in school.

Although he functioned overall in the borderline to low-average range on cognitive tasks, Nathaniel performed at age-expected levels on many of the neuropsychological tasks and on general information tasks if they did not resemble schoolwork. He also demonstrated the ability to learn when he was able to practice a task or was given feedback immediately about whether he was right. Memory for repeated trials of a word list, though, was significantly reduced. Abstract designs and hand movements were extremely difficult for him to copy. However, he was able to put together puzzles relatively well. He reversed letters and numbers,

Figure 8-1 Drawing of a boy by an 8½-year-old boy who had mild injuries at 2½ and 6 years of age.

omitted letters when he was spelling, had severe difficulty sounding out words, and often did not attend to operation signs while completing arithmetic problems. He was a dysfluent reader, starting on the right side of the page at times and demonstrated word reversals (*was/saw, on/no*).

Because of the specific nature of his deficits, with indications of average-level abilities but significant difficulties in academic learning, programming for children with learning disabilities was recommended. He especially needed a careful special education evaluation of his difficulty in learning to read, spell, and compute. However, equally as essential was intervention in emotional areas to give Nathaniel the confidence that he could learn in school and that his teachers were trying to find how to help him do this more easily. His parents worked with a psychologist in setting up a reward program for behavior with clear expectations for Nathaniel at home. A direct connection between Nathaniel's two mild head injuries, his seizure disorder, and his learning difficulties could not definitely be made. Because of his young age at the time of initial injury, it was not clear if he might have had learning difficulties without having been injured. However, at least some of the specific nature of his difficulties appeared to relate to the subtle effects of involvement of the right side of his brain.

INTRODUCTION

Despite the high incidence of mild head injuries, only within the past decade has there been increasing interest in the area of mild head injury. This interest began with the findings from research with adults that the effects of mild injuries could interfere significantly with employment and other areas of life satisfaction (Rimel, Giordani, Barth, Boll, & Jane, 1981). Research on the effects of mild head injuries in children has been very sparse, even though as many as 85% of pediatric head injuries could be classified as mild in nature (Kraus, Fife, Cos, Ramstein, & Conroy, 1986).

The most accurate way to define a mild injury is probably from a functional rather than a neurological point of view. Mild injuries occur when the head is struck, or is subject to a violent movement, resulting in a transient alteration in level of consciousness. Typically there is no hospitalization or hospitalization is brief, and the individual returns home to resume normal activities, such as school.

Many children who sustain mild injuries appear unimpaired until they attempt to return to school. At that point, memory difficulties, impaired concentration abilities, and a general decrease in their ability to learn efficiently may become apparent. Family relationships may also begin to suffer. Children may be seen as difficult, irritable, hyperactive, or stubborn. Many times these changes are seen as psychological and unrelated to the head injury.

Because of the high incidence and the recently recognized possible sequelae, mild injuries deserve consideration separate from moderate and severe injuries. The problem of mild head injury can be simply stated in that what appears to be a brief initial alteration in consciousness and functioning with quick physical recovery may have possible long-term effects cognitively, psychologically, socially, and educationally for children and adolescents. It is precisely in these circumstances that mild head injury becomes the epitome of the unseen injury or the silent epidemic.

In clinical and research literature, controversy continues regarding what is considered a mild injury versus a moderate injury as well as the nature and occurrence of postconcussion syndrome. In fact, the definition of these terms appears to be changing over time. There was very little delineation among the three in earlier literature. Currently there is growing respect for the sequelae of mild injuries as being separate from more moderate injuries and a bump on the head.

This chapter attempts to bring together current research and theory regarding mild head injury in children and adolescents and suggests some ideas for evaluation, treatment, and future research. In gathering information for this chapter, it was clear that only a few studies directly address the issues of mild head injury in general and even fewer deal specifically with children and adolescents.

INCIDENCE AND EPIDEMIOLOGY

The incidence of mild head injury is difficult to determine accurately. It has been estimated that nearly 75% of all head injuries are mild or moderate in nature (Langfitt & Gennarelli, 1982) and that this can increase to 88% of injuries in children under 15 years of age (Kraus et al., 1986). Many mild injuries never come to the attention of medical personnel; therefore the incidence is quite likely to be underestimated rather than overestimated. Contributing further to the difficulty in determining an accurate incidence of mild injuries is the inclusion of lacerations of the face and scalp, as well as contusion with no definite impairment of consciousness, in the category of mild head injury in medical diagnostic classification systems.

Accidents, including severe head injuries, are reported as the leading cause of death to infants and children between the ages of 1 and 14 (Klonoff

& Robinson, 1967). In addition, children and adolescents are also at high risk for mild head injuries stemming from accidents in the home and on the playground. Rutter (1977) has suggested a greater role of a child's preinjury behavior and temperament for placing them at higher risk for mild injuries. Child abuse may be a major cause of mild injury; however, the extent that child abuse plays in the incidence is not known. The shaken baby syndrome as typically reported results in much more severe injuries. Certainly milder forms of this syndrome exist; however, the consequences have not been investigated or reported.

Much has been reported regarding the epidemiology of head injury in general. Estimates of 5% of the U.S. population being at risk for craniocerebral injury were reported by Caveness (1979). Most of the epidemiological literature on head injury supports the idea that the factors underlying the etiology of mild head injury are the same factors that underlie all head injuries in general. This is likely to stem from the fact that most head injuries are of the mild type. For adults, the automobile, factors of life style and life cycle, and recreation and leisure activities play a significant role in the incidence of brain injury. For children, accidents at home account for a significant proportion of preschool cases, but for school-age children, falls regardless of where they occur constitute the most common cause of milder head injuries treated in hospitals (Klonoff, 1971).

MEDICAL DEFINITION AND SYMPTOMS

Mild head injury can occur from an actual blow to the head or from acceleration and deceleration injuries that do not necessarily involve a blow. Some researchers believe that the latter form of injury results in more significant cognitive and behavioral sequelae (Boll, 1983). Minor injury may also occur after a severe whiplash injury, even if the head is not struck, especially if the whiplash involves a rotation of the head in addition to linear movement. A concussion, typically defined as instantaneous diminution or loss of consciousness, was once believed to be completely reversible because no structural neurologic damage to the brain had occurred and in most cases recovery was relatively rapid and complete (Parkinson, 1977). Some researchers now believe that this may not always be the case.

In describing the pathophysiology of head trauma, disturbances of functioning at the level of the nerve cells appear to be the major area of investigation (Ommaya & Gennarelli, 1975; Jane & Rimmell, 1982). It was initially believed that no gross anatomic changes would be found even at a microscopic level. This apparent absence of structural pathology combined with the rapid recovery of function in mild brain injury led many to believe that the changes following mild injuries were due to secondary brain injuries (Symonds, 1962). The lack of signs from neurodiagnostic procedures, such as CT scans, also led some observers (McLaurin & Titchener, 1982; Bakay & Glasauer, 1980) to postulate that changes following head injury were of a nonorganic nature. However, other investigations (Ommaya & Gennarelli, 1975; Adams, Graham, & Gennarelli, 1981) have demonstrated that brain function can be severely impaired, even to the extent of death, with no observable pathophysiological evidence on diagnostic tests. The changes were observed only on autopsy and consisted of degeneration of the extensions of the nerve cells (axons and their branches) in various areas of the upper brain and the brain stem. Therefore it would appear that even in cases where no structural damage can be readily identified by neurodiagnostic techniques, the possibility of actual and significant physiological changes exists.

Beyond structural and physiological changes, alterations in level of consciousness are the behavioral hallmark of brain injury. The Glasgow Coma Scale (GCS) (Jennett & Teasdale, 1974) is generally accepted by most researchers as a standard for quantifying alterations of level of consciousness. The utility of the GCS for identifying milder brain injuries with adults has been established over the past 7 to 10 years (Rimel, Giordani, & Barth, 1982; Jennett, Teather, & Bernie, 1973). The general consensus appears to be that GCS scores of 9–15 comprise the range of injuries termed *moderate* (9–12) and *minor* (13–15).

In addition to initial determination of level of consciousness, duration of altered consciousness also aids in estimating severity. Observation of posttraumatic amnesic (PTA) states has proved a useful method for estimation of the end of altered consciousness with adults. PTA, also called *anterograde amnesia*, is usually measured up to the point at which the memory for ongoing events of daily life becomes continuous (Brooks, 1975). Length of PTA allows for a rough measure along a single continuum for both mild and severe head injuries. Jennett and Teasdale (1981) suggest the following scheme for classification of posttraumatic amnesia and mild injury:

less than 5 minutes	very mild
less than 1 hour	mild
1 to 24 hours	moderate

It is very difficult to determine PTA particularly in young children. PTA of less than 1 hour may not be easily observed because the child may not normally be accurate in reporting events in time sequence over such a short period. The young child also may simply not be asked relevant questions shortly after being injured. If new memory is not directly tested as soon as possible, it is not easy to detect a deficit. In very small children, crying, irritability, and lethargy may be a sign of alteration in consciousness. Therefore, use of PTA in mild head injuries to children may not be as helpful for determining severity as with more moderate and severe injuries. It also becomes less reliable depending on the child's age, with younger children less able to report events consistently than older children.

Level of consciousness should be one of many considerations in viewing head injuries. Other complications such as posttraumatic seizures, intracranial hematomas and infections, and the secondary effects of brain swelling, hypotension, and hypoxia can occur, although infrequently, with mild head injury (Reilly, Graham, & Adams, 1975; Jennett, 1976). Jennett (1976) has accurately stated that a description of any head injury should always distinguish initial severity from complications and posttraumatic sequelae, as well as document the duration of coma and posttraumatic amnesia.

In defining the nature and extent of changes with mild head injury, an interesting note is worth mention. In clinical lore there is reference to a symptom-free period following head injury in children referred to as *talk and die*. Snoek, Minderhoud, and Wilmink (1984) investigated this phenomenon and its possible etiology in a study conducted with many children seen by the neurology staff at University Hospital in the Netherlands. Forty-two children (of 967, or 4.34%), following a seemingly minor or trivial head injury, developed neurological signs after a lucid or symptom-free period. Only 1 of the patients had an intracranial hematoma, a condition that is commonly seen in adult head injury. The remainder of the children showed a transient syndrome consisting of either convulsive or nonconvulsive signs. One major conclusion of the study was that given the not infrequent deterioration following a mild head injury in children, hospital admission and monitoring should always be a consideration.

Although many mild head injuries require no medical management, some mild injuries do result in physical symptoms that are noticeable and disturbing in nature (vomiting and nausea, dizziness, vertigo), and individuals with these problems are typically seen in the emergency room or by family physicians. Young children who are less able to report subjective feelings of dizziness or vertigo may be irritable and lethargic. Medical management typically includes careful observation and examination. If there were a loss of consciousness, even of short duration, observation usually includes at least a 1-night admission to the hospital. Neurodiagnostic examinations are typically normal or return to normal within a short period.

At this point a detrimental mistake is often made. Parents may be informed that no neurological damage has occurred, and therefore recovery is or soon will be complete. Parents confidently return home and place their child back in school, unaware that the cognitive and behavioral changes that may shortly begin to appear can be directly related to head injury. Clearly intervention should begin at the emergency room or in the office of the family physician.

It is difficult to quantify mild injuries in general but particularly in small children. Clinicians need to be observant of behavioral, physical, and cognitive signs to make an accurate and needed diagnosis.

PSYCHOLOGICAL SEQUELAE AND OUTCOME

It now appears certain that neurobehavioral deficits following mild head injury are more extensive than initially believed. Some changes may be immediately observable, and others may appear days or weeks later. The following areas seem to be the agreed clusters of sequelae from work with adults: deficits in information processing and reaction time (Gronwall & Wrightson, 1974, 1981), intermediate and short-term memory difficulties (Benton, 1979; Logue & McCarty, 1982), problems with perceptual functions (Levin, Grossman, & Kelly, 1977), verbal and communication problems (Levin, Grossman, & Kelly, 1976; Reitan, 1982), and difficulties with concept formation and general reasoning abilities (Reitan, 1982). Boll (1983) pointed out that what may be relatively mild and perhaps clinically invisible decreases in cognitive capabilities may significantly alter a person's ability to perform tasks at a personally adequate level or in a fashion minimally acceptable to others. Individuals with mild injuries may also show personality changes, headaches, and irritability.

Typically rate of recovery is correlated with the severity of injury. It appears that the strength of this association between severity and recovery is somewhat weaker with mild and moderate injuries (Levin et al., 1976). Patient's typical complaints of decreased concentration, memory problems, and emotional lability are generally vague and may reflect only subtle subclinical differences on formal neuropsychological testing (Barth, Macciocchi, & Giordani, 1983; Sarno, 1980). Specific cognitive impairments evident upon formal testing appear more indicative of focal brain injuries and are often accompanied by neurological signs of focal brain injury (Benton, 1979). In addition, there is considerable variability between individuals in the nature and duration of specific complaints of neurobehavioral deficits they experience after mild brain injury. What becomes obvious is that recovery seldom follows a singular course. Boll (1983) has acknowledged the wide acceptance of a pattern of recovery involving rapid early improvement with gradual slowing over the early months following injury.

Following this rapid improvement there may be either a period of stability or one of gradual improvement.

Memory disturbances are the most commonly reported sequelae of all brain injuries (Levin, Benton, & Grossman, 1982). These disturbances of memory are likely to be complex. Gronwall and Wrightson (1981) found three effects of mild concussive injury reflecting the likelihood of multiple loci of damage: (1) attention and concentration difficulties reflected in the rate of information processing, (2) deficits in long-term memory storage correlated with the duration of posttraumatic amnesia, and (3) impaired ability to retrieve previously stored material that was uncorrelated with information-processing speed or PTA.

It is generally believed that recovery from mild brain injury may take considerably longer than previously thought. Whether the greater proportion of recovery occurs within the first few months postinjury remains to be documented completely, though it would seem that the greater the initial deficit, the greater the improvement during the initial phases of recovery.

Reports of clinical symptomology have described a wide range of sequelae associated with mild and moderate head trauma (Jennett & Teasdale, 1981; Cartlidge, 1981). However the basis of the sequelae has been debated in the literature; the argument centers around whether the symptoms have an organic basis or reflect psychological responses to the injury (McLaurin & Titchener, 1982; Lidvall, Linderoth, & Norlin, 1974; Rutherford, Merrett, & McDonald, 1977; Jacobson, 1969). It would seem likely that posttraumatic sequelae involve a combination of both organic and functional disorders. Explanations of the sequelae of mild brain injury have taken several forms. Organic interpretations may reflect pathological processes during recovery. Emotional responses to trauma in general or particular symptoms associated with head injury have been implicated. Historical understanding of mild brain injury has been that the set of symptoms commonly observed following such brain injury comprise a postconcussion syndrome that is most likely to be seen in the more mildly injured patient (Cartlidge, 1981; Caveness, 1979).

The subjective complaints of headache and dizziness, and sometimes poor concentration, memory, fatigue, and irritability, constitute the constellation of complaints termed *postconcussion syndrome*. This constellation is relatively consistent from individual to individual; however, there is some variation in degree and duration of the complaints. These complaints are reported by older children but less so by children younger than 9 to 10 years of age. The term *postconcussion syndrome* was first used when part of the definition of concussion was lack of organic damage, with only transitory functional disorder. The term remains in use today even with the knowledge that organic changes may actually occur in mild injuries. Some researchers believe that there may be very little evidence of a postconcussive syndrome (Lidvall, Linderoth, & Norlin, 1974; Rutherford, Merrett, & McDonald, 1977). This does not mean that definite symptoms do not follow concussive events but rather that individuals seldom exhibit more than one or two of the posttraumatic symptoms at any one time.

Regardless of the explanation used for causes of the sequelae, what matters in the final analysis is the behavioral and cognitive changes after brain injury. Most researchers now agree that even the most mild head injuries can produce permanent brain damage even though it may be of a relatively minor and seemingly insignificant degree. However, the clinical meaningfulness of this damage is not always clear.

OUTCOME RESEARCH ON INJURY EFFECTS IN CHILDREN

Common to all research in head injury and children are concerns regarding methodology. Much of the early outcome research on head injury in children was based on unreliable clinical observation. Studies that utilized comprehensive reliable neuropsychological evaluations have been few. Many early studies utilized a wide range in ages of children and wide ranges in severity and duration of coma. In addition, relatively few studies utilized adequate control groups, and many studies were retrospective.

In a longitudinal study, Klonoff (1971) and his colleagues attempted to overcome many of these problems by following a line of research that included prospective, long-term, and multidimensional designs that also took into account antecedent, clinical, and interactional factors. These works are among the most comprehensive investigating the effects of mild head injury over time in preschool and school-age children.

Klonoff collected data and grouped preschool and school-age children into five categories based on severity of head injury as follows: (1) minor—patients without evidence of loss of consciousness; (2) mild—no evidence of loss of consciousness but cerebral symptoms such as vomiting, dizziness, lethargy, nausea indicating concussion; (3) moderate—concussion with loss of consciousness less than 5 minutes; (4) severe—skull fracture or concussion with loss of consciousness from 5 to 30 minutes; and (5) serious—concussion with loss of consciousness greater than 30 minutes or depressed and compound skull fracture and other symptoms of serious injuries such as aphasia or posttraumatic psychosis. Medically speaking, children in the first three categories would most likely be considered to have had mild head injuries, and most would not have been hospitalized. While children in the fourth and fifth categories would possibly be hospitalized, the prognosis of children in all five categories in this study would be considered quite good, and most would be viewed as physically and neurologically normal within a short period of time. The findings of this series of studies allow for many reassuring statements regarding the generally excellent prognosis for recovery. In fact, approximately 60% of the children in the study did well rather quickly following the accident.

Most importantly, however, Klonoff found that a significant number of these children showed neuropsychological deficits on initial and 1-year follow-up evaluations. Two years postinjury 30% still demonstrated neuropsychological impairment on the tasks presented. A sizable percentage of these children continued to show patterns of recovery fully 4 years post–head injury. In fact, Klonoff pointed out that 23% of his head-injured children continued to demonstrate measurable neuropsychological deficits 5 years following injury. The ramifications of these deficits may be seen in that 25% failed a grade or were placed in remedial or slow learner classrooms at some time after their head injury; this differed from the child's preinjury educational course.

Gulbrandsen (1984) examined outcome in a study of 56 children who were between 9 and 13 years of age and had undergone evaluation between 4 and 8 months following their injury. They all had the diagnosis of concussion in the emergency room based on the presence of several symptoms including unconsciousness (not exceeding 15 minutes), amnesia, nausea or vomiting, drowsiness, and somnolence. When compared with control subjects, those children with mild head injuries were deficient on 29 of 32 test variables. It appeared that concussion explained most of the differences between groups. The differences between the groups tended to decrease with increasing age and to increase with increasing complexity of tests. She concluded by demonstrating that even with few subjective complaints following an injury, and even when no perceptible lags in academic achievement had been noted, neuropsychological sequelae could be demonstrated.

In an interesting outcome study by Lyons and Matheny (1984), cognitive and personality differences between identical twins following skull fractures were examined. In this study, 13 pairs of male identical twins, one of whom had suffered a noncompound skull fracture during one of two periods (between 12 and 36 months of age or between 36 and 48 months of age), were compared on the Wechsler Preschool and Primary Scale of Intelligence (WPPSI) and on a personality and temperament scale. These researchers found that twins injured between 12 and 36 months had no cognitive deficits but had higher scores on a factor denoting ratings of emotionality. The twins injured between 36 and 48 months, when compared with their co-twins, had significantly lower scores on four of the performance subtests of the WPPSI but did not differ on ratings of temperament. The authors point out that some caution should be used in interpreting the data because the nature and extent of the brain damage could not be specified and because the sample size was small. Relevant to the discussion, the duration of loss of consciousness for all but one subject was 1 to 2 hours and the length of unconsciousness was slightly higher in the older group. As with previously discussed studies, the severity of the injuries examined here may be in the mild-moderate or moderate range and may not be generalizable to mild injuries, where there is only a brief alteration in consciousness.

In an additional study of outcome, Levin and Eisenberg (1979), utilizing a comprehensive battery of neuropsychological tests as well as a standardized classification scale for a measure of severity of coma (Glasgow Scale), studied 45 children and young adolescents recovering from head injury. They found the degree of neuropsychological deficit was directly related to severity of injury measured by duration of coma. In patients with loss of consciousness less than 24 hours, residual impairment was found in the early posttraumatic period. However, persistent intellectual deficit after a longer postinjury interval was most predominant in the group of children with loss of consciousness longer that 24 hours, which would be considered in the moderate severity range. As predicted, the longer the period of loss of consciousness, the greater the deficits. However, even in the mildest group with the briefest loss of consciousness, residual impairment was noted.

In contrast to the preceding studies that found sequelae after mild head injuries in at least some of the children involved, a series of prospective outcome studies found little change in a 2-year follow-up of a mildly injured group when compared with a control and a severely injured group of children (Brown, Chadwick, Shaffer, Rutter, & Traub, 1981; Chadwick, Rutter, Brown, Shaffer, & Traub, 1981; Chadwick, Rutter, Shaffer, & Shrout, 1981; Rutter, Chadwick, Shaffer & Brown, 1980). The same relationship held true for psychiatric disturbance following injury. There was a marked increase in new psychiatric disorders following severe injury in their study group. However, in the mild group, a higher level of behavioral disturbance was noted before the injury but no significant increase following the injury. It was concluded that head injuries resulting in PTA of less than 1 week did not appreciably increase cognitive or psychiatric risk. (It can be argued that a PTA of less than 1 week may place these children in a moderate range of injury, and therefore the conclusions of the study may not generalize to mild injuries.) The authors concluded by agreeing with Benton (1973) that "cerebral lesions in children must either be quite extensive or have specific disorganizing functional properties in order to produce important behavioral abnormalities."

Their findings, though, need to be reconciled with the previous studies that found sequelae after mild head injuries in children. Possible sources for the differences may be that different groups of children are being studied, involving a different incidence of those children with a higher rate of behavioral and cognitive problems before injury. Also the number of children with sequelae after mild injury appears to be fewer than after severe injury, and therefore the effect of these children is more likely to be lost in group data.

Overall the outcome research demonstrates that with severe injury the results are straightforward. Duration of loss of consciousness is related to severity of cognitive deficits, particularly in older children and adolescents. Conclusions regarding those children with mild injuries are less discernible. The majority of children after mild injuries probably recover extremely well with little noticeable effect after a couple of months postinjury. But there is also a group of children with significant and persistent deficits after mild injury. However, it is unclear why some children experience more significant sequelae after mild injuries than others. Very young infants appear more likely to recover well on cognitive tasks but may demonstrate personality and temperament changes. Older children and adolescents appear to be more likely to sustain cognitive difficulties, sometimes with observable changes in school performance, as well as behavior problems that may be primary (organic) or secondary (in reaction) in nature.

INTERVENTION

Especially in the case of mild head injuries, intervention necessarily begins with awareness. Families as well as professionals need to be aware that when a child sustains a mild head injury, there may be subsequent effects of that injury despite the lack of physical symptoms and the lack of observable neurologic signs. Intervention requires the recognition of the problem and possible sequelae.

Medical personnel need to be aware of the presenting symptoms, immediate results, and longer-term sequelae that can occur with milder head injuries. This has been implemented in cases of severe injuries, and many excellent programs of early identification and intervention have been in place for the past decade. Emergency room personnel for the most part are aware of the need for careful observation and treatment following a more severe injury (observation that takes place for at least several hours and days following onset). Mild head injury now deserves the same attention and consideration, especially for children and adolescents. A set of pamphlets and videotapes (Kay, 1986) has been developed for use in training hospital personnel, as well as for educating adults who have sustained mild head injuries. However, no similar materials are available for children, adolescents, and their parents.

Intervention also involves education and information for the family members of children who have had mild injuries. This process aids them to understand the process of mild head injury, the possible effects, and possible strategies for managing difficult behaviors and other sequelae. This process reduces the chance of psychological stresses that can develop secondarily as a result of the injury and can thus indirectly aid in the child's recovery. Families need to receive support from professionals and from other families. Local support groups, state head-injury foundations, and area hospitals can assist in filling that need. Unfortunately, few of even these resources have had much focus on the possible effects of mild injuries.

Adolescents can also benefit from the education and support process. Teenagers who are already in the process of self-discovery face a particularly difficult time following a mild injury. The feelings of being invisibly different are intensified. Feelings of depression and anxiety may become more prominent. Some local head-injury groups may have meetings where the majority of those injured are in the teenage range. Individual counseling or psychotherapy with a therapist who is familiar with head-injury effects is also indicated for those individuals having a difficult time with adjustment.

Specific interventions can be applied for those with identified sequelae. Children and adolescents need to be thoroughly evaluated by a clinical neuropsychologist with pediatric experience and training, utilizing appropriate assessment methods to measure the subtle deficits that follow milder injuries. Tests that examine reduced attention, particularly sustained and selective attention, should be included. Testing for higher-level deficits in memory, planning, generalization, and organization skills should be employed.

Ideally evaluation should occur shortly after injury so that the proper classroom aids, programs, and other possible special needs of the child after mild injury can be met, even if needed only on a short-term basis. However, behavioral or learning difficulties may become gradually apparent in the classroom. If so, evaluation may occur only after the child demonstrates changes. A regular classroom program usually can be adapted to meet the special needs of the child after mild head injury. Reduction of course load and shorter school days may be appropriate, especially in the period immediately following injury. In general, any way in which pressure on the student can be reduced, thus decreasing stress levels, and monitoring frustration, are in the student's best interest.

For those children with persistent sequelae after mild head injury, special education evaluation of their learning in an academic setting and school-based intervention, involving tutoring and special teaching strategies, may be needed.

SUMMARY

Mild head injury is the most common type of head injury and is unfortunately the least understood. Care must be given to the specific issues that are involved; the attention that severe injury has received must now be focused on the milder counterpart. Relatively few studies regard mild head injury in general, and even fewer look at the specific considerations of children and adolescents. There needs to be an agreed definition of mild injury that is different from postconcussion and moderate injury. Work should also investigate how to predict specific extended sequelae in different subgroups of children. Research with children must stress the importance of learning in school and the effect of injury on development. Also the effect of multiple mild injuries (potentially from child abuse) needs further investigation.

REFERENCES

Adams, G.H., Graham, D.I., & Gennarelli, T.A. (1981). Acceleration induced head injury in the monkey: The model, its mechanical and physiological correlate. *Acta Neuropathologica*, Supplement, 7, 26–28.

Bakay, L., & Glasauer, F.E. (1980). Brain injury. In L. Bakay & F.E. Glasauer (Eds.). *Head injury* (pp. 97–114). Boston: Little, Brown & Co.

Barth, J.T., Macciocchi, S.N., & Giordani, B. (1983). Neuropsychological sequelae of minor head injury. *Neurosurgery, 13*, 529–533.

Benton, A.L. (1973). Minimal brain dysfunction from a neuropsychological point of view. *Annals of the New York Academy of Science, 205*, 29–37.

Benton, A.L. (1979). Behavioral consequences of closed head injury. In G.L. Odom (Ed.), *Central nervous system trauma research status report* (pp. 220–231). Washington DC: National Institute of Neurological and Communicative Disorders and Stroke.

Boll, T.J. (1983). Minor head injury in children: Out of sight but not out of mind. *Journal of Clinical Child Psychology, 12*(1), 74–80.

Brooks, D.N. (1975). Long and short term memory in head injured patients. *Cortex, 11*, 329–340.

Brown, G., Chadwick, O., Shaffer, D., Rutter, M., & Traub, M. (1981). A prospective study of children with head injuries: III. Psychiatric sequelae. *Psychological Medicine, 11*, 63–78.

Cartlidge, N.E.F., & Shaw, D.A. (1981). *Head injury*. London: W.B. Saunders.

Caveness, W.F. (1979). Incidence of craniocerebral trauma in the United States in 1976 with trend from 1970–1975. In R.A. Thompson & J.R. Green (Eds.), *Advances in Neurology*, Vol. 22. New York: Raven Press.

Chadwick, O., Rutter, M., Brown, G., Shaffer, D., & Traub, M. (1981). A prospective study of children with head injuries: II. Cognitive sequelae. *Psychological Medicine*, *11*, 49–61.

Chadwick, O., Rutter, M., Shaffer, D., & Shrout, P.E. (1981). A prospective study of children with head injuries: IV. Specific cognitive deficits. *Journal of Clinical Neuropsychology*, *3*, 101–120.

Gronwall, D., & Wrightson, P. (1974). Delayed recovery of intellectual function after minor head injury. *Lancet*, *2*, 605–609.

Gronwall, D. & Wrightson, P. (1981). Memory and information processing capacity after closed head injury. *Journal of Neurology, Neurosurgery and Psychiatry*, *44*, 889–895.

Gulbrandsen, G.B. (1984). Neuropsychological sequelae of light head injuries in older children 6 months after trauma. *Journal of Clinical Neuropsychology*, *3*, 257–268.

Isaacson, R.L. (1975). The myth of recovery from early brain damage. In H.R. Ellis (Ed.), *Aberrant development in infancy: Human and animal studies*. New York: Halstead Press.

Jacobson, S.A. (1969). Mechanisms of the sequelae of minor craniocerebral trauma. In A.E. Walker, W.F. Caveness, & M. Critchley (Eds.), *The late effects of head injury* (pp. 34–45). Springfield, IL: Charles C Thomas.

Jane, J.A., & Rimmel, R.W. (1982). Outcome and pathology of head injury. In R.G. Grossman & P. Gildenberg (Eds.), *Head injury: Basic and clinical aspects* (pp. 229–237). New York: Raven Press.

Jennett, B. (1976). Early complications after mild head injuries. *New Zealand Medical Journal*, *84*, 144–147.

Jennett, B., & Teasdale, G. (1974). Assessment of coma and impaired consciousness. *Lancet*, *2*, 81–84.

Jennett, B., & Teasdale, G. (1981). *Management of head injuries*. Philadelphia: F.A. Davis.

Jennett, B., Teather, D., & Bernie, S. (1973). Epilepsy after head injury: Residual risk after varying fit-free intervals since injury. *Lancet*, *2*, 652–653.

Kay, T. (1986). *The unseen injury: Minor head trauma*. Southboro, MA: National Head Injury Foundation. (Also videotape).

Kinsborne, M. (1974). Mechanisms of hemispheric interaction in man. In M. Kinsborne & W.L. Smith (Eds.), *Hemispheric disconnection and cerebral function*. Springfield, IL: Charles C Thomas.

Klonoff, H. (1971). Head injuries in children: Predisposing factors, accident conditions, accident proneness and sequelae. *American Journal of Public Health*, *61*, 2405–2417.

Klonoff, H., & Robinson, G.C. (1967). Epidemiology of head injuries in children. *Journal of the Canadian Medical Association*, *96*, 1308–1311.

Krause, J.F., Fife, D., Cox, P., Ramstein, K., & Conroy, C. (1986). Incidence, severity, and external causes of pediatric brain injury. *American Journal of Diseases of Childhood*, *140*, 687–693.

Langfitt, T.W., & Gennarelli, T.A. (1982). Can the outcome from head injury be improved? *Journal of Neurosurgery*, *56*, 19–25.

Levin, H.S., Benton, A.L., & Grossman, R.G. (1982). *Neurobehavioral consequences of closed head injury*. New York: Oxford University Press.

Levin, H.S., & Eisenberg, H.M. (1979). Neuropsychological outcome of closed head injury in children and adolescents. *Child's Brain*, *5*, 281–292.

Levin, H.S., Grossman, R.G., & Kelly, P.J. (1976). Aphasic disorder in patients with closed head injury. *Journal of Neurology, Neurosurgery and Psychiatry*, *39*, 1062–1070.

Levin, H.S., Grossman, R.G., & Kelly, P.J. (1977). Impairment of facial recognition after closed head injuries of varying severity. *Cortex*, *13*, 119–130.

Lidvall, H.F., Linderoth, B., & Norlin, B. (1974). Causes of the postconcussional syndrome. *Acta Neurologica Scandinavica*, *56*(50), 7–14.

Logue, P., & McCarty, S.M. (1982). Assessment of neurological disorders. In F.J. Keefe & J.A. Blumenthal (Eds.), *Assessment strategies in behavioral medicine* (pp. 133–163). New York: Grune & Stratton.

Lyons, M.J., & Matheny, A.P. (1984). Cognitive and personality differences between identical twins following skull fractures. *Journal of Pediatric Psychology*, *9*(4), 485–494.

McLaurin, R.L., & Titchener, J.L. (1982). Post-traumatic syndrome. In J.R. Youmans (Ed.), *Neurological surgery vol. 4* (pp. 2175–2187). Philadelphia: W.B. Saunders.

Ommaya, A.K., & Gennarelli, T.A. (1975). A physiopathologic basis for noninvasive diagnosis and prognosis of head injury severity. In R.L. McLaurin (Ed.), *Head injuries: Proceedings of the Second Chicago Symposium on Neural Trauma* (pp. 49–75). New York: Grune & Stratton.

Parkinson, D. (1977). Concussion. *Mayo Clinic Proceedings*, *52*, 492–496.

Reilly, P.L., Graham, D.I., & Adams, J.H. (1975). Patients with head injury who talk and die. *Lancet*, *2*, 375–377.

Reitan, R. (1982). Psychological testing after craniocerebral injury. In J.R. Youmans (Ed.), *Neurological surgery, vol. 4* (pp. 2195–2204). Philadelphia: W.B. Saunders.

Rimel, R.W., Giordani, B., & Barth, J.T. (1982). Moderate head injury: Completing the clinical spectrum of brain trauma. *Neurosurgery*, *11*, 344–351.

Rimel, R.W., Giordani, B., Barth, J.T., Boll, T.J., & Jane, J.A. (1981). Disability caused by minor head injury. *Neurosurgery*, *9*, 221–228.

Rutherford, W.H., Merrett, J.D., & McDonald, J.R. (1977). Sequelae of concussion caused by minor head injuries. *Lancet*, *1*, 1–4.

Rutter, M. (1977). Brain syndromes in children: Concepts and findings. *Journal of Child Psychology and Psychiatry*, *18*, 1–21.

Rutter, M., Chadwick, O., Shaffer, D., & Brown, G. (1980). A prospective study of children with head injuries: I. Design and methods. *Psychological Medicine*, *10*, 633–645.

Sarno, M.T. (1980). The nature of verbal impairment after closed head injury. *Journal of Nervous and Mental Disorders*, *168*, 685–692.

Snoek, J.W., Minderhoud, J.M., & Wilmink, J.T. (1984). Delayed deterioration following mild head injury in children. *Brain*, *107*, 15–36.

Symonds, C. (1962). Concussion and its sequelae. *Lancet*, *1*, 1–5.

Chapter 9

Outcome and Future Directions

Ellen Lehr

INTRODUCTION

The previous chapters of this book have dealt with outcome in an indirect but specific way by addressing the issues of how children and adolescents fare in many areas after traumatic brain injuries. This chapter discusses outcome issues more explicitly, especially in terms of what should be measured and how it should be measured. Outcome from head injury has become an area of increasing interest in the past 3 to 5 years. This interest has been driven by medical, therapeutic, and economic concerns, focusing on the most optimal management delivered as efficiently as possible for the least cost. Because the sequelae of head trauma can be life-long, especially with more severe injuries, this has major implications for medical, rehabilitation, and postacute management in educational and therapeutic settings. Outcome issues not only involve the child or adolescent and the family but also the providers of service and those who are responsible for paying for it.

Outcome essentially involves prediction, including prediction of whether the head injury has had an impairing effect on the child's or adolescent's functioning, as well as whether and how much functioning has improved over time after injury (Dikman & Temkin, 1987). It is hoped that outcome studies increase the ability to predict eventual physical, cognitive, and psychosocial behavior after head injury. They can also help in rationally allocating rehabilitation and other resources. However, this effort is at a preliminary stage at present. Even in work with adults, outcome issues are not very well understood. Even less is known about prediction of sequelae and effectiveness of treatment in children after head injury than in adults. Important areas of concern in studying the outcome of head injuries in children involve understanding the process of recovery and improvement. This includes questions such as which children recover and improve and

how much, when recovery occurs—in stages or only initially after injury—
how return to the child's previous developmental course can be determined,
and what factors and interventions influence the amount of recovery and
improvement that occurs.

Quality-of-life issues have been difficult to address with adults after head
injury and are even more problematic when dealing with children after
injury. Some of the factors that can be assessed as part of quality of life
after head injury include the ability to perform self-care activities at an
age-appropriate level, the ability to get around independently, quality of
social relationships with both adults and other children, the capacity to
learn both in academic and nonacademic settings, satisfaction with self,
and extent of future prospects (Jennett, 1984). Outcome issues have usually
focused on the individual who has been injured, but quality-of-life issues
also affect those immediately involved with the individual. With children,
it is essential to assess quality of life changes for their parents and siblings,
for these changes have not only an immediate family effect but also a
societal one.

From the earlier chapters of this book, it has become evident that head-
injury issues with children are highly complex and can not be approached
in a simplistic manner. This is not merely a comparison of who does better,
adults or children. Rather the effects of head injury in children require
direct attention. Findings do not necessarily generalize across the entire
pediatric age span in any one area that is evaluated. Outcome issues are
at the center of this complexity. Children and adolescents after head injury
are not a homogeneous group but include children with different levels of
injury severity, different types of injury, different medical management
approaches, and differential availability of rehabilitation and intervention
services. However, most of the outcome studies to date have included a
heterogeneous group of children, often through studying consecutive ad-
missions to hospitals. Most studies have also focused on children who have
had severe injuries where it is easier to evaluate possible impairment and
the relationship between sequelae and injury are more easily recognizable.

OUTCOME ISSUES

Because of the variety of factors that comprise the overall concept of
outcome, there are also multiple methods of measuring the effects of traumatic brain injury. The specific measures that are utilized depend upon
the unique questions that are being asked (Jacobs, 1987). Outcome questions can consist of the effect of factors such as age or severity of injury
on physical or psychological functioning, the effectiveness of different med-

ical management approaches and techniques, the effectiveness of rehabilitation and therapy interventions, and the role of preinjury characteristics such as differences in child behavior, parenting approaches, and the impact of environmental variables. Outcome measures can involve observations of the injured individual's functional abilities and disabilities, interviews with the individual or more commonly with family members, and performance on intelligence or neuropsychological tests. The information derived from these different approaches varies the perspective on outcome, depending on what the measures are designed to assess and how reliably and accurately they do so. Certainly no one measure can portray in detail the multiple sequelae of head injury in children and adolescents from their perspective, their families' perspective, their friends' perspective, and their teachers' perspective.

Another key issue in measurement of outcome involves timing of the assessment. The ultimate measure of outcome from head injury sustained in childhood is actual functioning as an adult. However, this involves long-term follow-up over many years, which is usually not feasible. Even if children were followed until adult years, prediction of the difference between their actual adult functional abilities and what they might have been like if they had not been injured is difficult if not impossible to determine. The strategy that has often been used with adults, though, is also inappropriate. Outcome from head injury with adults is often confined to a 6-month to 2-year period after injury, after which spontaneous recovery and improvement is considered basically completed. Even if this were true in children (and there are some data to show that it might not be) (Klonoff, Low, & Clark, 1977), the effect of injury on a child's subsequent development certainly has not been completed in a 2-year period. For children injured at an early age, the full effects of injury may not be apparent for many years due to the nature of brain development and injury interaction. Therefore the issues of timing in measurement of outcome of injury in children can be quite different than in adults.

One area that presents specific difficulty in assessing outcome with children and adolescents is measurement of baseline functioning, that is, the difficulty of evaluating change in functioning in children who are continuing to develop and have not yet reached even an approximation of what they will be like as adults. It can be difficult to obtain reliable and accurate information about the characteristics and level of children's preinjury functioning for comparison with postinjury functioning. Reports from parents and teachers after the child has been injured, even if they are elicted early, are affected by the stress that the respondents are under and fears that the child may not return to the normal level of functioning. Parent and teacher reports on such rating scales as the Child Behavior Profile (Achenbach,

1979) and the Hyperkinesis Index (Connors, 1975) can be useful as indicators of preinjury functioning and characteristics as long as the specialized use is recognized. School records, especially standardized achievement test results, can also give an indication of a child's learning and functioning in school before injury. However, a variety of these tests are used in different schools, and the results from different tests may not be comparable. Also, the tests are usually given only once a year and have the drawbacks of reduced reliability of group-administered tests. Procedures have also been developed to estimate performance on intelligence tests, which can be used in comparing how an individual functions after injury with how he or she might have functioned before injury. These procedures, though, are not as reliable when they are applied to children as they are to adults (Klesges & Sanchez, 1981).

OUTCOME MEASURES

Glasgow Outcome Scale

Like the Glasgow Coma Scale, the Glasgow Outcome Scale (GOS) was developed to increase comparability of information about patients after traumatic brain injury across different medical centers and across research studies (Jennett & Bond, 1975). It is a 5-category rating scale that focuses on the level of disability after injury.

1. Good recovery. At this level individuals are able to lead a full and independent life, although they may have minor physical or mental deficits. They demonstrate the capacity to resume normal occupational and social activities, but they may not actually have done so for a variety of reasons not related directly to injury sequelae.
2. Moderate disability. These individuals are able to be independent, to look after themselves at home, to get around outside of their home but are not able to do some previous activities because of mental or physical deficits.
3. Severe disability. These individuals are conscious but are totally dependent on others in order to accomplish daily activities. A wide range of disability includes those individuals who are totally dependent in all areas to those who need assistance only with one activity such as dressing or mobility. However, the individual's level of disability requires daily assistance; the person cannot be left alone for extended periods or overnight. Disability at this level usually is related to a combination of physical and mental disability.

4. Vegetative survival. Individuals at this level show no evidence of psychologically meaningful responsiveness. They are able to breathe spontaneously, may have their eyes open and may follow moving objects, may grasp reflexively and swallow food. However, none of these activities is done in response to commands or purposefully.
5. Death from injury.

To increase the senstivity of the scale, each of the higher three categories can be subdivided into two subcategories, one for higher-level functioning and one for lower-level functioning.

The Glasgow Outcome Scale was an initial attempt to assess the overall social outcome of head injury, without dealing with the multiple components of resulting disability. It can be useful in making basic predictions about gross outcome and in identifying gross effects of early management (Brooks, 1987). Therefore, at a crude level it can be used for predicting outcome, but it cannot measure the fine details of recovery and improvement nor was it intended to do so. Because of the GOS's limited categories, individuals may change considerably and yet not move from one category to another. Ratings on the GOS may not be directly related to findings from psychological or neuropsychological evaluation, nor applicable to predicting success in educational or vocational settings. At the upper end of the scale questions of the reliability of ratings have been raised (Eisenberg & Weiner, 1987). This is a major concern since discrimination between good recovery, moderate, and severe disability is essential in assessing outcome. The GOS is also limited in its application to children since it does not have a developmental base for determining the varying expectations for independent functioning at different age levels (Fletcher, Miner, & Ewing-Cobbs, 1987).

When the GOS has been used to assess outcome from traumatic brain injury in adults, two-thirds of patients had reached their highest level within 3 months of injury, and 90% within 6 months of injury. This finding has been utilized to draw the conclusion that little recovery continues to occur in adults after 6 months of injury onset and that further improvement is due to better social adaptation and adjustment rather than recovery (Jennett, Snoek, Bond, & Brooks, 1981; Jennett, Teasdale, Braakman, Minderhoud, & Knill-Jones, 1976). Because of the nature of the GOS, this conclusion appears to be unwarranted unless supported by research utilizing more discrete measures of functioning and outcome.

Functional Independence Measure and WeeFIM

Development of the Functional Independence Measure (FIM) was begun 5 years ago to attempt to document the severity of patient disability and the outcomes of medical rehabilitation (Granger, Hamilton, & Kayton, 1987). It was designed for use with all patients in rehabilitation settings from age 6 on regardless of etiology and was not designed specifically to assess outcome after traumatic brain injury. Documentation includes demographic characteristics, diagnoses, impairment groups, length of inpatient hospital stay, and hospital charges. The scale assesses self-care, sphincter management, mobility, locomotion, communication, and social cognition through 18 items that are rated according to what the individual actually does and the degree of assistance needed in each area.

It is being adapted for use with children from 6 months of age to 6 years. Although the WeeFIM is not yet completed, difficulties in utilizing this approach for assessing outcome of children after head injuries are already apparent in the FIM. Most of the self-care and physically related items of the FIM have been basically mastered by 6 years of age, but complete independence is not always appropriate in each of these areas. For example, a 6-year-old boy who wets his bed occasionally at night may be well within expected functioning for his age but would not be able to be rated so since normal developmental expectations have not been incorporated into the scale. This becomes more complex when dealing with the communication and social cognition areas. The normal functioning child at six years and older has considerable development to undergo before reaching the level of the normal functioning adult. However, there are no guidelines as to how to rate what is expected of children as compared with adults on these items. The downward extension of the FIM encounters significant difficulties in the areas of both normal physical and normal mental development. It should incorporate developmental milestones as a built-in feature of the scale in order to assess accurately the outcome of children over the span of 6 months to 6 years of age.

National Traumatic Coma Data Bank

The National Traumatic Coma Data Bank was organized to study specific questions concerning the medical management and outcome of individuals after traumatic brain damage across six centers in the United States (Marshall, Becker, Bowers, Cayard, Eisenberg, Gross, Grossman, Jane, Kunitz, Rimel, Tabaddor, & Warren, 1983). It is a computer-based data bank that includes comprehensive information collected in a uniform manner in each center including data about preadmission functioning, neurological evaluations including CT scan findings, and patient status and management in the emergency room, operating room, and intensive care unit. Baseline and follow-up neuropsychological and social adjustment measures are also utilized with all individuals, with specific protocols for adults and for children. The study was designed to answer specific questions such as whether the quality of emergency care, specific treatment procedures, or rapidity of patient transport has an effect on outcome from injury. Because the centers are in different areas of the country, the study can also indicate geographic differences in etiology and outcome. The amount and kind of outcome data being collected for the National Coma Data Bank therefore differ significantly from ratings on more simplistic outcome rating scales and should be more useful in determining appropriate treatment approaches and techniques, especially in medical management areas.

Summary

The evaluation of outcome after traumatic brain injury is an all-encompassing endeavor and certainly cannot be circumscribed by the existing outcome scales. It is the center of study involving how infants, children, and adolescents function after head injury in all areas throughout their life span. A simplistic conception and measurement of outcome after injury do a disservice to the field of head injury research and management, as well as possibly interfering with appropriate service delivery to head-injured children and adolescents.

FUTURE DIRECTIONS

As stated many times in this book, there is much that we do not know about pediatric head injury. This last section presents an agenda for both research and delivery of service to further our understanding of pediatric traumatic brain injury and to provide a system of care for its management. In this way many of the issues discussed throughout the book are summarized but in a format that moves forward the endeavor of understanding and treating children and adolescents after traumatic brain injury.

Research Agenda

General Research Needs and Characteristics

In comparison with the large body of research on the effects of traumatic brain injury in adults, very little is known about the effects of traumatic brain injury in infants, children, and adolescents. We need to know more about the effects of head injuries when sustained at different developmental periods, delineated more clearly according to neurological, neuroanatomical, and neurodevelopmental components. The relationship of age at injury to speed of recovery, patterns of deficits, delayed effects, and long-term impairment is not understood. A particular emphasis should be placed on understanding the effects of head injury in infants, toddlers, and preschool-age children because of the dearth of knowledge of the effects of injury sustained during the early stages of development. This should include evaluation of the short- and long-term effects of head injury sustained early in life, consideration of both generalized and specific deficits, as well as attempts at prediction and amelioration of delayed effects. Although the overwhelming majority of head injuries in children are mild or moderate in severity, little is known about their effects on immediate and subsequent functioning and development. Even though more is known about the effects of severe head injuries in childhood, the variation of outcome is not well understood, that is, why some children after very severe injuries recover or improve markedly and others do not. And last the effects of nonaccidental trauma related to child abuse or the shaken baby syndrome need considerably more attention. We especially know little about those infants who suffer repeated "minor" insults. Development of effective intervention and prevention approaches with the parents and families of these infants is clearly essential.

Because of the nature of child development, research on the long-term effects of traumatic brain injury in childhood needs to be conducted not only from a developmental perspective but also in a longitudinal manner incorporating the interaction of the process of recovery and improvement with the process of development. Since children often experience more adequate physical recovery and improvement, primary areas of focus are cognitive, behavioral, emotional, academic, psychosocial, and adaptive areas. Children, even more so than adults, are dependent on other people. The impact of a child's injury must be studied in terms of not only its effect on the child's functioning but also its effect on the child's family, friends, therapists, teachers, and community. All of these people are critical in aiding the child's recovery and development.

Research on intervention with children after head injury is in its infancy. The effectiveness of intervention approaches, techniques, and programs, including combinations of existing services and those designed specifically to enhance functioning after head injury, needs immediate and careful evaluation. Intervention design and evaluation proceed more rapidly and more usefully if children after head injury are delineated into more homogeneous subgroups according to such variables as age at injury, severity and type of injury, and acuteness of injury.

Medical and Therapeutic Research Needs

Developments in the medical management of infants, children, and adolescents after traumatic brain injury have been occurring at a rapid pace, especially in areas of emergency and acute care. Although the effect of various methods of management may be relatively clear in terms of immediate progress and recovery, the long-term implications of different medical management strategies are often less well-understood, especially in areas such as improved cognitive, behavioral, and social functioning. And yet it is likely that medical management techniques do impact on these psychological areas of functioning.

Although therapy often begins in the medical setting, the need for therapy almost always continues in the community and school. Integration of therapeutic and educational intervention is usually seen as essential, yet it is not clear how this can be most effectively accomplished. There are fewer therapeutic options for children after head injury than there are for adults. Although it has become clear that children often require specialized therapeutic intervention integrated with educational programming after head injury, models for accomplishing this are only now being attempted. The effectiveness of the various possible intervention program models should be evaluated in terms of which children they are appropriate for, at what ages and stages of recovery and improvement, with focus on transitions for children between one program and another as their needs change over time. It is also not known if children and their families function better after head injury if their management is coordinated by one person (case manager) or a team, instead of being planned piecemeal by each agency or facility and coordinated by the child's parents.

Cognitive and Learning Research Needs

The effects of traumatic brain injury on cognitive processes such as attention and concentration, memory, and reasoning as well as the effect of disruption of cognitive processes on learning are not well understood. Research in this area should involve study of the ways in which learning is altered in children after head injuries and exploration of how learning after injury can be fostered. It is unlikely that the course of cognitive recovery and improvement is the same for all children after head injury. However, we know little about the variation of cognitive processes and patterns in head-injured children. If we could more accurately predict which children will experience significant long-term learning impairments, then specific interventions could be designed to help remediation efforts for those children who are the greatest risk. We also do not know if early intervention is effective in avoiding or ameliorating cognitive deficits. That is, do children who are identified, evaluated, and receive intervention soon after injury do better than those who receive services only after cognitive and learning difficulties arise? There has been considerable effort made in the past 5 to 10 years in the development of specific cognitive intervention approaches with adults who have had head injuries. However, it is not clear if these approaches are directly applicable to children and adolescents or how they should be altered to meet their developmental cognitive needs. Because of the critical nature of fostering and maintaining the ability to learn in children, questions such as whether to address strengths or weaknesses and whether to train to task or teach general strategies become even more important than with adults after head injury.

Although there are many traditional measures of cognitive abilities in infants, children and adolescents, there are fewer well-developed and well-standardized measures of the specific cognitive processes that can present significant concern after traumatic brain injury. The one area in which this is most striking is memory. There are few equivalents for children of the measures utilized to evaluate memory in adults. Those memory measures that do exist for children assess only limited aspects of memory and are usually standardized for only a limited age range.

Educational Programming Research Needs

A child's functioning in school is as or more important than an adult's functioning at work, and yet relatively little emphasis has been placed on the educational deficits and needs of children after head injuries. For those children who have significant loss of school time subsequent to their head injury, the transition to school must be carefully planned. However, we know little about how this transition can be most effectively facilitated both in terms of the child's needs and the educational system's needs. Determining the appropriateness of educational programming for children after head injury is often quite difficult, especially due to the frequent need for alterations as the children recover and improve in functioning. However, we do not know whether children whose school programs are managed carefully and flexibly perform better in school than those who return with little or no adaptations or services. In terms of teaching, we do not know the relationship and interaction between cognitive abilities and academic learning in children after head injuries. Because of the critical nature of school learning in children after head injury, we also need to explore how educational personnel can be most effectively taught to manage the educational needs of these children.

Emotional and Behavioral Research Needs

Little is known about how children understand, react, and cope with the emotional and behavioral aspects of traumatic brain injury. Therefore many issues need to be focused on in this area. We do not know what the precursors of emotional and behavior sequelae are in terms of whether specific types of injury are more likely to give rise to emotional and behavioral manifestations in children, whether preinjury personality and behavioral characteristics increase the risk of emotional and behavioral deficits, nor the expected characteristics of the natural history of the emotional and behavioral components of head injuries in children. There is some evidence that the behavioral and emotional components of head injury in children increase rather than decline with time after severe injury (Rutter, Chadwick, & Shaffer, 1983). However, it is not known how long this increase persists and if it does so equally whether the child is involved in intervention directed toward reducing the emotional and behavioral aspects of injury or not. Nor do we know the likelihood of delayed emotional and behavioral effects in children who have sustained injury at very early ages, long before they are aware of the impact of their deficits. Rarely have the children themselves, even at ages when they can be expected to be aware of injury and deficits, been utilized to give their perceptions and experiences in this area. We do not know how their reports would differ from the observations of the childrens' emotional and behavioral sequelae by parents and other adults. Some children may be at heightened risk both for sustaining head injury in general and for emotional and behavioral sequelae of injury. However, we know little about how to identify these children, both to aid in prevention of injury in the first place and in prevention of emotional and behavioral sequelae after injury.

Intervention approaches are less often focused on emotional and behavioral aspects of head injury than they are on the cognitive aspects, despite the importance of both of these areas for adequate functioning. It is not known what specific therapeutic approaches and strategies might be most helpful in avoiding, reducing, and ameliorating the emotional and behavioral sequelae of head injury in children and adolescents. As with school-based intervention, there is also a need in the emotional and behavioral area to train community mental health personnel and other professionals in the possible emotional and behavioral sequelae of head injuries in children and adolescents and the approaches that are likely to be successful in working with them.

For those children and adolescents with severe emotional and behavioral needs after head injuries, research into effective management approaches will not only increase their ability to function appropriately but also reduce the societal burden on their families and their communities. These children and adolescents often require extensive and expensive intervention, at times in residential programs, either through the mental health or the juvenile justice system. It is critical to be able to identify which children and adolescents can benefit from which intervention approaches. Legal and justice system personnel need to be alerted to and taught about the needs of those head-injured children and adolescents who come into their jurisdiction in order to most appropriately manage their care.

Family Research Needs

Currently we know considerably more about the effect of various kinds of intervention directly involving head-injured children and adolescents than we do about the children's effect on their families and their families effect on them. Since children spend most of their time with their families and since their families are essential to their functioning and development, this area needs immediate research attention. Initially this could entail an analysis of parent perceptions of their children after injury, effects of their perceptions on their child's functioning, their child-rearing behaviors and characteristics of parent-child interaction. This should be explored both initially after injury and then over a longer period to understand the effect of the crisis of a child's injury on the family and how the family subsequently reorganizes. To understand fully the familial effects of head injury, the siblings and extended family should be included, depending on their involvement in family functioning.

Family-focused intervention approaches of necessity differ from those approaches utilized with individual children and adolescents. Interventions should be designed to help reduce family stress and support family coping. Preparation of family members in terms of possible effects of head injury for their injured children, the nature of the recovery process, and approaches for dealing with head-injury sequelae are approaches that can be used but also must be evaluated for their effectiveness in terms of improving both the family's and the head-injured child's functioning. Especially for those children and adolescents who present significant management difficulties, creative approaches such as in-home teaching for family members and a variety of respite alternatives should be explored, not only in terms of improving the head-injured child's functioning but also in terms of maintaining and increasing the family's functioning. Some families may be at high risk for having members prone to more frequent accidents and injuries. Prevention and intervention approaches designed specifically for these families may have significant benefits in terms of injury reduction and avoidance.

Social System Research Needs

This area has received relatively little attention in terms of the effect of traumatic brain injury on social functioning in children and adolescents. The relationship between cognitive and social deficits after traumatic brain injury in children is not well understood. This involves research into such areas as social perception and social cognition changes and impairments after head injuries in children and adolescents. Research on the effect of traumatic brain injury on social functioning and social development over a long-term period should focus on both the disruption of social skills after injury and the impact of injury on the development of social skills that have not yet been acquired or mastered. Effectiveness of social skills–based intervention approaches that have been utilized with children and adolescents with other disorders should be explored with head-injured children. The focus of intervention should be on fostering catch-up in social areas related to lost developmental time after injury, teaching of specific social skills that will help lead to independent social functioning, reduction of social vulnerability, and increasing ability to engage in recreational and leisure activities.

Further study also needs to focus on the very small but highly visible group of children and adolescents who develop socially dissanctioned behavior and significant adaptive behavior deficits after traumatic brain injury. These behaviors include alcohol and drug abuse, inappropriate sexual behavior, and violent or criminal behavior. The role of head-injury factors, preinjury characteristics, and environmental variables are not clearly understood in these individuals. Nor do we know how to contain or treat their significant behavior disorders, which can present threats not only to themselves but also to others.

Prevention Research Needs

Prevention of accidents and injuries including those involving brain injuries is probably the highest priority for anyone who has sustained a head injury or for those who work with and care for individuals after head injury. Because of the incredibly high incidence of injuries in infants, children, and adolescents, research in prevention is beginning to receive national attention as a funding priority. However, prevention of traumatic brain injury in the developmental age period is a very complex undertaking that intimately involves the adults who care for them as well as the results of adult behavior in general. Therefore prevention efforts must involve not only analysis of child variables related to increased incidence of injury but also adult and environmental variables such as parenting styles, parental stress, design of the environment (e.g., playgrounds and traffic intersections), and adult behavior (e.g., child abuse and drunken driving).

System of Care

It has become evident since 1980 that for many if not most individuals after head injury, the impact of injury extends throughout their lives. This is even more so for those infants, children, and adolescents with sequelae after traumatic brain injury. And yet our current system of care is very fragmented and heavily focused on the initial medical aspects of treatment rather than on the life-long nature and needs of individuals and their families (Johnston & Cervelli, 1987). The need for long-term functional systems of service delivery with an emphasis on community integration is beginning to be implemented for adults after traumatic brain injury. However, efforts in this area for children and adolescents after head injury have barely begun. The emphasis of all of our efforts in working with head-injured children and adolescents must be on ensuring their functioning in all areas of life so that they can be contributing members of society to the best of their capacity. To accomplish this goal, a coordinated system of care with a clear emphasis on functioning over an extended period is essential.

At present, there is no such system for individuals after traumatic brain injury. Rather than creating a complete array of services only for head-injured children and adolescents, existing services and programs should be utilized as much as appropriate. Programs designed specifically for children and adolescents after head injury are necessary but not all-inclusive. Rather designated programs can be designed not only to meet the unique needs of head-injured children and adolescents but also to coordinate other appropriate community-based services. For example, the head-injury programs could explore and identify school programs and recreation programs, help to train their personnel in head-injury management, and serve as problem solvers and overall case managers as the head-injury experts. In this way existing services and programs can be effectively and efficiently utilized, costs can be reduced, and the head-injured child or adolescent can be integrated more fully into the community. However, without the coordination and planning services of professionals experienced in head-

injury management, existing services are unlikely to be identified appropriately, personnel are unlikely to be comfortable in working with head-
injured individuals, and integration is unlikely to be successful.

REFERENCES

Achenbach, T.M. (1979). The child behavior profile: An empirically based system for assessing children's behavioral problems and competencies. *International Journal of Mental
Health*, 7, 22–42.

Brooks, D.N. (1987). Measuring neuropsychological and functional recovery. In H.S. Levin,
J. Grafman, & H.M. Eisenberg (Eds.), *Neurobehavioral recovery from head injury*. New
York: Oxford University Press.

Connors, K. (1975). *Parent and Teacher Hyperkinesis Index*. North Chicago, IL: Abbott
Laboratories.

Dikman, S., & Temkin, N. (1987). Determination of the effects of head injury and recovery
in behavioral research. In H.S. Levin, J. Grafman, & H.M. Eisenberg (Eds.) *Neurobehavioral recovery from head injury*. New York: Oxford University Press.

Eisenberg, H.M., & Weiner, R.L. (1987). Input variables: How information from the acute
injury can be used to characterize groups of patients for studies of outcome. In H.S. Levin,
J. Grafman, & H.M. Eisenberg (Eds.), *Neurobehavioral recovery from head injury*. New
York: Oxford University Press.

Fletcher, J.M., Miner, M.E., & Ewing-Cobbs, L. (1987). Age and recovery from head injury
in children: Developmental issues. In H.S. Levin, J. Grafman, & H. M. Eisenberg (Eds.),
Neurobehavioral recovery from head injury. New York: Oxford University Press.

Granger, C.V., Hamilton, B.B., & Kayton, R. (1987). *Guide for use of the Functional
Independence Measure for Children (WeeFIM) of the uniform data set for medical rehabilitation*. Buffalo: State University of New York, Research Foundation.

Jacobs, H.E. (1987). The Los Angeles Head Injury Survey: Project rationale and design
implications. *Journal of Head Injury Rehabilitation*, 2, 37–50.

Jennett, B. (1984). The measurement of outcome. In N. Brooks (Ed.), *Closed head injury:
Psychological, social, and family consequences*. Oxford, Eng.: Oxford University Press.

Jennett, B., & Bond, M. (1975). Assessment of outcome after severe brain damage. *Lancet*,
1, 480–487.

Jennett, B., Snoek, J., Bond, M.R., & Brooks, N. (1981). Disability after severe head injury:
Observations on the use of the Glasgow Outcome Scale. *Journal of Neurology, Neurosurgery, and Psychiatry*, 44, 285–293.

Jennett, B., Teasdale, G., Braakman, R., Minderhoud, J., & Knill-Jones, R. (1976). Predicting outcome in individual patients after severe head injury. *Lancet*, 1, 1031–1035.

Johnston, M.V., & Cervelli, L. (1987). *Systematic care for persons with head injury*. Position
paper presented at the National Invitational Conference on Traumatic Brain Injury Research, Tyson's Corner, VA, November 2–4 (cosponsored by the Office of Special Education and Rehabilitation Services and the National Institute on Disabilities and Rehabilitation Research).

Klesges, R.C., & Sanchez, V.C. (1981). Cross-validation of an index of premorbid intellectual
functioning in children. *Journal of Consulting and Clinical Psychology*, 49, 141.

Klonoff, H., Low, M.D., & Clark, C. (1977). Head injuries in children: A prospective five
year follow-up. *Journal of Neurology, Neurosurgery, and Psychiatry*, 40, 1211–1219.

Marshall, L.F., Becker, D.P., Bowers, S.A., Cayard, C., Eisenberg, H., Gross, C.R., Grossman, R.G., Jane, J.J., Kunitz, S.C., Rimel, R., Tabaddor, K., & Warren, J. (1983). The National Traumatic Coma Data Bank. Part 1: Design, purpose, goals, and results. *Journal of Neurosurgery*, *59*, 276–284.

Rutter, M., Chadwick, O., & Shaffer, D. (1983). Head injury. In M. Rutter (Ed.), *Developmental neuropsychiatry*. New York: Guilford Press.

Index

241